Higher Education as A Moral Enterprise

Edward LeRoy Long, Jr.

GEORGETOWN UNIVERSITY PRESS / WASHINGTON, D.C.

Georgetown University Press, Washington, D.C.   20057
© 1992 by Georgetown University Press. All rights reserved.
Printed in the United States of America
10 9 8 7 6 5 4 3 2 1   1992
THIS VOLUME IS PRINTED ON ACID-FREE OFFSET BOOK PAPER.
Library of Congress Cataloging-in-Publication Data

Long, Edward LeRoy.
    Higher education as a moral enterprise / Edward LeRoy Long, Jr.
    p.   cm.
    1. Education, Higher—Moral and ethical aspects.   2. Education,
    Higher—Aims and objectives.   I. Title.
LB2324.L66   1992
378'.014—dc20   92-13886
ISBN 0-87840-531-3

In memory of
CLYDE AMOS HOLBROOK

Colleague of many years whose sudden death
occurred during the major work on this manuscript.

His early treatment of these issues was among
the first things I ever read on this subject and
during our long association he exemplified for me
the scholarly craft and the pedagogical art at
its most perfected human level.

Contents

Contents

PROLOGUE

On the Nature of a Moral Perspective

In this book I argue that higher education is fundamentally a moral enterprise that needs to be guided by commitments to what is morally right and fundamentally good. I therefore take issue, both explicitly and implicitly, with prevailing tendencies to give attention merely to what is intellectually warranted, operationally feasible, or superficially attractive to students who consider themselves more as consumers of educational wares than as aspirants to membership in a special guild.

Across the years some of the best minds have been intrigued with the challenge of defining the purposes of higher education. Books such as John Henry Cardinal Newman's *Idea of the University* have become staple items in almost every library, being shelved together with a host of similar efforts. More recently there has been a spate of writing about the university that has attracted considerable public attention. Most of this recent writing has shown a critical, even polemic, tone. It has attacked the shortcomings of the university with vehemence, contending that higher education is failing to achieve its goals. Allen Bloom's *The Closing of the American Mind* is only one, perhaps the most widely known, of a series of sharp attacks on the academic enterprise that have aroused enormous public attention in the last few years.

The public response to such polemics against the university indicates a deep discontent with the present state of the academic enterprise. While people still pursue higher education because they deem it essential for gaining access to most of the desirable professions, they often feel that college education is a dread necessity rather than an exciting venture. The academic guild is often tolerated more for its foibles than honored for its accomplishments. The campus has been of interest more as a locus of controversy and tension than as a uniquely attractive community. Interest in higher education is exceedingly high, but confidence in higher education is disturbingly low.

While polemics can help us to realize that something is amiss and can even help us to diagnose what is wrong with the contemporary academic enterprise, only positive statements can provide the vision with which the academy can seek its intended destiny. Instead of more polemics, we need a moral reconceptualizing of higher education. Instead of focusing attention on what is wrong, we need to articulate what the academy looks like when it functions aright.

Alas, the very discontent with the academy that prompts attacks upon its present condition makes the prospect of moral reconceptualizing enormously difficult. People can respond to attacks without having to forge any understanding of what ought to be the guiding goals of learning, but they cannot move toward constructive alternatives without espousing a set of guiding ideals to which they are committed. While it seems contrary to the spirit of the time to make a compelling case for a positive vision of educational purpose, we must enter into creative conversation to arrive at a perspective that will enable the academic guild and the wider public to embrace the goals of higher education as it ought to be pursued. Only as we discuss these matters within a community of dialogue will higher education become a moral enterprise that people cherish as a foundational element for social well-being.

Higher education is a tremendous cultural asset. Society is enriched by the presence of institutions devoted to preserving a sense of its heritage, extending an awareness of other cultures, searching for a knowledge of reality, honoring truth as an intrinsic value, developing a zest for working with ideas, and providing for the training and maturation of citizens. A willingness to reassess foundational premises is essential to sound education and equally salutary for social well-being. Where there is no vision, the people perish, and where there is no higher education, there is less likely to be vision.

Every person concerned with higher education must make concrete decisions about policy and strategy in specific contexts. Devising such policies and strategies is crucial to the nurturing of a moral enterprise. It is most likely to be done wisely, however, if ethicists set forth a vision of what is good both for individuals and for institutions, warn against the blockages both of ignorance and malfeasance that can thwart the achievement of that good, and delineate both the personal and corporate commitments that are characteristic of agents capable of facilitating needed transformation. The discussion that follows attempts to do these things in a way that will inspire those who are related to the educational venture in any of several roles to rededicate themselves to what is potentially the most sublime of callings.

Acknowledgments and Appreciations

I want to acknowledge financial assistance given many years ago for the initial research and drafting of this project from the Danforth Foundation (which provided an Underwood Fellowship for release time) and from the Hazen Foundation (which provided grant money for travel to a number of campuses with diverse and intriguing features).

I also want to express my appreciation to the many individuals who have helped in a great variety of ways in the preparation of this book. Some have merely listened to me talk about it and encouraged me to keep working on it; others have read manuscript and made suggestions which have been incorporated into the text with considerable benefit. The list is too long to mention everyone and the difficulty of drawing distinctions between casual and more substantive help is too hazardous to make the naming of selected individuals prudent. I trust all who helped in whatever way will take satisfaction in the final appearance of this book.

CHAPTER ONE

Defining Educational Purpose: Crucial Task and Elusive Goal

Many years ago Ortega y Gasset emphasized the importance of having a clear idea of educational mission. "An institution," he wrote, "cannot be built of wholesome usage, until its precise mission has been determined."[1] Almost half a century later, A. Bartlett Giamatti, former president of Yale, made the same point perhaps even more forcefully by warning that an institution of higher learning is in special danger when marked by a "smugness that believes the institution's value is so self-evident that it no longer needs explication, its mission so manifest that it no longer requires definition and articulation."[2]

Institutions that are experiencing declining applications, diminishing financial support, and a loss of public confidence may not suffer from the smugness criticized by Giamatti, but neither will they necessarily have the sense of purpose called for by Ortega y Gasset. While it may be hard for those who are in the throes of retrenchment to sense the importance of deliberating about their purposes, they should realize that a controlling vision is more likely than logistical gimmickry to help an institution marshall its resources for maximum accomplishment.

SOME DIFFICULTIES IN DEFINING EDUCATIONAL PURPOSE

To set forth the basic goals of higher education is a complex and difficult task. The academic world has never achieved unanimity concerning its aims, purposes, and methods. There have been times, however, when the differences have been less confounding than they seem to be at present. Today, many an academician can recount, for instance, the problems encountered in trying to draw up a statement of institutional purpose in anticipation of the visit of an accreditation team. Such an assignment is complicated in part because so many

2   ideas, from both the past and the present, vie for allegiance. Moreover, on any contemporary campus many conflicting interest groups seek to make their special agenda the controlling reason for the university's existence.

Lack of agreement is not, as a cynic might suggest, evidence that educators have no idea what they are doing. Rather it indicates that the task of higher education is so complex, so challenging, and so contextual that its purposes must be described in a way that encourages diversity of implementation. Perhaps the mission of higher education has never been so well defined as to eliminate tensions between various ways of understanding its tasks, but it ought to be possible to dialogue about the issues more fruitfully than is the case in many circles today.

The percentage of those in the academy who think and write about the meaning and purposes of higher education is small in comparison with the total number of those who engage in pedagogical and governance roles. Many academicians tend to work without giving considered attention to the underlying premises that give their efforts legitimacy and meaning. Others, worn down by the pressures of daily responsibility, economic stringency, public suspicion, and cultural anti-intellectualism, lose interest in foundational questions. They feel swamped by the avalanche of pragmatic immediacies demanding their attention in order to keep the enterprise afloat.

The major trends in academic life in the last forty years have done much to concentrate attention upon cognitive dimensions of learning and to render them more deliberate and supposedly more precise. The intellectual side of higher learning has received the lion's share of notice during this period. The so-called academic revolution[3] that has taken place since World War II has resulted in unprecedented developments in the scope of and self-consciousness about knowledge, particularly within the separate disciplines. It has also brought with it heightened academic professionalism. Pressures to master a field of specialization and to contribute to its growth have become increasingly great. The "ivory tower" has become a "pressure cooker" of the mind, while many teachers have become academic versions of the jet-setter.

In this process, other concerns that have frequently been associated with higher education have been shunted to the periphery, if not abandoned altogether. This increased concern about cognitive competence has been achieved by slighting, even perhaps ignoring, the formation of personal selfhood within the campus experience and the claims of social responsibility beyond the campus gates. Both of these have been acknowledged ingredients of higher education in its historical odyssey, particularly in its British and American forms. An important task facing higher education today is to take fresh looks at these neglected concerns and bring them to a level of articulation and sophistication comparable to the attention that has been more recently given to the cognitive aspect of intellectual life.

SOME ALTERNATIVE WAYS TO DEFINE EDUCATIONAL PURPOSE

Despite the voluminous literature on "the university question"—as the discussion of educational philosophy has often been called—there is no agreed-upon pattern by which all parties reflect on educational purpose. That in itself is one of the problems confronting the contemporary academy.

It is possible to think of educational purpose in at least three different ways. One of these ways, once associated with the religious worldview that dominated Western life at the time the idea of the university arose, is based on a concern about orthodoxy, or right belief. It depends upon a set of guiding convictions that the university is committed to espouse. When orthodoxy is the touchstone for giving direction and purpose to education, intellectual endeavors are likely to be judged by their conformity to a system of convictions that are authoritatively imposed. Unity is sought in terms of substantive agreement about the ultimate nature of things.

In many periods of western culture religious belief and the intellectual quest have shared much in common. Under such circumstances right belief may have functioned helpfully to define the mission of the university. But as tension and even hostility have developed between certain ways of doing theology and the main premises of the scholarly enterprise, the use of right belief as a defining criteria for the academy has become less viable. In some instances insistence on right belief has resulted in the establishment of institutions with a separatist academic stance that is quite at odds with much intellectual life. Right beliefs that lead to sheer fideism are bound to be suspect as the basis for defining the mission of the academy. Ironically, those who insist upon adhering to theological beliefs that prompt the repudiation of modern scholarship have often accepted social practices that are quite modern in origin and secular in nature. The result is that considerable attention has been given, for example, to condemning the teachings of Darwin in the classroom while at the same time social outlooks in economics and politics that are outgrowths of social Darwinism have been endorsed.

4   The orthodox way of defining educational mission does not appear only in religious form. In Communist countries, Marxism has often been used as the guiding right belief for colleges and universities. A few private institutions in our country make allegiance to a particular economic ideology, such as free enterprise, a litmus test for measuring the guiding perspective for correct teaching.[4] An analogous phenomenon, usually appearing on a departmental level rather than as overall institutional policy, is seen in demands for various forms of political correctness.

Another way of defining educational purpose, this one associated with the Enlightenment, is to think in terms of orthognosis, or right knowing. Orthognosis focuses attention on a body of information that is considered central to the intellectual life. Some expressions of this approach, for example, hold that there is a "canon" of information and understanding that undergirds Western society. Every individual who would claim to be learned is expected to be familiar with this body of material. Instead of a single scripture treated as a measure of proper belief, a group of Great Books—usually the so-called Western canon—is treated as the compendium of necessary knowledge. Orthognosis may also occur as insistence on a particular way of knowing. In place of faith it stresses reason and experience. In most instances it is heavily committed to the empirical method, emphasizing the priority of observation. A great deal of what has happened in the academy since the Enlightenment can be understood as a consequence of the struggle of orthognostic thinking against orthodox commitment.

Many current discussions of higher education illustrate a concern for orthognosis. Alan Bloom's *The Closing of the American Mind*[5] and E. D. Hirsh's *Cultural Literacy*[6] are cases in point. Both seek to delineate a body of knowledge that should be mastered by every student who would claim to be adequately informed. Not only those who defend a classic perspective make the acquisition of a particular body of knowledge the chief focus of the academy. Advocates of multicultural understanding often utilize an orthognostic approach, insisting that knowledge about many cultures is educationally necessary. There can be sharp debates between those who embrace one understanding of what constitutes proper knowledge and those who embrace a different understanding. Such debates often include, but are not confined to, considerations of what is an appropriate way to judge knowledge claims.

Institutions with a religious heritage whose working premises have become heavily influenced by the attitudes associated with the Enlightenment often find themselves achieving their modern identity by chafing against their religious heritage—particularly if that heritage demands an orthodox approach. They play down the religious factor as much as possible and attempt to achieve autonomy in matters of intellectual and cognitive import. Religion may even come to be looked upon as counterfunctional to sound thinking about educational matters. Such institutions, particularly those with continuing ties to church bodies, acknowledge their ecclesiastical identity for purposes of public relations, but except for requiring courses in religion and having a chaplain, embrace the orthognostic approach very much as do secular institutions.

There is still a third way to define educational purpose, for which it is possible to use the term orthopraxis, or right practice. This approach sets forth the nature and purposes of higher education by focusing on how it functions. The way a community of learning lives and thinks becomes as much an object of attention as the beliefs that it espouses or the body of knowledge with which it is concerned. The focus shifts from the substantive to the procedural. Ground rules for interaction become more important than correctness either of belief or of knowing. Orthopraxis permits more diversity about belief than it is possible to have when using orthodoxy as the touchstone for defining the nature and purpose of the university. It also permits more modesty about knowing than it is possible to have when using orthognosis. Indeed, the very purpose of defining a university in terms of right practice is to create a situation in which it is possible to examine—for the purpose of both comparing and sharing them—the diversity of beliefs that mark the human lot and the varieties of ideas that constitute the intellectual enterprise.

Because they were concerned with defining the university as a special kind of community with unique qualities of life, some classic attempts to think about the university are probably closer to the approach of orthopraxis than that of either orthodoxy or orthognosis. They focus on the academy as a place where things are done in a particular way rather than on the academy as a place where only particular things are done. For instance, they are less concerned with what makes ideas correct than with what makes the embrace of ideas perceptive, broadening, and liberating.

Religious concern about the university question can take the form of orthopraxis. Those schools in which religion is used as an engendering impulse to cultivate richer human relationships, to keep the spirit of inquiry uppermost, to hold up importance of service, and to extend mutual concern between all segments of the campus community, demonstrate an approach to educational issues in which a particular way of doing things provides the basis for making educational policy.

6   While many have given extended thought to the various grounds that give the university cohesion, others have questioned the very concept of the university, indicating that it suggests a unity of purpose and direction that it is no longer possible to achieve. Clark Kerr, for instance, has argued that the university has become a multiversity,[7] suggesting that the search for a set of defining purposes is possibly misplaced, particularly if that search is dominated by a conception of knowledge to which all persons are expected to ascribe. But even Kerr does not propose to open everything up for grabs and he makes suggestions for thinking about the purposes of the multiversity that in their own way constitute a basis for policy.

To think in terms of orthopraxis is not to abdicate the effort to achieve a definition of educational purpose. Rather it is to focus on those qualities of openness, human compassion, fairness, and intellectual integrity that characterize a particular kind of community. In such a community different beliefs and different understandings of the natural and social world can dialogue with one another. To portray such a place is the thrust of books like A. Bartlett Giamatti's *A Free and Ordered Space: The Real World of the University*[8] and Ernest L. Boyer's *College: The Undergraduate Experience in America*.[9] The very nature of such an approach makes irenics more important than polemics; the building of community at least as important as the delineation of a proper body of knowledge. While such irenic treatments have not received the popular attention that polemic attacks on the university have recently attracted, in the long run they furnish a profounder basis for a contemporary rethinking of the academic enterprise.

THREE ASPECTS TO A FUNCTIONAL DEFINITION OF EDUCATIONAL PURPOSE

Right practice in higher education involves concern about three dimensions of the campus experience, all of which must be addressed in appropriate ways by any college or university. These three functions, for which the term "responsibilities" is more appropriate, are: (1) the responsibility of the college or university for the identification, maturation, and enrichment of selfhood; (2) the responsibility of the college or university for the discovery/construction, extension, and dissemination of knowledge and culture; and, (3) the responsibility of the college or university for the well-being of society. Each of these is an ingredient of helpful practice—potentially of an orthopraxis. The heart of thinking about educational purpose is the examination of the conditions under which these concerns are best embodied, and how

they get balanced in relationship to each other in the life of any given   7
institution.

a. Selfhood: The first of the sections that follow explores the responsibility of the college or university for the identification, maturation, and enrichment of human selfhood. This may seem a strange point of departure for the discussion of institutions that nowadays are commonly regarded as primarily concerned with intellectual matters. But institutions do not live by minds alone; each of them has an individual "character," and each can have a profound effect upon the lives of those who attend it. They tend to be distinguished to the extent that each of them appeals to potential students because of that "character" and are effective to the extent that they influence those who attend them to share certain aims and values. Many things that institutions do, even today, are related to the development of selfhood, although these things are often not explicitly acknowledged as a part of the institution's intentional concern.

Although there is a growing call for colleges and universities to teach ethics and to demonstrate concern for values, the idea of shaping character is likely to be met with suspicion on the contemporary campus. That should not, however, mean that the academy's responsibility for identifying individual selfhood and its concern for the growth and maturation of persons need to be equally suspect. Knowledge and learning, which are the assumed priorities of the academy, like other human potentials and achievements, are embodied in persons. If people are not properly curious, adequately motivated, concerned for truth as an object of personal commitment, and prepared to pursue learning with zest, they cannot function well in an institution of learning. Education will be creative and fruitful only if the individuals upon whom the activities of colleges and universities depend are functionally productive as persons.[10]

Colleges and universities that consider the development of selfhood incidental to intellectual achievement imperil their full effectiveness. Those aspects of the college experience that form and shape selfhood—character and personality—are proper foci of attention for educational policy, if not indeed its foundation. A. Bartlett Giamatti, citing a fifteenth-century treatise by Pietro Paulo Vergerio of Padua, put it succinctly by suggesting that Vergerio was, "like all *wise* writers on education, interested in the whole person."[11]

An adequate educational philosophy must give the same serious attention to student life-concerns as it gives to curricular matters, as much attention to how students live and interrelate socially as to what they study and how they learn. Residential colleges, and even learning

8   centers for commuters, are more than sets of classrooms and other formalized arrangements for dealing with purely cognitive matters. They are groupings of varied involvements, some of a cognitive nature, but many of an interpersonal quality, that exert profound— even traumatic—influences upon those related to them. Communal arrangements often exert a far more decisive influence on the way and the extent to which students learn and the kind of persons they become than does formal course work. Many of the memorable odysseys enjoyed by graduates of American colleges and universities have occurred as a result of their relationships to peers and mentors. Group activities and public ceremonies often influence students as decisively as anything they encounter in formal learning. This is not to suggest that the curriculum has no role in the formation of the self. It is only to point out that what goes on outside the classroom may well be of pivotal significance and should not be relegated to a secondary role or dealt with as an afterthought—the province only of officers of student life (whose faculty status is often problematic) or of business managers (who may treat student life arrangements as merely a set of logistical details to be cared for at minimal cost).

John Henry Cardinal Newman is often cited as an exponent of the view that the attainment of knowledge should be the sole controlling consideration in education. Included in his famous work *The Idea of a University* is a chapter entitled "Knowledge Its Own End." This chapter even declares it to be a mistake to burden the educational institution with the cultivation of virtue or with training in the mechanical arts.[12] However, in this very same chapter Newman wrote: "It is well to have a cultivated intellect, a delicate taste, a candid, equitable, dispassionate mind, a noble and courteous bearing in the conduct of life—these are the connatural qualities of a large knowledge; these are the objects of a University."[13] That language suggests that Newman realized that learning is related to the formation of character and that the educational venture is about the development of a total selfhood and not merely about the narrow acquisition of information. Because this function of education is so pivotal, it is explored in the first section of this book.

b. Scholarship: The most generally recognized function of the university is to discover/construct, to extend, and to disseminate knowledge and culture. Colleges and universities are called to be catalysts and guardians of intellectual achievement. They are stewards of a body of discovered data and devised constructs that abstract reality into meaningful and manageable conceptual entities. They are specifically charged with both the custody of intellectual achievement and the exploratory research or creative originality that continuously extends it. Many other institutions in society utilize the results of this concern, but in an ancillary rather than in a pivotal way. The college or university, however, would lose a crucial distinguishing feature of its life if it did not explore the intellectual heritage of the past and make contributions to the insights and achievements that enrich the present and contribute to the future.

But despite the fact that the academic guild has made this function so pivotal, it still lacks a common mind about it. Indeed, arguments about the sources, grounding, and nature of knowledge are growing increasingly complex and intense. With respect to this cognitive function, some scholars have been impressed with the importance of a conserving role for the academy, with the importance of knowing thoroughly what has been previously thought or already accomplished.[14] Others have put the emphasis the other way around, pleading for the continual discovery of new information and forward-looking change rather than for reliance upon wisdom gleaned from the past.[15] This difference is not a simple function of the movement from the past to the present. The conserving view continues to have staunch defenders, just as the view that all knowledge must change as circumstances demand would have had sympathetic hearing from many in the past.

But more than this difference between the conserving view and the innovating view of knowledge must be taken into account in discussing the moral implications of scholarship. Prevailing approaches to knowing are under attack. A harsh and brittle approach to knowing, whether evidenced as dogmatic traditionalism, positivistic empiricism, or negativistic relativism, has been declared wanting by many contemporary observers. They feel it yields no humility, no compassion, no self-transcending perspective on the human situation. This challenge raises the issue as to what manner of working with ideas is appropriate for the pursuit of knowledge, not merely what is the proper content of knowledge.

Debates about the proper scope and content of knowledge continue to be important. Everyone familiar with the academy knows how lengthy and sometimes bitter debates about curriculum matters can become. Should the curriculum consist of an entirely (or largely) fixed set of offerings that require students to become acquainted with a broad range of human knowledge as embodied in a certain combination of the disciplines, or should students be able to chose any pattern of studies they find most useful for their contemporary purposes? Interestingly, academic moods come and go with respect to this issue. For instance, in the mid-1800s the undergraduate at Harvard was

10   required to pursue a relatively standardized curriculum composed of studies that introduced the historical and conceptual roots of Western civilization; it was presumed that such a regimen provided insight into the factors basic to understanding the human situation, and that it was beneficial in "the disciplining of the mental faculties." The furnishing (i.e., the imparting of information and providing of perspective) and the disciplining (i.e., the training of memory and the capacity for analysis) of the mind associated with such a curriculum were accepted as important objectives by many educators. The course of instruction was heavily loaded with the ancient languages of the Mediterranean world since the ability to read Western classics in their original language was considered a mark of both cultural attainment and intellectual accomplishment. The curriculum was influenced in large measure by English antecedents, and combined the best elements of medieval arts and sciences with an interest in literature and belles-lettres promoted by the Renaissance. Logic, rhetoric, Hebrew and Greek, natural philosophy, and moral philosophy were its forebears, but the passage of time and changes in the world had begun to bring increased attention to the sciences.

Then, as now, there were those dissatisfied with a prescribed curriculum as a device for assuring educational adequacy. Moreover, the essentially required curriculum was by no means universal in higher education, even in seventeenth- and eighteenth-century universities. Thomas Jefferson had not instituted it at the University of Virginia—which was patterned on the French model. Nor was it to be characteristic of the Germanic research university that was later to be adopted as a promising pattern for American higher education.

In 1869 Charles William Eliot was installed as president of Harvard University. Drawing upon a basic philosophical view of the human situation set forth in the literary works of Ralph Waldo Emerson, Eliot succeeded in replacing the prescribed curriculum at Harvard with an elective system that permitted the student to choose courses "according to the inclinations of his own bent." The influence of this change was widespread for American education, particularly for liberal learning in the arts and sciences. Two eminent historians of American higher education, John S. Brubacher and Willis Rudy contend that the free elective system reached a heyday between 1870 and 1910.[16] However, such an elective system was not copied in every center of learning, nor was it to be permanent even at Harvard. The same institution that adopted the free elective system under the tutelage of Eliot modified it in the early 1900's. Moreover, during the World War II, after careful soul searching and academic self-scrutiny,

Harvard again instituted a core regimen of required courses designed   11
to guarantee a balanced "general education."

Movements from a structured to an open curriculum and back again have taken place sufficiently often in a number of institutions to merit a mild skepticism about the academic community's ability to be permanently satisfied (perhaps it should not be) with any one way of dealing with curricular matters.[17] To be sure, such movements do not occur with the regularity of pendulum swings; changes seem prompted at times more by a discontent with existing patterns than by concern about the nature or the structuring of knowledge. Sometimes, as in the case of Eliot's reforms at Harvard, an articulate philosophy embodying a view of the human situation furnishes the impulse for change. But at other times, an iconoclasm is at work—an iconoclasm better characterized as a psychic mood than as a thoughtful agenda. One student with experience in an experimental college of the 1960s, describing his second thoughts about the dominant individuality that infused the campus, remarked, "We did not know what we wanted. We knew only what we did not want."[18]

Both the perpetuation and the changing of existing practices can be advocated for reasons that have little to do with the substance of knowledge. Requirements and prescriptions are often kept in place by special privilege and departmental self-serving. They can also be adopted mainly for the sake of novelty or for publicity purposes. Educators should prefer to maintain existing procedures or to make changes on the basis of a guiding purpose, but that requires a sense of mission and an underlying philosophy about the nature of knowledge and the conditions for its most adequate transmittal. The middle section of this book discusses the underlying factors upon which a sound conception of the nature and functions of knowledge can be constructed and through which the professional responsibilities for discovering and extending knowledge and culture can be carried on with a solid sense of direction.

c. Society: Finally, if we are to think clearly and deeply about the nature and purposes of higher education, it is necessary to examine the role that learning plays in the society from which it seeks support. Next to concern about curriculum matters this may be the focus of the most fervent debate on the modern campus. Is the life of the mind responsibly related to the well-being of the public order? Are institutions of learning beholden in any sense to the societies of which they are a part (and by which they are often supported), or are they special voluntary associations dedicated to specific values of their own and

12   furnished sponsorship and support in order to foster a nonutilitarian independence?

Throughout much of its history, American higher education has reflected a tension between views of education professing an allegiance to scholarly attainment for its own sake, and views of education that see it as something more properly dedicated to the preparation of people to serve society with specific skills and learned talents.[19] Irving Babbitt, a colleague of Eliot at Harvard, championed an education that is detached and removed from the concerns of the marketplace. He saw detachment as the guarantee of a cherished independence essential to scholarly reflection. He opposed many of Eliot's reforms because they fostered a shift away from education for wisdom and character toward training for service and power.[20] Alexander Meiklejohn, whose career included faculty positions at Brown and Amherst and administrative roles at Wisconsin, considered the cultivation of intelligence to be the central task of liberal learning. He wanted the college and university to concentrate on promoting knowledge, not on adapting it to immediate practical consequences. His goal, stated bluntly, was to make scholars rather than plumbers.

Robert Hutchins was a subsequent advocate of "higher learning" as a pursuit of something valuable for its own sake.[21] Hutchins criticized vocationalism and professionalism because they diluted learning with a concern about social service. He denigrated efforts to foster personal growth as a form of social polishing unworthy of true learning. He felt so-called training in character was little more than teaching students how to make the right social contacts. Most of what Hutchins said had been enunciated somewhat earlier by Thorstein Veblen in his defense of esoteric knowledge and the right of the scholar class to determine its own destiny.[22] Veblen's prescription for severing vocational and professional education from the true university did not become decisively controlling in American higher education, even though discipline-oriented cognition has achieved an importance during the academic revolution of the past several decades that might well have surprised even such a staunch defender of pure learning.

The opposite perspective has also had its thoughtful defenders. If Amos Eaton's view is any guide, the impulse to found schools of the practical arts, like Rensselaer Polytechnic Institute, was not intended to provide an alternative to intellectual activity. Such schools combined the most rigorous available grasp of theoretical knowledge—usually of a scientific nature—with a concern for applications useful to the industrial and agricultural needs of an expanding nation. The Morrill Act of 1890 furthered public support of institutions designed to train students for meeting the social needs deemed impor- tant at that time. The rise of institutions dedicated to the service of society through the preparation of skillful doers rather than reflective thinkers changed the focus of intellectual attainment without seeking to downgrade the importance of either thought or understanding.

In many ways the difference between practical courses of study and the learning that designated itself with the adjective "pure" has tended to decrease, especially since the World War II. Schools of liberal arts have increasingly introduced courses with vocational overtones. Conversely, engineering education, to cite but one example, has been much concerned to broaden and expand its curriculum to include subject matter generally associated with liberal learning, and several of the best-known polytechnic institutes of the country now offer majors in the liberal arts. Their move in this direction has been prompted by a twofold thrust: first, to broaden the outlooks of the technically trained individuals they usually prepare; and second, to offer those so interested a liberal education that is thoroughly in touch with what is perhaps the most distinctive dimension of the modern world: its technological accomplishments.

But the practical arts and service-oriented professionalism, while clearly designed to contribute to society's well-being through the applica- tion of learning in practical ways, do not by themselves furnish a suffi- ciently creative model for relating the college or university to the social order in these times of great social need. Those who would be of greatest service to society must be its prophetic critics, not merely its technical or its professional servants. They must learn to employ the fruits of learning as the means of calling their society to greater achievements, particularly of fairness and justice, than have yet been made. We are still groping for insight as to what this may mean; many efforts to become clearer about the social responsibility of higher education in these respects are embryonic, controversial, and in need of still further cultivation.

There are, to be sure, limitations on what institutions of higher education can appropriately do in affecting society. It is not enough merely to argue that they must accept social responsibility as a part of their agenda. It is equally necessary to indicate appropriate ways for doing this—ways that are compatible with the other foci of institu- tional concern and with the freedom and openness that are essential for academic health. These considerations are the focus in the third section of this book.

THE ELUSIVE IDEAL

Complete agreement or an enduring consensus about the meaning and purposes of education will always elude our grasp. We should not expect everyone to think the same way about these matters, but

14 we should want everyone to devote some thought to them and to struggle to attain satisfactory balances between the claims of many different perspectives. There is value in the process of reflection itself, not merely in the reaching of immutable conclusions. Near the end of his report on the undergraduate experience in America, Ernest Boyer expresses the hope that, "with determination and effort, the undergraduate college can make a difference in the intellectual and personal lives of its graduates, in the social and civic responsibilities they are willing to assume, and ultimately in their world perspectives."[23] That expression of hope points to the same three concerns that generate the discussion that follows, and embodies the same cautious trust that higher education is enduringly significant despite the vicissitudes, the changing emphases, and the many modalities through which it does its work. Boyer holds, as do I, that a self is too precious a thing to deal with casually; knowledge is too complex and important to trivialize; and social well-being is too crucial to our very survival to shunt to the periphery of scholarly attention. Because in all these concerns values are involved so crucially, they are ultimately matters of morality and not merely of pedagogy. They call us to the best reflection and the most informed commitments of which we are capable.

NOTES

1. Jose Ortega y Gasset, *Mission of the University* (London: Kegan Paul, Trench, Truber and Company, 1946), 36.

2. A. Bartlett Giamatti,*A Free and Ordered Space: The Real World of the University* (New York: W. W. Norton, 1988), 25.

3. This term has been used by Christopher Jencks and David Riesman; see their *The Academic Revolution* (Garden City, N.Y: Doubleday, 1968).

4. It is probably more of a danger to have the state impose a uniform orthodoxy on all institutions than to have voluntary groups create institutions primarily devoted to promulgating their particular convictions, but that does not make orthodoxy any more satisfactory as a way of controlling the outlook of institutions that ought to be devoted to open inquiry.

5. Alan Bloom, *The Closing of the American Mind* (New York: Simon and Schuster, 1987).

6. E. D. Hirsh, Jr. *Cultural Literacy* (Boston: Houghton Mifflin Company, 1987).

7. Clark Kerr, *The Uses of the University* (Cambridge: Harvard University Press, 1963).

8. See Note 2.

9. Ernest L. Boyer, *College: The Undergraduate Experience in America* (New York: Harper and Row, 1987).

10. Understanding this, Arthur E. Morgan, a former president of Anti- **15** och College, once pointed out that the intellectual element is subordinate to and dependent upon the qualities of self. According to Morgan,

The major controls of life are not intellectual, but emotional. Intelligence implements emotions, but does not take its place. A scientist will never be a great scientist unless he cares greatly, and caring is an emotional state. A teacher will never be a great teacher unless he cares about life and destiny, and also unless he cares for students and associates as brother does for brother. Caring is not transmitted by reasoning so much as by contagion from those who care. Reason can inform, enlighten, and direct caring, but rarely if ever create it. ("Developing Community Responsibility," in *The Goals of Education*, Willis D. Weatherford, Jr., ed., [Cambridge: Harvard University Press, 1960], 114.)

11. Giamatti, *A Free and Ordered Space*, 133; my italics.

12. John Henry Cardinal Newman, *The Idea of a University* (London: Longman's Green, 1898), 120.

13. Ibid., 120f.

14. Nicholas Murray Butler emphasized the importance of continuity this way:

Only the scholar can realize how little that is being said and thought in the modern world is in any sense new. It was the colossal triumph of the Greeks and Romans and of the great thinkers of the Middle Ages to sound the depth of almost every problem which human nature has to offer, and to interpret human thought and human aspiration with astounding profundity and insight. Unhappily, these deeplying facts which should be controlling in the life of a civilized people with an historical background, are known only to a few, while the many grasp, now at an ancient and well documented falsehood and now at an old and well-proven truth, as if each had all the attractions of novelty. (Quoted in Robert Maynard Hutchins, *The Higher Learning in America* [New Haven: Yale, 1936], 80.)

15. The importance of recognizing change has been stated this way:

It is essential that we now pay far more attention to the need for cultural change because the pace of growth is so rapid that we can reasonably assume that all cultures are suffering from obsolescence. Failure to identify the areas of obsolescence will therefore ensure the end of our societies.

The basic disagreement on educational issues today, therefore, is about the methods that can be used to help people identify the necessary changes in patterns of thinking. It is generally recognized that this task must be accomplished because a culture will always pass on to its children its own present understanding of the appropriate social frameworks. If we fail to understand the necessity for change we will provide the next generation with a set of attitudes which were appropriate for the past but which will not be appropriate for the future. (From a "Dialogue-Focuser" in *Dialogue on Education*, Richard Kean and others, eds. [Indianapolis: Bobbs-Merrill, 1967], 16.)

16. John S. Brubacher and Willis Rudy, *Higher Education in Transition: A History of American Colleges and Universities 1636–1976*, 3rd ed. (New York: Harper and Row, 1976), 114.

17. For an extensive account of curricular changes see Frederick Rudolph, *Curriculum: A History of the American Undergraduate Course of Study since 1636* (San Francisco: Jossey-Bass, 1977).

18. Gary B. MacDonald, "Fairhaven College," in *Five Experimental Colleges* (New York: Harper and Row, 1973), 204.

19. For an impressively documented history of two strands in the entire history of Western education, one favoring learning for its own sake and the other stressing public usefulness see Bruce A. Kimball, *Orators and Philosophers: A History of the Idea of Liberal Education* (New York: Teachers College Press, 1986).

20. It is ironic that the character in Sinclair Lewis's novel by the same last name should represent a somewhat contrasting phenomenon, namely an unthinking conformity to middle class values and mores.

21. He stated the premises on which that position rests as follows:

If education is rightly understood, it will be understood as the cultivation of the intellect. The cultivation of the intellect is the same good for all men in all societies. It is, moreover, the good for which all other goods are only means. Material prosperity, peace and civil order, justice and moral virtue are means to the cultivation of the intellect. So Aristotle says in the *Politics*; "Now in men reason and mind are the end toward which nature strives, so that the generation and moral discipline of the citizens ought to be ordered with a view toward them." An education which served the means rather than their end would be misguided. (Robert Maynard Hutchins, *The Higher Learning in America* [New Haven: Yale, 1936], 67.)

22. Thorstein Veblen, *The Higher Learning in America: A Memorandum on the Conduct of Universities by Businessmen* (New York: B. W. Huebsch, 1918).

23. Boyer, *College*, 284f.

PART ONE

The Identification, Maturation, and Enrichment of Selfhood

CHAPTER TWO

Education and Selfhood

The view that higher education is properly directed toward a cultivation of total selfhood and not merely a training of the mind has a strong legacy. Many institutions have traditionally thought of themselves as engaged in the development and cultivation of a complete range of selfhood. Institutions of every type—some with religious origins and others without—have included the idea of personal growth in their statements of purpose. "The function of a university," one liberal arts college declared in its catalog, "is to encourage the earliest and fullest development of maturity in its students. This means not merely the stimulation of intellect, but the encouragement of social and moral growth as well. A university passes on much of what it teaches through example, and by such indirect means as intellectual climate, social atmosphere, and prevailing custom."[1] Nor are statements that emphasize the importance of whole personhood characteristic only of schools of liberal arts. A military college with a heavy concentration of studies in professional and technical fields has for many years summarized its statement of objectives with a phrase like this: "The College seeks also to provide activities, services, and facilities which will contribute to the development in its students of character, physical fitness, and moral and spiritual principles, thereby preparing them to meet the requirements of citizens and especially of leaders."[2]

When speaking of their concern about these matters some educators comment on the cultural situation of the time, which is frequently described as direly in need of a certain kind of person to bring it to a more healthy state. A former president of a prestigious polytechnic institution once wrote in the catalog, "The contemporary multicrisis we face is basically the consequence of an ever-increasing disparity between man's growing mastery of the physical world on the one hand, and his lack of understanding of the profound impact of his actions on himself and on his social institutions, on the other."[3] A

20   college noted for its educational experimentation and nontraditional structuring of education, making a diagnosis of contemporary culture in the process of defining its educational objectives, once described contemporary American life as follows:

> Perhaps the most serious accusation American young people make about the culture in which they live is that it robs them of a sense of self. The term is not easily definable, but it implies wholeness or integrity; a match between what one experiences and what one is told, between yesterday and today, and between the various reflections of oneself one gets from the "significant others" in one's life. From such congruence an individual receives an assurance of continuity on the one hand; on the other, basic feelings of trust, relatedness, competence, and adequacy. That such characteristics are hard to come by in urban American life is taken for granted by many social psychologists, cultural anthropologists, and educators, an agreement which is itself frightening.[4]

Professions of this genre, which presume that education is concerned with the cultivation of selfhood in its fullest dimensions, have been too widespread to be dismissed merely as either peripheral or antiquated. They have found their way into presidential statements and institutional catalogs because they have articulated, however diffusely, a prevalent assumption about what collegiate education should be about.

THE EROSION OF CONCERN ABOUT SELFHOOD

Those with doubts about this way of defining the educational task are increasing in number. Language about character building, human development, whole personhood, and the like, seems increasingly remote from the nitty-gritty of educational policy making and the pressures of cognitive learning. Hence, this emphasis upon the development of selfhood has tended to be eclipsed by other matters in recent years. The same university whose catalog a generation ago provided the first of the several quotations given above has subsequently put far more emphasis in its mission statement on a discussion of learning as an intellectual concern and as preparation for achieving an economically productive existence. The college from whose publication that extended quotation about the problem of American culture was taken has since cryptically suggested to the prospective student that its "mission may be summarized as helping you make a good life and a good living."[5] In contrast to the concern of the former president of the polytechnic institute who stressed the need to increase our understanding of how to control selves and social institutions for human betterment, a subsequent president of the same institution now indicates why a public awareness of, and appreciation for, science and technology is important.[6]

These examples suggest that a subtle change has been occurring in thinking about educational objectives. Many academics now regard character development as quite beyond their purview, and would be sympathetic to the contention that "the great-man theory and character-building theory amount to a denial that there is or should be content to education."[7] The triumph of the research model, which makes the discovery and transmission of knowledge the primary legitimation of education, shunts concern about the selfhood of students to the periphery.

Moreover, pressures from outside the academy push concerns elsewhere. Today, higher education has to sell itself as a means to improve a person's prospects for earning a living and succeeding in a workaday world. Such pressures put the stress on competence rather than on character. But efforts to hone competence apart from the cultivation of moral selfhood can make "the best and the brightest" into merely the smartest and the most scheming.

In addition to the economic factors working against a concern for the growth of the self, there has been increasing disagreement about the proper way to define a self. The value of pluralism of which we have all learned to breathe so deeply has made us suspicious of efforts to define a single kind of personhood which all institutions should regard as normative. Many worry that making matters like the development of character central to the academy will introduce arbitrary and extrinsic requirements into the educational equation.

A number of other factors may have contributed to the shift away from a concern about the development of selfhood. Douglas Heath points to one of these factors—though it is not clear whether he regards it as the cause or the consequence—when he charges: "To believe that most faculty are psychologically oriented, sensitive to the inner lives of their students, motivationally personally equipped, and effective in helping a young adult explore himself is a magnanimous but unrealistic view of most faculty."[8] Philip E. Jacob, in a study that proved quite provocative at the time it was written, argued that colleges are not especially effective in changing student values: "[There is] no specific curricular pattern of general education, no model syllabus for a basic social science course, no pedigree of instructor and no wizardry of instructional method which should be patented for its impact on the values of students.[9]

22   The difficulty of keeping the development of the self central in educational practice has still other causes. One is the ever-present tendency for the noncurricular side of campus life to be nonintellectual or even anti-intellectual. A faculty that struggles to maintain the primacy of intellectual attainment will look upon what transpires in the stadium, or what takes place in some forms of activism, or the capers that occur at weekend social events, as thwarting, or certainly as working at cross-purposes with, its primary goals. It will be likely to dismiss all aspects of collegiate life that are not centered in the classroom as unworthy of its attention.

Still more deeply, the emphasis we place on the cognitive can be traced in part to a one-sidedness in the Western intellectual tradition. John Macmurray, charging that much western thinking is based on the premise that the mind alone is self-sustaining and directive of all other human endeavors, finds this outlook mistaken.

> The traditional point of view is both theoretical and egocentric. It is theoretical in that it proceeds as though the Self were a pure *subject* for whom the world is *object*. This means that the point of view adopted by our philosophy is that of the Self in its moment of reflection, when its activity is directed toward the acquirement of knowledge. Since the Self in reflection is withdrawn from action, withdrawn into itself, withdrawn from participation in the life of the world into contemplation, this point of view is also egocentric. The Self in reflection is self isolated from the world which it knows.[10]

Such a model of the self—one of pure intellect working largely in detached isolation—does little to feed human yearning for community. It can turn the ivory tower into a competitive scramble and exclude the experience of collegiality from the meaning of the word collegiate. In a culture that often extols the importance of autonomy and the value of individualism, it is easy to fall into the trap of thinking about the self as "within each person, the core and substance of his experience as a human being."[11] In such a view the self remains the subject while all else is object.

With such a philosophical base it becomes easy to regard the self as a given subject that need not be an object of educational concern. In his study of uncommitted youth Kenneth Keniston remarks, "Alienation, estrangement, disaffection, anomie, withdrawal, disengagement, separation, non-involvement, apathy, indifference, and neutralism—all of these point to a sense of loss, a growing gap between men and their social world. The drift of our time is away from connection, relation, communion, and dialogue, and our intellectual concerns reflect this conviction."[12] Although the forms through which privatism expresses itself differ from time to time and from place to place, the fundamental stance is quite the same.

A sense of isolation is a problem for many people associated with academic endeavors. Training that cultivates critical acumen to razor sharpness, attitudes that assume one's own views are vindicated to the extent that other points of view can be demolished, and exposure to interaction under conditions that are largely controlled by the subject matter being explored, lead to a condition in which it can be said of academic types that they often show impatience with the inept and consider many ordinary folk to be unworthy of attention. Kenneth Keniston, once described the alienated in a way that could also be applied to many academics: They "do not suffer fools gladly, and they consider most of their fellows stupid. Above all, they have contempt for those who 'blind themselves' to the 'realities' of existence by 'pious optimism,' shallow consolations, and the easy acceptance of the traditional verities of society."[13]

Philip Slater, examining the inadequacy of solely autonomous conceptualizations of the self, has shown that our entire culture, and not merely its academic branches, has taught us to suppress instincts that prompt engagement with each other and the creation of community: "The belief that everyone should pursue autonomously his own destiny has forced us to maintain an emotional detachment (for which no amount of spiritual gregariousness can compensate) from our social and physical environment, and aroused a vague guilt feeling about our competitiveness and indifference to others."[14]

BEYOND MERE AMENITIES

Although institutions of higher learning have commonly professed a concern for total selfhood, they have been increasingly concerned about the intellectual agenda and given less and less attention to the development of selfhood and the nurturance of community. Students often complain that they are treated as less than persons, as units of cerebral matter on a production line of mental competence. John Hersey, in writing to his fellow Yale alumni about their school's educational policies and intellectual climate, cited the overemphasis on the purely cognitive. He reported a statement made by the Coalition for a New University, a statement reflecting a deep discontent with an education that had become too much of a head trip. "Yale," said the statement, ". . . provides intellectual furniture for your mind but gives you no food for the soul."[15]

24   The protest movements of the 1960s frequently decried the plight of the self in the academic milieu. But most protestors had little sense of the depth of the problem and of the scope of concern needed to address it. By emphasizing the importance of "doing one's own thing" radical innovators in the sixties actually continued the individualistic bias of the Western view. In turn, academic traditionalists, while resisting innovative pressures to make learning more responsive to individual desires and objectives, continued to refuse to subordinate their posture as scholars to any extrinsic claims of the communities in which they work or which they might potentially serve. They resonated with David Riesman's declaration, "that no ideology, however noble, can justify the sacrifice of an individual to the needs of the group."[16]

As colleges have given up or lost their commitment to develop the fullness of selfhood, some of them have tried to counteract that loss by speaking of themselves as being friendly places, or places where everyone is urged to speak to everyone else. One college president, writing to prospective students, after outlining the program, resources, and characteristic features of his campus, expressed this wish: "I also hope that I'll get a chance to know you, whether during a formal program, or walking across the green, or as a student in one of my classes."[17] In another institution, a student at her commencement, musing about the event and her experiences during the previous four years, revealed a similar appreciation for the personal element. As she listened to the commencement address, she thought,

> Hohum, I think, the "Now we are about to embark on the ship of life" routine [is] coming up. But then I'm surprised by what the president is saying—a personal goodbye to our class. He speaks of how he knows only a few of us well, but through these few he has a knowledge of all of us. He mentions some of our names, and the traits and events he remembers these people for. . . . [He says] "I know who you are, and what you care about. You are all valuable individuals, and I like you, and I will remember you." Suddenly I lose the feeling of being a performer in a movie, and begin to feel as if this is my day, my ceremony, a celebration for my classmates and me, and not an extravaganza put on for the benefit of parents and alumni. Things come to focus again. I relax and begin to enjoy myself."[18]

Such concerns to be friendly have preliminary significance, but to reduce the identification and maturation of selfhood to interpersonal niceties is to trivialize it. A concern about selfhood is not a frosting of the personal element put on the cake of an otherwise impersonal intellectual endeavor, but a dedication to making the entire process concerned with the enrichment of personal existence. Certainly, it involves paying attention to how persons relate to one another, but it also requires questions about pedagogy and what consequences learning has for those who are involved with it. It means being concerned for the growth that can result from learning and not merely with how well students master subject matter. Professors should take stock of their teaching using criteria such as these: What kind of persons does this treatment of the subject matter cultivate? Does it lead to their humility in the face of mystery, poise in the treatment of conflict, and sensitivity in relating to others? "Whole persons are developed," one author has wisely observed, "by placing them in a community where they may interact with older whole persons and their own peers over significant problems of the past, the future, and the present, and where they must make decisions about their own conduct and involvement in society that requires ethical reflection and growth in responsibility."[19] To do all this well necessitates deliberate attention to the creation of situations in which personal growth is paramount. Such situations do not arise by default, nor do they remain forever viable regardless of past accomplishments unless continual attention is given to keeping the essential ingredients alive.

Not all expressions of concern for personal meaning provide an adequate impulse for educational ventures. A leader in the "freedom movement" at the University of California once told a reporter that he had participated in civil rights work in Mississippi because "he wished to find himself." Kenneth Underwood, taking notice of this statement, quite rightly observed the danger in focusing attention mainly on private feelings. Asking whether the action in which the student had engaged fit the situation and whether it had, in fact, produced greater justice in a situation of need, Underwood commented:

> The absorption of [the sixties] generation in problems of personal identity, its introspective preoccupation with personal guilt and freedom, needs to be balanced by mature intellectual and faithful concern with discernment of the occasions for action, and the convergence of change and influence in whole complexes of institutions, with the presence of God already in the larger transformation of culture to be seen in the acts of courage and responsibility to bring personal meaning and purposes to the major institutions of society.[20]

26   THE IMPACT OF BOTH THE CLASSROOM EXPERIENCE AND CAMPUS LIFE

The primary task of higher education is to avoid the split between talk about personal growth and finding ourselves, on the one hand, and attention to the cognitive, structural, and systemic dimensions of learning, on the other. Concern about the identification and cultivation of authentic and enriched selfhood, and concern about corporate life and public achievements, are not mutually exclusive alternatives. Selfhood has both private and public meanings; education has both curricular and extracurricular elements. All of these must interface in an adequate educational experience.

There are at least two faces to selfhood: the autonomous face and the allocentric face. There are features of the self that are private and there are features of the self that relate to others in communities of dialogue and interaction. The modern college or university tends to concentrate curricular attention on the wholly autonomous self. It cherishes independence from external pressures and extraneous activities. But this excessively private self—such as an individual learner working autonomously—shies from social interchange in order to pursue its own way. A world consisting solely of private acting selves would have no communal dimensions; indeed, it could cultivate very little knowledge (for which the public dimension is important) and still less culture (which is essentially corporate in nature).

The allocentric self, in contrast to the autonomous self, is responsive to others, is capable of human interaction, and makes community possible. Douglas Heath correctly describes the individual as engaging in a wrestling process between allocentrism and autonomy. Noting the contrast between these two aspects of the personality, he argues that they must reinforce each other in any mature self: "allocentrism makes a man aware of others' views and motives, including those views about him; he is able to understand and converse with others, tentatively taking the position of the other. But his autonomy permits him to retain command of his own decisions, to accept selectively what the other person may say."[21]

Another way of probing the contrast between the autonomous and the allocentric self is to reflect on the difference between what it means to be a knowing subject and what it means to be a known subject. The autonomous self is usually imagined as a knowing subject. But community develops more adequately between known subjects—between those who have become capable of interaction precisely because they can share their own identities with others. What is known about us, or is capable of being known about us, reveals and embodies our selfhood at least as much as what we know about other things. We can live in friendship and community with others only to the extent that we know them and are in turn known by them. Some of the most important aspects of religious experience involve, not what persons know about God, but what they come to realize God knows about them. Religious maturity is not developed wholly by achieving mastery of certain ideas or concepts and solidifying them into doctrinal formulations no matter how correct, but evolves from the realization that we are known in both our worth and our shortcomings. Just as communion with God is open to the persons who feel known by a divine power perhaps even more than to those who feel knowledgeable about the holy, so community with others is most open to those known by others even more than to those who possess a knowledge about others as objects of mere curiosity. If this be true, it means that the educational enterprise cannot concentrate merely on the creation of knowers; it must also focus on the arts and skills of becoming knowable.[22] Character as an expression of selfhood is that aspect of our being that is knowable.

On many campuses the cognitive needs of the autonomous self are being deliberately cared for in the curriculum, while the needs of the allocentric self are presumed to be served—sometimes in only a haphazard manner—by the extracurricular aspects of campus life. The learning experience is thus bifurcated into intellectual growth (a "head trip") centered in laboratories and classrooms and a concern about personal growth that is supposedly cared for in a plethora of living patterns and campus doings that often work at cross-purposes with the education of the mind. When the recreational and social dimensions of campus life are totally divorced from the intellectual concerns of the curriculum, an appalling discrepancy develops. College learning becomes increasingly specialized and college life degenerates into capers such as stuffing telephone booths, getting drunk, even destroying property, in order to demonstrate machismo.

This means that educational strategies that concentrate mainly on the curriculum, particularly when the curriculum concentrates only on the development of the autonomous cognitive self, can never be adequate. It also means that educational innovations and those criticisms of traditional pedagogy that by concentrating mainly on the allocentric self would subordinate cognitive curricular concerns to affective learning may be equally inadequate, particularly if they are attended by excessive privatism in campus living. The divorce between the autonomous self and the allocentric self that is found when the curriculum is treated as a purely cognitive matter and the

28   extracurricular aspects of campus life are viewed as anti-intellectual (or nonintellectual) is not overcome by a reversal that crowds the curriculum primarily with affective kinds of learning and further privatizes the other aspects of campus life.

Ernest Boyer's treatment of the undergraduate experience in America devotes a whole part of the discussion to campus life,[23] and emphatically asserts that at a truly healthy institution "the curricular and cocurricular are viewed as having a relationship to each other."[24] Boyer discusses how living arrangements and learning atmospheres affect each other, and why community service projects often help students to understand the relationship between what they learn and how they should want to live. He notes with approval the condition of the early America college in which classroom, chapel, dormitory, and playing field were considered to be connected. Any wise discussion of higher education must do the same.

THE SEVERAL DIMENSIONS OF MATURITY

Concern for the cultivation of selfhood does not require acceptance of a single definition of maturity. It need not result in a stifling conformity. Indeed, colleges and universities should be places that are concerned with exploring what constitutes selfhood in all of its viable forms, just as they discuss what constitutes knowledge in its many variations. Moreover, they can understand the many different forms of selfhood. Robert J. Lifton has criticized the assumption that "fixity and permanence" are necessary to selfhood. His idea of "Protean man" suggests that any one individual is a complex of different and changing selves in tension and interaction with each other.[25]

Many years ago, addressing the Antioch College community, Samuel B. Gould declared, "We are beginning to see that education is not merely the development of the mind, but rather the creation of a mature personality."[26] As a prognosis Gould's observation was probably too optimistic; the generations since he made that observation have not witnessed an ever-expanding attention to the development of the self as part of the educational enterprise, and have quite possibly witnessed pressures in the opposite direction. But as an indicator of a proper focus for educational concerns, his outlook has perennial validity. The next four chapters will explore more fully what is entailed in making the development of selfhood a central aspect of the educational task.

1. "A Tradition of Innovation," *The Catalog of Connecticut Wesleyan University 1969–70*, 11.

2. *The Bulletin of The Citadel, 1987–88*, 12f.

3. Jerome B. Wiesner, "An M.I.T. Education for Our Times," *The Catalog of the Massachusetts Institute of Technology, 1971–72*, xlviii.

4. *Education and Freedom: Catalogue Part I* (Plainfield, Vt: Goddard College, March 1971), 15.

5. "An Introduction to Campus Study," *Goddard College Bulletin 1987–88*, 27.

6. Paul E. Gray, "An MIT Education for Our Times," *MIT Bulletin 1987–88*, 5.

7. Robert Maynard Hutchins, *The Higher Learning in America* (New Haven: Yale, 1936), 30f.

8. Douglas H. Heath, *Growing Up in College: Liberal Education and Maturity* (San Francisco: Jossey-Bass, 1968), 258.

9. Philip E. Jacob, *Changing Values in College: An Exploratory Study of the Impact of College Teaching* (New York: Harper and Row, 1957), 11.

10. John Macmurray, *The Self as Agent* (London: Faber and Faber, 1956), 11.

11. Arthur T. Jersild, *The Psychology of Adolescence* (New York: Macmillan, 1957), 17.

12. Kenneth Keniston, *The Uncommitted: Alienated Youth in American Society* (New York: Harcourt Brace and World, 1960), 3.

13. Ibid., 66.

14. Philip E. Slater, *The Pursuit of Loneliness: American Culture at the Breaking Point* (Boston: Beacon Press, 1970), 25.

15. John Hersey, *Letter to the Alumni* (New York: Knopf, 1970), 30f.

16. David Riesman, *Individualism Reconsidered and Other Essays* (Glencoe, Ill : Free Press of Glencoe, 1954), 38.

17. John G. Kemeny, quoted in *Dartmouth College Catalog, November 1972*.

18. Heidi McClellan, "The End of Something Special," *Oberlin Alumni Magazine*, July/August 1973, 6.

19. Charles S. McCoy, *The Responsible Campus: Toward a New Identity for the Church-Related Campus* (Nashville: Division of Higher Education, Board of Education, United Methodist Church, 1972), 110.

20. From a mimeographed paper "The Ethical Question of the University," 10f. This paper is located in the Archives of the Danforth Study of Campus Ministries, Record Group 62, Box 71, Folder 860 in the Library of the Yale Divinity School. The quotation is used with permission.

21. Heath, *Growing Up in College*, 17.

22. The inspiration for the foregoing formulations came from the title of the book by Parker J. Palmer, *To Know as We Are Known: A Spirituality of Education* (San Francisco: Harper and Row, 1966).

30   **23.** Boyer, *College: The Undergraduate Experience in America* (New York: Harper and Row, 1987), Part V.

24. Ibid., 195.

25. See Robert J. Lifton, *Boundaries: Psychological Man in Revolution* (New York: Random House, 1967), especially the chapter entitled "Self."

26. Samuel B. Gould, in an address before an Antioch College Assembly, 5 June 1956, from *Knowledge Is Not Enough* (Yellow Springs, Ohio: Antioch, 1959), 92. The title for the address is not given.

CHAPTER THREE

Cognitive, Affective, and Kinesthetic Skills in the Wholeness of Selfhood

In discussions of educational policy, a distinction is commonly drawn between cognitive and affective aspects of experience. These terms denote a comparison that is popularly made between the "head" and the "heart." The cryptoslang of the sixties utilized labels such as "subject-matter types" to denote those interested in former, and "touchy feelies" to denote those interested in the latter. While those epithets are largely things of the past, the contrast between cognitive and affective learning is still with us. Faculty members and students are often thought to fall into one of two contrasting camps: those whose main preoccupation is with books, computer printouts, empirical surveys, and "hard" data; and those attracted to sensitivity training, group encounters, transactional analysis, and an interest in personal growth.

While this distinction has some analytical worth, it does not exhaust the alternatives that need to be considered. A third kind of learning has to be recognized if education is to foster the achievement of a fully developed self. In addition to cognitive and affective skills, kinesthetic skills are also crucial in a surprising amount of learning.

COGNITIVE ELEMENTS IN SELFHOOD

It is important to train the intellect cognitively. A mind that is informed about both the empirically discoverable and the conceptually devisable dimensions of human experience, a mind aware of the alternative ways of thinking about and portraying that experience, and a mind trained to evaluate the validity of data and test the cogency of both abstract theories and mythopoetical expressions of meaning is an enviable possession. Such a mind can guard the self against infatuation with glib answers, against the adoption of agendas that have been previously tried and found wanting, against commercialized slickness

32   and ideological oversimplification. Such a mind can assess a wide body of information with candid fairness and honest openness. The conceptual inventory of an educated person, says Richard McKeon, should "take into account the conception of the world developed by science and the influence of scientific ways of thought, the operation and history of social and political institutions and the judgment required for their effective operation, the values expressed in art, philosophy, and religion, and the perceptive appreciation that opens up their significance."[1]

The connotations associated with the term "cognitive" underwent a subtle metamorphosis during what has been described as "the academic revolution."[2] Whereas the term once denoted a broad sense of humane fullness, as it does for instance in Newman's *Idea of the University*, it has come to imply propositionally (sometimes called linearly) formulated modes of thought. For instance, the use of the term by Adam Ulam in *The Fall of the American University*,[3] seems to suggest a form of intellectual endeavor pursued for its own sake and characterized by disregard for attention to the whole person and the potential contribution of learning to individual and social well-being. Used in this sense, cognitive competence may be viewed as reaching a kind of zenith in the modern university with its strict definitions of intellectual accomplishment and single-minded pursuit of learning for its intrinsic conceptual value.

An overemphasis upon the cognitive can produce an academic elitism that reserves the fruits of learning for those peculiarly blessed with the talent, stamina, and opportunity to pursue it. Albert Jay Nock, for example, sharply distinguished between instrumental knowledge, which aims at doing something or getting something done (and which produces "mere Edisons") and formative knowledge, which enlarges appreciation and broadens understanding (and produces "Emersons").[4] According to such a view, cognition tends to define itself in counterdistinction to vocationalism. Robert Hutchins eliminated everything except cognitive elements from his vision of "permanent studies"—the main embodiment of which was reading the Great Books. Hutchins's approach, prompted as it was in part by a legitimate disgust with the mediocre and tawdry level of attainment characteristic of much American higher education in his time, nevertheless helped to set the cognitive into isolated preeminence as the measure of learning. Jacques Barzun, partisan of intellect though he has been, is not unaware of the ambivalent response that such an esoteric approach to cognitive learning has produced. He has attempted to account for this ambivalence:

The deep, universal distrust of Intellect rests upon its hostility to what is felt as the pulse of life. Common language records this opposition in a dozen ways: Life is warm, hot, glowing; Intellect is cold and dull. Life is its own mover, impetuous, heedless of reasons and obstacles, intent upon a few elemental goals which are not to be argued with—food, shelter, love, survival. Intellect is static, calculating, aimed at purposes clear to a few, but uncertain in their results, and vague or invisible to the multitude. Intellect observes rules of its own making that no one enforces, and is full of scruples in private, though in public it speaks confidently of itself and callously of life. The classic instance of Intellect's inhumanity is Voltaire's remark after he had asked why someone wrote bad books and was told that "the poor man had to live": "I do not see the necessity."[5]

Despite the preeminence that intellectual learning has attained in the modern academy, rather than furnishing a rallying cry that unites all academics, the term "cognitive" elicits mixed responses. Those many educators engaged in vocationally oriented instruction are not likely to applaud its use to read them out of the academy. Those who see the cognitive interpreted as antithetical to the personal element will turn to other touchstones for describing the focus of education. In the judgment of Harold Hodgkinson, the stress placed by traditional teaching on the cognitive to the exclusion of other considerations was behind much of the protest of the sixties. He observed at the time, "The undergraduate academic program with its assumption that only the cognitive matters and the affective is evil or unimportant, is a source of much student protest, at least as a hidden agenda item."[6]

Consider, for instance, how closely the term "cognitive" has come to associated with the term "excellence." The latter has gathered around itself a host of connotations related to high achievements in subject-matter skills, culminating in high scores on tests that largely measure informational attainment and mental agility. The use of the term "excellence" apart from a more careful delineation of its broadest implications has often been "like a magical incantation with a many splendored thing."[7] When misused in this way, "excellence" becomes a slogan that tends merely to emote about cognitive achievement rather than to be an informative description of carefully defined skills.

When the cognitive is set in contrast to the affective—whether by its friends or by its foes—all academics should be concerned. Hard-nosed competence should not lead to a strangulation of the feelings, nor should attention to the affective dimensions of education imply that cognition has only a secondary place. Moreover, the cognitive

34   need not be associated only with the precise formulations that are divorced from creative and leisurely reflection. We should all be concerned, as was Daniel Bell, who once made this analysis of why the cognitive becomes suspect:

> The culture of the Western intelligentsia in the last hundred years has been largely anti-institutional and even antinomian. By celebrating the self and the individual, it established the polarity of the individual versus society. It exalted the idea of the genius, or the artist, who was exempt from social convention. But these impulses, as expressed by the romantics to the surrealists, have been contained by the developing discipline of form in art. What one encounters today is a double movement; an attack not only on form itself but on any effort to find meaning in art—that is, the breakdown of boundaries and the end of genres—and what Karl Mannheim once called "the democratization of genius," the idea that self-expression and self-fulfillment, without any regard for boundaries and limits, are open to everyone. In the "cult of experience" all realms of experience must be open and explored. Everything is under attack; authority, since no man is better than any other; the past, since learning tells us nothing; discipline and specialization, because they are constricting. What results is a fierce anti-intellectualism, since what counts is feeling and sentiment, not cognition. Education, then, is not the transmission of learning, but a search for "meaningful identity," to be gained by "dialogue," "encounter," and "confrontation."[8]

To be sure, there are forms of cognitive learning that are truncated and confining. There are also reactive stances concentrating on the affective such as Bell identifies and decries. Pressures to increase the informational load of the curriculum can exacerbate such consequences. But, as William G. Perry, Jr., has pointed out, growth can be aided by cognitive learning in much the same way that growth takes places in moral development. There is an enormous difference in the type of cognition that depends upon authority and presumes that bits of information as set forth by that authority are final, and a cognition that is aware of ambiguity and the complexities involved in constructing a conceptual understanding of life.

Cognitive skills at the most mature level not only enable us to grasp the grand and magnificent contours of human efforts to understand reality, but also help us to be aware of the persistent ambiguities and absurd hiatuses in the human effort to perceive it. The self that is as cognitively informed as it ought to be passes beyond the tendency to evaluate reality only within one framework of meaning, beyond the unreflective embrace of the latest fad that claims to be innovative. The importance of the cognitive must not be downgraded, no matter how necessary it is to recognize that other skills are constitutive of the full self.

AFFECTIVE ELEMENTS IN SELFHOOD

Susanne K. Langer identified feeling as the unique ingredient that distinguishes the human species from animals:

> His departure from the normal pattern of animal mentality is a vast and special evolution of feeling in the hominid stock. This deviation from the general balance of functions usually maintained in the complex advances of life is so rich and so intricately detailed that it affects every aspect of our experience, and adds up to the total qualitative difference which sets human nature apart from the rest of the animal kingdom as a mode of being that is typified by language, culture, morality, and consciousness of life and death.[9]

Such an emphasis on the importance of feeling suggests that no conceptualization of the self that ignores its need for affective skills is pedagogically adequate. Indeed, some of the most cherished assumptions of a heavily cognitive academic enterprise are seriously challenged, such as the assumption that the more data is kept in sterile isolation from the consequences of personal involvement the nearer one gets to truth.

Bernard Meland has given us another terminology for embracing a concern about feeling within the parameters of the academy's agenda. He has developed a philosophy of education utilizing the term "the appreciative consciousness." In Meland's view there is a unity between the cognitive and the affective self:

> [The appreciative consciousness] invites a sense of wonder and an awareness of the depth of relations that inform thought and judgment. This view presupposes that sensibilities, being seminal to the nature of thought and formative even in critical inquiry designed to be objective, need to be acknowledged, disciplined, and nurtured within the educational process. Education of the mind, conceived simply as an instrument for problem solving, will hardly serve the human needs now arising in modern cultures; nor will it evoke in man the full measure of his humanity.[10]

36   In some discussions of these matters a contrast is drawn between the Enlightenment and the Romantic movement. Nathan Adler, for instance, describes the respective emphasis of these two roots of modern culture in sharply contrasting terms.

> If the Enlightenment valued clarity, rationality, and order, the Romantics sought the allusive and the synesthetic, the intuitive, and the passionate. The Enlightenment confirmed the social man, but the ideal of the Romantics was the isolated wanderer, the lone melancholy rebel. If the Enlightenment embellished thought with ceremony and activity with ritual, the Romantics opposed rules and regulations. If the Enlightenment asserted the primacy of the group and the civility of life, the Romantics repudiated the mediocrity of the herd and affirmed the impulsive, the spontaneous, and the novel.[11]

Adler's characterizations of the Enlightenment reveal that he himself does not think of it as a preoccupation only with the cognitive, and so warns against letting it be seen that way. Both the Enlightenment and the Romantic movement were richer than contemporary efforts to be either purely cognitive or purely affective. Jacques Barzun, not least among the appreciators of cognition, knew this, and flatly disassociated himself from those who create a dichotomy between the head and the heart. "Popularly," he notes, "the Romantics are said to have revolted against Intellect and avenged its crimes by substituting everywhere the heart for the head. This is untrue because impossible. Feeling cannot long subsist without thought (though the thought may be ill chosen), and thoughts, however dry, express feelings, however weak."[12]

Although these many and varied remarks affirm the equal importance of cognitive and affective skills in different ways, contemporary higher education is frequently charged with having neglected the affective. For instance, Kenneth Keniston once observed:

> Not only have academic pressures mounted in the past generation but these pressures have become more and more cognitive. What matters, increasingly, to admission committees and college graders is the kind of highly intellectual, abstracting, reasoning ability that enables a student to do well on college boards, graduate records and other admissions tests, and—once he is in college or graduate school—to turn out consistently high grades that will enable him to overcome the next academic hurdle. And while such intellectual and cognitive talents are highly rewarded, colleges increasingly frown upon emotional, affective, non-intellectual, and passionate forms of expression.[13]

To the extent that Keniston's charges accurately describe a prevalent academic perspective, they identify a problem to be faced. The academy has periodically experienced displeasure with the sterility of a purely cognitive agenda, as well as displeasure with other depersonalizing forces and the insensitivities associated with technological culture. Many consider the established academic world too objectivized, too detached, and too materialistically preoccupied. The counterculture of the sixties, for instance, took that disdain with which many academics had always viewed the commercial sector and turned it upon the academic world itself.

But the counterculture did more than merely re-emphasize the affective in contrast to the cognitive. It gave a peculiar flavor to the emotive, dominated by a new informality, a stress on romantic attachment to the natural, and a willingness to enjoy casually formed groupings created by accidental circumstances. Thus it nourished not only a stress upon the affective in contrast with the cognitive, but certain styles for the expression of the affective that were often as patterned and frequently as stereotypical as those that it rejected as too cold, stiff, and structured.

The counterculture often tended, therefore, to associate the affective with freewheeling independence and anti-institutional iconoclasm. George B. Leonard, a defender of the affective dimensions of education, characterized them as "free wheeling rather than rigorously scientific" and as feeling "that the first big step we could take toward increasing human ability and happiness would be merely to remove the artificial societal restraints that now bind us."[14]

Among the counter-cultural advocates of affective learning it was popular to refer to traditional education as "survival learning," suggesting that it consists merely of overcoming a perniciously created obstacle course. Lewis B. Mayhew may have overreacted, but in exasperation with the hostility to rationalism that was present in some movements of the sixties, he lashed out:

> One of the frightening arrogances of this minority [the protestors] is their rejection of rationality. Their embracing of the mystical folk idea of pure feeling and emotion is indeed sinister to one who saw what reliance on folk tradition did to German youth in the 1920s and 1930s. They believe that if faith can be put in participatory democracy, in the goodwill of the common people (whom students do not like—witness hatred of the police, who are working people), and in the race, all will be well. This view flies in the face of the long struggle between rationalism and the jungle. If man has a unique role, it is to exercise his reason and make conscious choices. But the militant young say, "Feel! Feel! Feel!" just as German youth said, *"Blut! Blut! Blut!"*

Modern man is still too much a child of Aristotle to reject feeling. But feeling is the twin power of cognition, which should also be put to the service of the organism. To reject reason is to reject reality. And this the militant young sometimes seem to do.[15]

Belief in the importance of the affective does not require a repudiation of either tradition or structure. It may call, rather, for opening the eyes to see how much the traditional patterns of campus life and learning have, in fact, cultivated the feelings, produced a sense of belonging to community, and genuinely nurtured the very qualities of selfhood that higher education ought to care about. The affective needs of students have been cared for in the college experience for generations. Think, for instance, of the personal satisfactions and growth that resulted from the service students performed in outreach projects sponsored by such agencies as campus YMCA's and YWCA's. Think of campus living, such as sit-down dining, which had communal dimensions and a gracefulness about it that cannot be found in a cafeteria run only according to considerations of efficiency. Serious conversations over meals are important to the assimilation of ideas, and are not encouraged by conditions in campus eateries where the jangle of dishes is ever present and where even food fights may occur.

Rollo May, analyzing the Victorian mood, has complained that it swamped out the capacity to love by placing excessive stress on willpower. He has shown how parents molded in the Victorian style sought to dominate all vitalities, including those of their children. But May has also suggested that it is possible to make the reverse error, to vitiate the will by emphasizing the unstructuredness of love. He charged the hippie movement, engaged as it was in an understandable revolt against its Victorian parents, of ending up with "a love that is fugitive and ephemeral." "Victorian will power," he wrote, "lacked the sensitivity and flexibility which goes with love; in the hippie movement, in contrast, there is love without the staying power that goes with will."[16] May's sense of the proper symbiosis between love and will is a suggestive paradigm for the relationship that ought to exist between cognition and affection. Each needs the other.

KINESTHETIC ELEMENTS IN SELFHOOD

Clarity about the mutual importance of cognitive and affective skills for the development of the self is an important ingredient in developing an adequate morality of education. But the importance of these two factors must not become so encompassing as to overlook a third and equally important dimension of selfhood with which the college or university must be concerned. The educated person must have skills of a kinesthetic nature as well as those of a cognitive and affective nature.

When kinesthetic development is mentioned we too often assume that the physical education department is alone and exclusively concerned with that aspect of the self. But consider the training in manual technique that a laboratory course involves. Such a course often requires learning how to do careful manual manipulations of delicate instruments and fragile specimens. To be sure, laboratory instruction creates skill in the organized presentation of material—in the sifting and combing of data to discover relationships—but it also involves making charts with attractive formats to show things graphically. Similarly, drafting skill as taught to students of engineering or architecture calls for the development of manual dexterity. In the liberal arts, both art and drama classes require dexterity in the use of the body. Instruction in music performance depends to a large degree upon the training of kinesthetic capabilities.

All professional schools must insist upon competence in certain manual skills associated with practice. A teaching hospital with surgical interns would be foolish to regard manual dexterity as unimportant. All medicine, for that matter, depends to a considerable extent on learning how to "lay hands" upon those in need of healing. Preachers with something brilliant and probing to say will be better communicators if they have mastered certain skills in the use of the voice and gestures of the body. The conduct of liturgy requires kinesthetic training. Lawyers must learn that winning trials before juries is not solely dependent on logical rationality but is affected by subtle techniques that are often matters of body language.

The use of the bodily members is not merely a grubby necessity of the workaday world. Using the hands—and tools, which are often only the extensions of the hands—is no less a distinctive dimension of what it means to be human than utilizing conceptual abstractions or having feelings. A self that cannot use its bodily members to serve the desires of the mind and the expression of the emotions has not reached its fullness. Just as Susanne Langer has pointed to feeling as the attribute in us that most distinguishes us from the animals, so Daniel Callahan has suggested that manual dexterity is an important aspect of what it means to be human:

> The fashioning of tools and implements, the essence of technology, has provided, from a zoological and anthropological perspective, an essential criterion for distinguishing humans from animals. It is, also, from a philosophical perspective, a key sign that one is dealing with intelligence and rationality. If one wants

40   to look for the ultimate source of the technological fallacy—that
            man must by nature become technological—then one could find
            no better place than to start with the assumption that the making
            of tools and implements is *sui generis* to man, part of what it
            means to be *Homo sapiens*. Yet there is every reason to think that
            this is no less than the literal truth of the matter. This truth is by
            no means hostile to the parallel truths that to be human means
            to think abstract thoughts, write poetry, experience emotions,
            paint pictures, compose music, and build cultures. But to empha-
            size all of the latter while ignoring the former is simply not to
            have in hand the full truth, part of which is that *man is by nature
            technological.*[17]

In light of Callahan's observation, it is sobering to realize how
much hostility or suspicion has existed in the academic tradition
toward the manual arts or toward those who use their hands for
technological purposes. How often have land grant schools been
dubbed "cow colleges?" The attitude seems to have a long history:

            Plato assigned mechanics and farmers to the lowest order of his
            utopia, and he recommended that unruly soldiers be disciplined
            by demoting them to it. Aristotle agreed with him. Both of them
            approved of athletics, politics, and war, which they did not
            consider to be work. Farming, technical crafts, and commerce,
            however, they deplored as both banausic and brutalizing. Their
            point of view, shared by their aristocratic contemporaries,
            remained strong in the West until the recent past; and it still
            dominates many Oriental, African, and Hispano-American soci-
            eties as well as the thinking of American academic breast-
            beaters.[18]

In the same mood, a commencement speaker at Harvard once noted
that if the Puritan settlers had not founded the college "the ruling
class would have been subjected to mechanics, cobblers, and tailors
[and] the gentry would have been overwhelmed by lewd fellows of
the baser sort."[19] Such snobbish disdain for those who work with their
hands does nothing to enhance the stature of the intellectual. After
all, what teacher of arts and letters has not wished at times for students
with better handwriting?
        There are values intrinsic to the self in the possession of kines-
thetic skills. In Western monasticism, manual work has played an
important role in providing a symbiotic rather than a dichotomous
relationship between the body and the spirit. Moreover, a manual-
labor component to education has often been evident in those institutions of learning founded, as was Oberlin College, with religious

purposes. For other reasons Ezra Cornell included it among the formative ideas for the university that bears his name.[20] William Smith, early provost of the College of Philadelphia, visualized a dual track according to which the mechanical arts were to parallel the liberal arts. His proposal was rejected by the trustees, who opted for a program of instruction involving only the latter, but they would probably have been wiser to insist both elements belong together. Booker T. Washington placed great importance on the value of manual skills and wrote a book entitled *Working with the Hands*.[21] The book presents a rationale for manual work as a part of education, stressing its value for the self quite apart from its usefulness as means to rise up the ladder of opportunity.

A very few institutions still consider manual work to be educationally valuable. Others utilize a work program as a means of enabling students to keep tuition down by providing some sweat equity toward the support and maintenance of the institution. One college actually builds most of its physical facilities with student labor, but it is a rare exception. Some of the innovations that emerged in the sixties revived interest in this kind of activity. At one West Coast college, flower and vegetable gardens covered a whole hillside on the campus; at a liberal arts college distinguished for its academic quality, one of the most widely elected courses in the experimental program was auto mechanics; in the learning center of a major Ivy League college, the basement has long been replete with equipment that is useful in all kinds of manual crafts. Such equipment may be employed for both recreational purposes and for curricular projects that involve several modes for learning and communication.

While public athletic events clearly cultivate kinesthetic skills for those on teams the majority of students do not participate in them. Spectator sports, while providing publicity for the institution, do little to enhance the development of kinesthetic skills in the majority. Sports events that entertain the public bring large returns to local entrepreneurs and arouse the excitement and stimulate the donor instinct of many alumni and alumnae, but do not broadly serve the need for kinesthetic development in all students. Success in spectator sports, built (as it often is) by attracting to campus a cadre of individuals for whom other aspects of learning are at best only secondary concerns, can attract attention and create institutional visibility. But spectator sports are more like bread and circuses than holistic in their nature. They are often just as dysfunctional in relationship to the general kinesthetic development of the student body as a whole as an emphasis solely upon the mind.

42   Kinesthetic development should be geared to the needs and capabilities of each person. Appropriate levels of attainment may vary greatly from one person to another. Not all students need to become professional or paraprofessional in a performing art or sports; not all need to achieve some special level of artistic or athletic accomplishment. But they need not sense defeat if they are not stars. Just as intramural sports proceed with a comfortable level of athletic skill, so the campus version of artistic work, drama, manual craftsmanship, and the like, can be modest and enjoyable aspects of the educational experience. The proper balance gives an activity a sense of rigorous endeavor yet does not push expectations so high as to make it a source of frustration and rancor to all except the group for which it is a special interest. Moreover, kinesthetic activities provide opportunities to assess the range of one's skills and to live gracefully within the perimeters of acknowledged limitations.

Just as sports can teach persons to be good competitors, so manual arts and other kinds of doing with the hands can teach many lessons. They teach respect for the given qualities of natural media. Working with wood, or clay, or the soil teaches a kind of patience. Long periods of time may be needed to complete a single work of enduring significance. Similarly, those who work with their hands are often well aware than imperfection is an inevitable corollary of human achievement. Mistakes cannot be obliterated by wishful thinking or pawned off as the fault of others. Many accomplishments are irreversible. The board is cut; the clay is glazed and fired; the produce that is harvested too early cannot be put back to ripen further. Learning to live with the satisfactions and the dismays that attend human creativity is driven home most emphatically by these kinds of undertakings.

Moreover, engaging in one's own manual activities can help to counteract the commercialism that has made price the key factor in determining the worth of things. Prices measure demand, not quality. Then too, pride of craft is in no danger of becoming a major American obsession, and its rarity too often compels us to rest content with the poorly made product. The lewd and the base consist not of work with the hands per se, but of that shoddy productivity that floods the marketplace with junk and serves the public with construction that is irresponsibly tawdry because it is cheap. Should not becoming liberally educated mean developing skills and sensibilities that can help to counteract this blight?

MAINTAINING THE INTERACTION

Arthur W. Chickering's massive anthology of essays, *The Modern American College*, has placed us in his debt for a thorough examination of the educational needs of students.[22] It goes a long way toward

exploring the interplay between cognitive and affective, between cog-   **43**
nitive and moral, learning. Pleas for the development of skills that
promote both intimacy and empathy appear throughout the book. But
the apparent absence from that book, as from much discussion of
these matters, of any mention of kinesthetic skills as an important
aspect of the self, may reveal a serious deficiency in contemporary
thinking about the nature of higher education. We need a still broader
sense of the self.

Chickering's book does remind us of another truth: that learning
cannot be merely individualistic. All skills are nurtured in interaction
between peers and between peers and mentors. In *No Time for Youth*
Joseph Katz and coauthors speak about the importance of doing
tasks—any tasks—together.[23] We can only do things together—
whether cognitively, affectively, or kinesthetically—to the extent we
are members of communities. The next chapter will consider the significance of community for the experience of education.

NOTES

    1. Richard McKeon, "Universities in the Modern World," in *Issues in
University Education: Essays by Ten American Scholars*, Charles Frankel (ed.)
(New York: Harper and Brothers, 1959), 16.

    2. Christopher Jencks and David Riesman, *The Academic Revolution*
(Garden City, N.Y.: Doubleday, 1968).

    3. Adam Ulam, *The Fall of the American University* (LaSalle, Ill.: Library
Press, 1973).

    4. See "Albert J. Nock," in Michael R. Harris, *Five Counterrevolutionists
in Higher Education* (Corvallis: Oregon State University Press, 1970), 97.

    5. Jacques Barzun, *The House of Intellect* (New York: Harper and Broth-
ers, 1959), 162f.

    6. Harold L. Hodgkinson, "The Next Decade," in *Power and Authority:
Transformation of Campus Governance*, Harold L. Hodgkinson and L. Richard
Meeth (eds.) (San Francisco: Jossey-Bass, 1971), 143.

    7. I am indebted to Charles S. McCoy for this phrase. *The Responsible
Campus: Toward a New Identity for the Church Related College* (Nashville: Division
of Higher Education, Board of Higher Education, the United Methodist
Church, 1972), 142.

    8. Daniel Bell, "By Whose Right," in *Power and Authority*, Hodgkinson
and Meeth(eds.), 161.

    9. Susanne K. Langer, *Mind: An Essay on Human Feeling*, 2 vols. (Balti-
more: Johns Hopkins Press, 1967), 1:xvii.

    10. Bernard E. Meland, *Higher Education and the Human Spirit* (Chicago:
University of Chicago Press, 1953; rpt, (Chicago: Seminary Cooperative Bookstore, n.d.), ix.

44   **11.** Nathan Adler, *The Underground Stream: New Life Styles and the Antino-mian Personality* (New York: Harper and Row, Torchbooks, 1972), 40.

12. Barzun, *The House of Intellect*, 164.

13. Kenneth Keniston, "Drug Use and Student Values," in *Religion for a New Generation*, Jacob Needleman, A. K. Bierman, and James A. Gould (eds.) (New York: Macmillan, 1973), 26.

14. George B. Leonard, *Education and Ecstasy* (New York: Delacorte Press, 1968), 46.

15. Lewis B. Mayhew, *Arrogance on Campus* (San Francisco: Jossey-Bass, 1970), 6f.

16. Rollo May, *Love and Will* (New York: W. W. Norton, 1969), 279.

17. Daniel Callahan, *The Tyranny of Survival and Other Pathologies of Civilized Life* (New York: Macmillan, 1972), 59f.

18. Michael R. Harris, *Five Counterrevolutionists*, 9.

19. Cited from Brubacher and Rudy, *Higher Education in Transition: A History of American Colleges and Universities, Revised Edition* (New York: Harper, 1976), 10.

20. Brubacher and Rudy, *Higher Education*, 92; Andrew D. White, as president of Cornell, espoused the same ideal. See ibid., 161.

21. Booker T. Washington, *Working with the Hands*, (New York: Double-day, Page, 1904).

22. Arthur W. Chickering (ed.), *The Modern American College: Responding to the New Realities of Diverse Students and a Changing Society* (San Francisco: Jossey-Bass, 1981).

23. Joseph Katz and Associates, *No Time for Youth: Growth and Constraint in College Students* (San Francisco: Jossey-Bass, 1968), 438.

CHAPTER FOUR

The Significance of Community for the Institution of Learning

From one perspective education is an intensely personal thing. Learning must be done individually. Students are graded one by one. Faculty members are promoted for their own achievements. Even if they work on team projects—which is more the exception than the rule—their attainments are measured by what they have personally contributed. It is a major breach of scholarly integrity to present as one's own work anything done by another.

But from another perspective education involves doing things together. The idea of a college is communal in meaning. Even if applied to a single institution, the term "college" designates a corporate activity. The word can even be used to refer to a group of nonacademics working on a common agenda, a meaning preserved, for example, in the term "College of Cardinals." Mark Hopkins's log—the symbol of the most intimate pedagogy possible—has a person at each end, and is therefore already a community. Moreover, knowledge is considered to be public. Scholars are expected to publish the results of their investigations so that others may know what they have thought or have discovered, and in turn build upon the foundations laid by others. Words can be copyrighted, ideas are to be shared, acknowledgments are expected to be given.

THE TENSION BETWEEN THE PRIVATE
AND THE COMMUNAL

This ambivalence between privatism and community is continually present in higher education. It was once highlighted by two contrasting evaluations of the multiversity made by people associated with the University of California after the disturbances on the Berkeley campus in 1963. A select committee was appointed to take a fresh look at the educational situation on that campus. Its report, informally

46   known as the Muscatine Report (after the name of the committee's chairman), concluded that one root—perhaps a chief root—of student disillusionment with the university was the absence of a sense of community in the campus environment. The report attributed the difficulty to numerical size, curricular and vocational diffusion, scattered and isolated living arrangements, and an impersonal quality in the relationships between faculty and students. According to the report, a student enters the university with certain expectations:

> He expects it to fill his need for a community in which he can participate, find satisfactory communication with adults, and enlist their support in his struggle to right the wrongs of society. With such high, if unformulated, expectations, this kind of student is bound to be disappointed. Communication with the older generation often fails to materialize in large lecture courses. Few, if any, of his teachers even know his name. He comes to believe that his worth is measured in answers to mass examinations, not in personal assessment of his work and ideas.[1]

In contrast to the assessment made by the Muscatine Committee that the Berkeley campus had become too impersonal and lacked the necessary sense of community to service its students well, Clark Kerr, the one-time chancellor, contended that the multiversity quite rightly places its attention elsewhere. He argued that an emphasis on the importance of community could prevent the university from preparing students for modern life. Writing after the Muscatine Report was issued, he said:

> The cry for community, the cry for integration of thought and action, are cries that call backward to a smaller, simpler world. The revolutionary visions of today are of the old, not the new, of ancient Athens and medieval Paris and not of modern New York. It is a sad commentary when the new revolutionary goal is the old past, not the future. . . . The standard model for the University is not the small, unified, autonomous community. Small intellectual communities can exist and serve a purpose, but they run against the logic of the times. . . . The longing for community, for this fantasy, for this pie-in-the-sky, can actually impede efforts to make better that which must be. . . . The campus consistent with the society has served as a good introduction to society—to bigness, to specialization, to diffusion of interests; to problems, to possibilities.[2]

THE IMPORTANCE OF COMMUNITY FOR LEARNING   47

Some learning may go on when participation in a community is missing or significantly curtailed. But learning done under such conditions may not be nearly as fruitful as that done in open and supportive interaction with others, and may even be painful. Probably the most thoroughgoing instance of deliberate exclusion from a campus community is the practice known as "silencing" as it used to be employed at West Point. Cadets suspected of an honor violation were brought before a committee of their peers. Those judged by the committee to be guilty of an honor violation were expected to resign, even though the evidence against them may not have been sufficiently strong to sustain a legal proof of guilt leading to an official discharge. Until the practice was modified in 1973, cadets who did not resign when the cadet committee deemed their behavior questionable (but the official review board did not judge the charges serious enough to warrant discharge from the academy) were penalized by deprivation of peer acceptance. Unofficial in its status, such "silencing" included restriction of conversation with other cadets to necessary official communications, limiting of associations to official functions, eating at a separate table and assignment to a single occupancy room (the last two obviously requiring quasi-official involvement). The "silencing" was not infrequently exacerbated by overt harassments. It was even applied—as it was against Benjamin O. Davis, Jr., a black cadet in the 1930s—to individuals who were considered unacceptable to the cadet community on other grounds.

It is not enforced silence as such that is the devastating factor in this form of punishment, for the very silence that was used as an instrument of exclusion in this instance can also be an instrument of community, as it is in a Cistercian monastery. It is intentional exclusion from community that hurts. When Amish communities impose the ban, which is a form of exclusion for an infraction of their mores, it is intended as a therapeutic device, tempered with mercy and reasonableness, and aimed at bringing the offender back to good standing. Even though the ban involves a refusal to associate normally with the member being punished, this practice involves quite different dynamics than those of silencing.

These illustrations are drawn from special situations—ones in which membership within a community has been already defined and therefore can be clearly and explicitly repudiated or temporarily suspended. In other settings we have an absence of community. Some wag has suggested that there is about as much community on some campuses as there is between the persons whose names are found on

48   the same page in the telephone book. If community has never been a central feature of academic life in a particular setting or has simply eroded from neglect, its absence may not be as keenly felt as when it is explicitly denied, but this does not mean there is any less of a problem.

Joseph Katz and his associates have reminded us how much mentorship enhances learning.[3] It is their conclusion that many educational methods do not provide sufficient interactional enrichment, that interaction between students and mentors should be increased and that faculty should be trained and encouraged to engage in those personally supportive encounters with students that are now assigned to ancillary student staffs. According to their view several modes of learning are necessary in higher education. Only two of these—the academic-conceptual and the ability to deal with inanimate, man-made, objects—can effectively occur without communal interactions. A third—the aesthetic-artistic—might occur without communal interaction. The others—people-oriented activity (whether service-oriented or commercially/politically-oriented), motor expression (such as athletics), and sociability—require that students interact with a wide range of persons. Moreover, they contend that the kind of learning that requires sociability is a major part of what college education is about.

Katz and his associates are professionals who are especially concerned about student life and its consequences. But Robert Nisbet, who has been primarily concerned about the intellectual aspect of the educational venture, has also pointed to the importance of community. Although he occasionally inveighs against searching for "togetherness" and "belongingness" almost as strongly as does Kerr,[4] Nisbet opposes such tendencies only in so far as they are sought as ends in themselves or as touchstones of an educational philosophy that undercuts what he calls "the academic dogma." That dogma is a belief that "knowledge within the learned disciplines . . . [is] good in and for itself, irrespective of any discernible practicality, relevance, or demonstrable capacity for binding up wounds to the ego or fractures of one's identity."[5]

Nisbet brings academics and community together in a special way. He sees the academic guild as a special and particular kind of community. That community, according to Nisbet, will be built on a dogmatically delineated purpose—which Nisbet defines cognitively. It is one in which faculty exercise authority over curricular matters and appointments, in which individuals are admitted only after proving themselves capable of learning or masters of teaching, and in which the role of students is "to do or depart, not to advise, lead, guide, or govern." Moreover, such an academic community is (or was before the degradation of its defining dogma eroded the quality of its life) given coherence by a sense of honor (deriving from the high esteem accorded the professor's role) and a sense of its superiority over lesser cults (deriving from the pride taken in scholarship). Even this highly traditionalist profile makes one thing clear: the scholar is entitled to enjoy a sense of belonging in a special guild. Concern for community need not be considered a matter appreciated only by innovative types.

In another work, bearing the subtitle *Community and Conflict in Western Thought*, Nisbet draws heavily upon Cardinal Newman's *Idea of a University* to suggest that "the university is far more than a place of research only, of teaching only, or of study only. Its essence is intellectual fellowship; only through such a fellowship at all levels, with fruitful communication among all levels, can there be a university."[6] Nisbet certainly reads Newman correctly, for Newman gave much attention to the importance of community as an essential dimension or quality of the academy. "A University is," he wrote, "according to the usual designation, an Alma Mater, knowing her children one by one, not a foundry or a mint, or a treadmill."[7] Newman declared that if forced to choose between a university consisting of formally structured arrangements (residence and tutorial superintendence, examinations and degrees) but lacking communal dimensions, and a university merely bringing together young minds to explore with each other the bent of their intellectual curiosity but lacking formal structures, he would choose the latter.[8] Newman held that tradition is the reality through which the sense of community acquires a natural (rather than forced) structure.[9] He envisioned a "bond of union" between the members of an academic guild. This bond has not become progressively stronger and stronger with the passing of the years. There has been no "communal explosion" in the last few decades comparable to the "knowledge explosion."

Vociferous cries about the lack of community on campus have been common in the last several years. One student has written, "The university is at war with itself."[10] A professor has declared, "It has become . . . pointless to try and figure out what has happened to turn the campus into a wasteland."[11] A journalist, reflecting on the situation he found some years ago while a visiting fellow at a distinguished institution, reported, "Students often feel they are no more than passing numbers in the institution's scheme, unknown by name or distinguishing characteristics to those who lecture them in lots of two hundred or more, strangers even to their classmates, with little voice in student government."[12]

50   It is easy to bemoan the lack of community on the modern campus—doing so has even become something of a communal orgy in some circles! But the problem runs very deep, and is by no means a merely peripheral one. Indeed, a national study issued in the spring of 1990 suggests that the fabric of contemporary campus life is badly rent, that traditional academic and social values have eroded to an alarming extent, and that a breakdown of civility threatens the very essence of the educational process.[13]

COMMUNITY IS POSSIBLE IN ALL CAMPUS SETTINGS

It is misleading to think of community as something that is experienced only in the extra-curricular aspect of college life. It is wrong to assume that what goes on in the dormitories, at fraternities or sororities, on "big-bash" weekends, or at the stadium, are the only things that can embody community. Granted, these are the places where the idea of sociability is given lip service and where rites of passage are most often experienced, but they do not exhaust the possibilities for the achievement of community.

        Classroom activities provide an opportunity for community just as potentially important, although different in form, as what happens outside the classroom walls. It is frequently assumed that a class is merely a group of entirely private individuals having obligations only to their teacher. If this is the assumption, students will logically conclude that they feel free to postpone doing assignments without harming others, or that they must do them on time only because the professor can penalize delinquency. But if a classroom is viewed instead as a learning community, students will see doing assignments on time as crucial to the dynamics of learning. A class reaches its lively possibilities as a community of learning only if each member accepts its routines as a moral obligation. Students are most likely to ask illuminating questions that benefit everyone if they have been regular and punctual in both preparation and attendance. An elan develops when a group pursues learning on the same schedule that seldom appears in classes where each individual works at a self-determined speed or where many lag behind because they sense no reason for meeting deadlines other than to avoid the penalties imposed privately on individuals by the instructor. Taking a course is not simply fulfilling a private contract; it is a commitment to a process of creating a community for inquiry, receptivity, and discussion.

        Much has been written about the shift in faculty orientation from campus loyalty to disciplinary identification. Many commentators have pointed to this feature of the modern academic scene, noting that instead of spending time acting as guides, mentors, and sources of inspiration for students, faculty are jetting from one place to another to give lectures that enhance their prestige or are doing consulting work to supplement their income. This development has been widely and even popularly decried.

While it is conceivable that the off-campus preoccupation of some faculty members detracts from the sense of community on the campus, the highly visible academician does not always ignore responsibility for the local community. There are teachers of wide reputation whose contacts with students are exemplary and whose excitement and contacts with the discipline and with the world of wider affairs are shared productively with those who study with them. Reinhold Niebuhr, to cite but one example, held regularly scheduled open houses for members of the Union Seminary community and in so doing not only created community but shared with students the insights that were his because of his wide-ranging travels. Conversely, there are campus-bound locals who hardly know how to treat a student civilly.

Still another set of influences bears adversely upon the effort to create and sustain community. The residential pattern of the traditional residential campus, marked by high homogeneity and by ongoing association, is giving way in many places to the commuting campus. People attend school while carrying on duties and maintaining identities in other settings—such as families, neighborhoods, and workplaces. Such persons naturally tend to see the demands of academic involvement as peripheral to their main identity. Moreover, they may well be taught by adjunct faculty members, themselves associated with other communities rather than with the life of the institution in which they teach part-time. If community is experienced only in the extracurricular side of things, such developments all but exclude its possibility for such persons. But if community is understood as a potentially present in the very curricular process itself, these persons will be able to contribute to its formation. Such students often make classes especially exciting because of the wide experiences on which they can draw to enhance discussions.

We must overcome the assumption that while the training of the mind requires a deliberate sense of purpose, hard work, and the acceptance of discipline, community comes about through more casual efforts. Community is not arrived at easily, least of all by wishfully hoping for it to appear. Community requires having a shared purpose or purposes and the wisdom to articulate those expectations through institutionalized forms and procedures. The abolition of rules does not of itself make community possible. Easy-riding is very different

52   from formation flying, and much less likely to yield the satisfaction of being on a team.

More recently the creation of community in the educational process has been made problematic by the shift of paradigm from one that portrays the relationship between student and teacher as that between apprentice and mentor to one more analogous to the relationship between a consumer and a provider of services. There are several underlying causes for this shift of paradigm—including the changing of governance patterns in response to student demands for an academic "product" to their liking and the marketing efforts of institutions to attract students from a shrinking pool of candidates. But trustful and personal interaction is more commonly found, and works in profounder ways, between a mentor and an apprentice than between a seller and a buyer. The mentor/apprentice relationship is not always salutary, but it surely has a potential for providing a greater interpersonal sense of support than do marketplace dynamics.

Many changes are occurring in the wider culture that make the achievement of community difficult in any place. The university is by no means the only contemporary social institution that finds it difficult to create and maintain a sense of community. The business community has experienced many of the same changes, and may indeed have undergone them in more extreme forms because of its frequent transfer of key personnel. Residential life in the suburb whose citizens move periodically is distinctively different from residential life in the old, small-town America. Life in communities that surround military bases shows some of the same problems in even more acute ways. Vance Packard referred not merely to the campus but to the culture as a whole, when he described us as *A Nation of Strangers*.[14] In a nation of strangers it requires special intentionality to achieve community.

Since every form of human interaction has both ways of reinforcing and ways of threatening those who are involved, it is possible for different people to experience the same conditions in opposite ways. Consider, for instance, two readings of the same set of campus dynamics. One describes the changes being felt at a major university several years ago.[15] The article is accompanied by two pictures, probably put there by the editor. In one picture, four white male undergraduates in ties and jackets are shaking hands with a male faculty member and seeming to enjoy pleasantries under the college banner in pleasant surroundings; in the other picture, a heterogeneous group, mixed sexually and racially, and attired with casual individuality, is struggling to make its way through a registration line. The message the pictures suggest is "What ever happened to the college way?" But a different reading of the campus scene from the same period, coming from John Hersey, reported that the desire for community was one of the strongest of fifteen traits that made life meaningful for the Yale students even during the period when traditional patterns were being challenged.[16]

It is quite possible that the students on the hectic registration line experienced more community than did those in the sedate parlor. The trauma of battling registration lines may give people a sense of togetherness that is more real than that created by the formal open house. Surely, registration chaos is remembered by almost everyone who has ever graduated from an institution of higher education. Moreover, for all its attractiveness to some, the all male reception in the formal parlor was a myopic form of community. The external polish tended to cover up the problems involved in failing to have women and minorities included. In this regard, it is appalling to realize how often quotations used in this present book—many taken from serious and even distinctive books on the meaning of higher education—use the third person masculine.[17] Such language reveals more than dated modality of speech; it suggests an ethos in which the male element has been overpowering and hence one that is not felt as community by women to the same extent it is experienced as community by men. The struggle to open higher education more equally to both genders and to move to inclusive language is a battle on behalf of community and not merely for justice.

Likewise, the struggle to open higher education to members of minority ethnic groups is a battle on behalf of community as well on behalf of justice. It may entail the laying aside of practices believed to be communal in the past—a process that can involve trauma and rancor. It will not do simply to open doors to selected minorities subsidized on scholarships only to expect them to enter into an ethos that is blind to their heritage and insensitive to their identities. Only as an experience of inclusiveness is given substance by putting together the contributions of each constituency will the collegiate experience become embracing of all.

Struggles for both justice and for more inclusive community bring profound changes. Past forms of community, while they stimulate nostalgia in some, may not have been as valuable as is frequently supposed. It still remains to be seen whether colleges and universities can make interpersonal and intergroup pluralism as functionally operative as a source of community as they have made a large and enlarging vista of intellectual complexity (even of cognitive dissonance) acceptable and productive.

ADDITIONAL DIMENSIONS TO COMMUNITY

I have introduced the debate about the role that community plays on campus. I have examined the consequences of denying community and the less obvious implications of never having achieved it in the

54   first place. I have looked at some possible explanations as to why the elements of community have not been enriched to the same extent as concern about knowledge has been expanded in the recent developments of higher education. In all of this I have treated community as something that should be found in each and every aspect of the educational setting and not merely in the extracurricular side of things.

In concluding, I will cast the discussion more positively by indicating briefly some of the necessary ingredients of community. Community depends upon objective realities as well as psychological moods. Structure and ethos are necessary for its achievement. Structure takes shared values and translates them into agreed-upon expectations—not least by the articulation of the rules by which a group agrees to live. An ethos provides symbolism as well as articulates purposes. It transforms the basis for belonging from a mere happenchance into a sense of covenanting with an ongoing reality. An ethos provides an overarching sense of the fitting by which all members of a group measure their participation (and contribution) by something they cherish more than their immediate advantage. An ethos even possesses a power to transform hierarchies, in which differentiations of attainment and status are acknowledged, from elitist instruments of repression into realities in which the achievement of standing is attended by the progressive acceptance of ever-greater responsibility. In reporting on what enables first-year students to succeed in college, Douglas Heath contends that "the most powerful support is an institutionalized vision of a way of life that is consistently manifested in the lives of both faculty and upper classmen."[18] Heath also suggests that if an institution does not furnish guiding expectations and the faculty does not offer intimate support, first-year students will find these elsewhere—often in ways that are dysfunctional to liberal learning.

There must also be some sense of passage associated with coming into a community. Cadet corps and Greek-letter societies have recognized this truth and have long used rituals of initiation to mark the transition to full membership in the community. When these are detached from academic values and left without adult involvement they may become harsh, brutal, or irresponsible, but they still persist because they give evidence of an intentionality to community. "Plebes" and "pledges" know that someone cares about them even as they undergo rituals of passage, and they feel a pride in belonging that cannot be had from merely signing in. There are similar rituals of passage, less formally defined and far profounder, in those institutions that have reputations for unique success in producing graduates with especially high academic orientations or a unique social concern. In such schools students internalize a set of values upheld by the entire

institution and struggle to learn how to express and embody those 55
values.[19] This involves an experience of passage less dramatically
expressed than "hell weeks" or "rat years" but no less indicative of
entrance into a community that is selfconsciously aware of its reason
for being.

While not all institutions of postsecondary education will be able
to achieve a sense of community in the same way or to the same
degree, none are exempt from the need to ask how to do so within
the setting in which they find themselves. The next two chapters
explore aspects of life in community that have special significance for
the academy.

NOTES

1. *Education at Berkeley: Report of the Select Committee on Education* (Berkeley and Los Angeles: University of California Press, 1966), 33.

2. Clark Kerr, "The University and Utopia," *Daily Californian*, 11 May
1967, 7–9.

3. Joseph Katz and Associates, *No Time for Youth: Growth and Constraint
in College Students* (San Francisco: Jossey-Bass, 1968), 428ff.

4. Robert Nisbet, *The Degradation of the Academic Dogma: The University
in America 1945–1970.* (New York: Basic Books, 1971), 42f.

5. Ibid., 47.

6. Robert Nisbet, *The Social Philosophers: Community and Conflict in Western Thought* (New York: Crowell, 1973), 229.

7. John Henry Cardinal Newman, *The Idea of a University: Defined and
Illustrated* (London: Longman's Green, 1896), 144f.

8. Ibid., 146.

9. Ibid., 147f.

10. Thomas Murray quoted in "The Campus Scene," in *Community on
Campus: Its Formation and Function*, Myron B. Bloy (ed.) (New York: Seabury,
1971), 12.

11. Roye Wates, quoted in *Community on Campus*, 13.

12. Larry L. King, "Blowing My Mind at Harvard," in *Harper's Magazine*,
October 1970, 102.

13. *Campus Life: In Search of Community*, A Report by the Carnegie Foundation for the Advancement of Teaching (Princeton: Princeton University
Press, 1990).

14. Vance Packard, *A Nation of Strangers* (New York: David McKay,
1972).

15. "Tradition No Longer Walks Princeton's Hallowed Halls," *New York
Times*, 15 September 1973, 25.

16. John Hersey, *Letter to the Alumni* (New York: Knopf, 1970), 72f.

56   17. To change the wording of such quotations would violate the cardinal responsibility of a scholar to cite the work of others just as it originally appeared. Perhaps many of those who are quoted would, given the opportunity to do so, opt to use more inclusive language. Many of us will do that mentally as we make use of these materials to furbish our own understanding.

18. Douglas H. Heath, *Growing Up in College: Liberal Education and Maturity* (San Francisco: Jossey-Bass, 1968), 262.

19. See David Riesman, *On Higher Education: The Academic Enterprise in an Era of Rising Student Consumerism* (San Francisco: Jossey-Bass, 1980), chapter 1.

CHAPTER FIVE

Frolic and Celebration in the Academy

Our waking hours are devoted to activities that we tend to classify either as work or as play. Work is supposedly productive; play is frequently regarded as trivial. Work is hard and demanding; play is often easy and generally relaxing—even when it requires strenuous physical exertion. Work usually warrants remuneration; play very frequently involves the outlay of money. In work we create; in play we presumably are "re-created." In work we frequently seek to exercise control over persons or objects; in play we are more often content to interact with and to enjoy people for what they are in themselves.

What is done in school is generally classified as work. Not many children carry "homeplay" in their bags, but millions carry "homework" and perform it with that sense of begrudging duty that parents often see as a healthy preparation for life in the "real" world. This process carries over to college and university life, where compulsive attainment is often as central as it is in the worlds of commerce and industry. At Oberlin College an admonition in an early student handbook read, "Drones will not be tolerated in this beehive of industry!" Faculty research and scholarship (which, in a very important sense, should be forms of re-creation) are sometimes referred to as "productive work."

When the claim of work is allowed to become all-encompassing, then the monotonous grind is often relieved by outbursts and escapes. While we know the adage that "all work and no play makes Jack a dull child," we have not been as articulate about the significance and importance of campus play as we have been about the significance and importance of campus work. In the educational enterprise, play (and a related phenomenon designated "celebration") should be cared for as deliberately and as intentionally as work.

ALTERNATIVE PERSPECTIVES ON WORK AND PLAY

Much thinking has been done in recent years about the way in which work and play are interrelated. The "work ethic" has come under

58   review, if not under total attack. Harvey Cox has pointed out that
sobriety, thrift, and ambition have diminished the importance of
myth, play, and festivity for many moderns (if not, indeed, eliminated
celebration all together). Describing the consequences, Cox observes:

> Mankind has paid a frightful price for the present opulence
> of Western industrial society. Part of the price is exacted daily
> from the poor nations of the world whose fields and forests
> garnish our tables while we push their people further into pov-
> erty. Part is paid by the plundered poor who dwell within the
> gates of the rich nations without sharing in the plenty. But part
> of the price has been paid by affluent Western man himself.
> While gaining the whole world he has been losing his own
> soul. He has purchased prosperity at the cost of a staggering
> impoverishment of the vital elements of his life. The elements are
> *festivity*—the capacity for genuine revelry and joyous celebration,
> and *fantasy*—the faculty for envisioning radically alternative life
> situations.[1]

Because the value of work was overstressed for so long it is
natural to react against the work ethic. One example of the movement
away from the work ethic and the entire style of life that it engendered
was penned some years ago by a Yale professor of law. Charles Reich
wrote a declaration of independence from the striving and dedication
to productivity found in the prevailing cultural styles of American
experience and presented as an alternative a new life-style more akin
to play than to work. Reich's ideas initially attracted a great deal of
interest.[2] Although much of that interest has now faded—the "hippie"
has given way to the "yuppie" as the focus of media hype—the issues
posed by Reich's book are not moot, but simply muted.

Reich believed in the possibility of replacing a work-oriented
consciousness with a play-oriented consciousness. He has not been
alone in that hope. David L. Miller, in a playfully provocative book,
calls to our attention the extent to which the metaphor of the game
has come to be used, not merely for the peripheral and ephemeral
aspects of the academic experience, but to describe the very handling
of knowledge itself.[3] Rubem Alves has argued that the joke, the jest,
and the process of debunking were used by Jesus to turn society
upside down. Alves urges his readers to employ the various aspects
of play for the same purpose. The production/consumption syndrome
of our culture, which diminishes the freedom and spontaneity of
selfhood by making productivity the only warrant for an activity, can
be broken down, argues Alves, only by play. Play becomes a means,
therefore, to subvert the dominant values of an existing society. Play

implies a radical refusal to abide by the logic of the contemporary adult world.[4] Even politics would be recast according to Alves. Speaking as a Christian, he contends that play embodies love. "My neighbor is always an end in himself. He is therefore, to be enjoyed. I play with him."[5]

Robert E. Neale has provided us with a psycho-theological study of these matters in his book *In Praise of Play*. Outlining the factors in our culture that have discredited leisure and created a sense of shame in those who play rather than work, he develops a concept of play that presents a truly different life mode from that of a production-minded culture. Play, according to Neale, is the psychic condition in which a harmony is experienced between our need to discharge energy and our need to design experience. In play, a person finds the discharge of energy following the design, whereas in work there is a conflict between discharge and design. Play is activity that is pursued without a felt need to resolve inner conflicts, whereas work is always interconnected with tension. If you have to do something when you do not want to do it, the result is drudgery; if you want to do something that you also realize you ought to be doing, it becomes joy. Thus play becomes a condition for doing all things without "hang-ups" rather than doing any particular kind of thing.[6]

Many of the foregoing proposals imply that it is possible to replace a condition in which everything has been dominated by the idea of work with one in which play becomes the controlling experience. While it is natural to resonate sympathetically with the motivations behind such thinking, such proposals do not provide the only way of dealing with the relationship between work and play, and may not be the most convincing diagnosis or compelling prescription. An alternation between work and play may be more helpful than the dominance of either.

Among some Amish groups a "frolic" is a special occasion when the entire community engages in an act of neighborly aid, such as rebuilding a house or barn for the victims of a fire or storm. In such an undertaking much work is done, but under different conditions than those that accompany the doing of routine chores. In the special event the discharge of energy becomes harmonious with design because there is a unique occasion, a special need, a different purpose. Amish daily life is disciplined and structured—more so than the life of many other groups. It has confining dimensions and firm discipline. It acquires a different significance when it rallies to support its members in need.

The Old Testament vision for Israel's life embodied the idea of alternation between arduous requirements and rest. The Mosaic law

60   provided for cessation from work on a weekly basis, for relaxation of more oppressive patterns of social control every seven years,[7] and for a general righting of social and ecological relationships every fifty years. Other instances of alternation are worth examining. In many parts of Western Europe during the Middle Ages on a given day each year the lower clergy and common people donned masks, sang songs of revelry and satire, and mocked the pretensions of churchly rituals and courtly procedures. They made sport of the customs and conventions of their world, subjecting even sacred practices and institutions to public jesting. Though higher clergy and ruling officials were discomfited, the public and minor officials got something off their chests.

This "Feast of Fools" has contemporary counterparts, like the annual Gridiron Dinner in Washington. A society has to be spiritually healthy to engage in these sorts of roasts. Roasts cannot take place if the officials are too insecure or the people are too victimized to treat their condition lightly. Schools with cadet corps sometimes have a "turnabout day" when the "rats" or "plebes" assume the functions of upperclass officers for a short specified period. Sometimes these play events are recaptured by a works rationale. A "turn about day" has often been designed to raise money for a campus charity by auctioning rank to bidders—something that gives it a productive purpose and to some extent alloys its quality as a kind of play. Nevertheless, it lightens (if only briefly) the burdens of a rigid authority structure. Other campuses have a long-standing tradition of the spoofing skit, providing a therapeutic ridicule of those who usually make the policies. Such skits are possible only in situations secure enough to tolerate spoofing and healthy enough to know it is a matter of jest. If deep, unresolved disagreements smolder on campus, it is too dangerous and/or embarrassing to ridicule them. The spoofing skit either becomes a heavy, vitriolic expression of rancor that conveys only hostility and displeasure or else it quietly fades away.

FROLIC AND LEARNING

Realizing that an overabsorption with work has frequently characterized academic life, proposals have been made from time to time to introduce play into the life of the academy. Some people would introduce play into the academic context using the model of replacement; others, the model of alternation. George B. Leonard, arguing that education should be pure delight, belongs with those who feel play can replace work altogether. According to Leonard, education is destroyed when dominated by the idea of work. The child, like so many great people who have been persons of discovery and thought, starts with joy in learning. Such joy is squelched when the coercive mold reappears, as it does when education is likened to work.[8]

Jacques Barzun, in contrast, while praising the value of work also suggests the importance of play. While Barzun recounts how work becomes satisfying when it is motivated by passion—under which conditions it become "fun"[9]—he appreciates the need for symbiosis between work and play:

> Unlike the Greeks whom we so much admire, with our lips, for their taste and their reason, we make no provision in society for the bacchanalian part of being. We do not know how to laugh or revel. We are serious thinkers and serious alcoholics. Like the late Wolcott Gibbs, we "lie with a hard ball of panic in our stomachs." We read Freud's *Civilization and Its Discontents* and approve but do not hear. The Middle Ages, for all their fits of Puritanism and supposed fears of eternal punishment, knew how to wash away panic in laughter and make room in civilization for the dionysiac as well as for its sublimation in work. We have lost all three forms of release, and can only look for "relaxation," wondering why we are timid and tired, afraid of power and looking for shelter in little huts—art, the home, the religions of the East—like sufferers from agoraphobia.[10]

While there is a sense in which all activity should move as much as possible toward the harmony of discharge with design, there is also a sense in which play must be different from ordinary undertakings. If the Feast of Fools ran all year long, it would cease to be a festival. If spoofing were the only activity of the campus it would become a bore. Scholarly learning should be fun, though to expect it will be only fun is to make significant attainment unlikely. A life without some tension between discharge and design is not for ordinary mortals—or at least not for ordinary mortals this side of utopia. If you make a business out of clowning, you diminish the likelihood of having fun from it. If you take all formative discipline and tension out of the academy, you reduce pedagogy to a whimsical indulgence of interests that is little more than intellectual narcissism.

The educational world will do well to ponder the value of alternation between work and play. A sense of renewal and release can be experienced by moving from one activity to another. Student play has not always been constructive. Play, as a reaction against, rather than a complement to study, may be escapist, even destructive. But patterns are changing. Hell-week has become "help-week" on many campuses; the weekend marked by the drunken binge can be replaced

62   by a service project; the dormitory water fight, by a cookie- or bread-baking event or the preparation of a special meal. The principle of alternation still works in these patterns, but it is an alternation between contrasting forms of constructiveness rather than between constructiveness and wastage.

Any group that has forgotten how to play is in trouble, but perhaps no less so than a group that knows nothing but play or that can "goof-off" only in destructive ways. Constructive play is a safety valve that prevents chores, which are intended as the tools of creative productivity, from becoming compulsive goads and the driving masters of all vitality. It is not, however, an end in itself or a pattern that can be made all-encompassing. Play, because it embodies joy and humor, allows the pathos of seriousness to be exposed without the value of seriousness being destroyed. It keeps creativity from truculence, mastery from arrogance, achievement from presumption, and learning from being a crushing weariness. The institution that fails to cherish and plan for frolic as part of its life-style, invites by its neglect, the alternatives to work that often relieve pressures in escapist and even uncivil ways.

LEARNING AND CELEBRATION

If frolic has suffered neglect in the modern academic context or has taken the form of unworthy "antisense" engaged in only as diversion, how much more has celebration come into eclipse? Celebration includes not merely activities specifically designated as religious observances, but any community's use of symbolic action for the purpose of defining its life or rejoicing in its reason for being. The eclipse of frolic has made the play life of the many academic environments escapist and destructive, but the eclipse of celebration has left their routines pedantic, even sodden. The transformation of frolic into antics represents the triumph of the anti-intellectual over the cultured; the demise of celebration represents either the triumph of a sterile rationalism over richer conceptions of selfhood and community, or the privatization of enjoyment over the sense of common purposiveness in the academy as a whole.

In frolic we have the festive possibility of lightness; in celebration we have the festive possibility of grandeur. Both have a relationship to joy, either the releasing joy of laughter or the sustaining joy of recollection. Both joys are important to the fullness of human selfhood. Ross Snyder has pointed to the importance of celebration:

We were meant to enjoy, to delight, to celebrate. To be fascinated by Presence, Mystery. To be wonder, amazement, surge of realization. To be so sensitive to patterns of beauty that they instress us and dwell in us from that time on.

To be fully human is to have consummatory experience—when many lengths of experience come into conjunction, and the worth of them hits us all at once. Instead of continuing to rush about, we take in, appreciate, we sense what it all means. We feel the flowing generosity of communion and consummation. The altogether lovely is present, not merely longed-for. We cleave to that which is good, until we become one body with it.

There are evils in the world which must be fought and problems which must be worked on. And they must not be ignored. But if our attention is constantly only upon them . . . we become eroded, rigid, drained of warmth, dehumanized.[11]

If the demise of frolic from the life of the academy occurred because play was discredited by the triumph of a work ethic, how shall we account for the eclipse of celebration? The explanation is more complex and quite possibly extrapolatory. But some conjectures merit examination.

One possible cause for the eclipse of celebration is the triumph of the utilitarian. This is a development associated in part with the rise of technology. Nature has been desacralized and history debunked. Both have come to be viewed as without mystery and without sanctity. They are "stuff," not foci of meaning and mystery. They are raw material for control and manipulation rather than sources of gratitude and wonder. The same temper that has allowed, if not indeed encouraged, the rape of the earth in the pursuit of productive efficiency has eclipsed the sense of mystery and heritage that is essential to celebration.

Another possible cause for the eclipse of celebration is the loss of, if not indeed antagonism toward, liturgy in the largest and most indigenous of the American religious bodies. This has two roots. The first lies in the Puritan's distrust of anything that would detract from the sense of God's sovereign holiness. The Puritans so feared the holy ultimacy of God as to be suspicious of efforts to embody holiness in forms or rituals. They worshipped in "the beauty of holiness" and shunned complicated rituals. When the deep and rich sense of God's intrinsic majesty, which Puritans cherished, eroded, their non-ritualistic forms were bequeathed to us shorn of significance. While not all traditions have been affected by this process, enough American life has been so affected as to make liturgy more likely to be suspect than to be honored.

64   The other cause for the eclipse of liturgy was the frontier. Here the rugged and highly individualistic life-style and marginal conditions of existence were incompatible with the continuation of sensibilities toward historic forms and practices. The evangelistic harangue conducted in a tent became more typical than a *missa solemnis* performed in a cathedral. At the beginning of the twentieth century almost all religious groups in America using formal liturgies were more identified with the Old World than with the New. While the subsequent assimilation of these groups into a pluralistic mainstream has undercut the validity of this generalization from one end, and the interest in liturgy that has made some inroads into all religious bodies makes it less categorically true from the other, the most typical American psyche remains suspicious of liturgy rather than responsive to it. Those who are uncongenial toward liturgy are likely to be ill at ease with institutionalized forms of celebration.

In a somewhat different analysis of these matters, Philip Slater has identified a generational difference in attitudes toward ritual: "For the older generation rituals, ceremonies, and social institutions have an intrinsic validity which makes them intimidating—a validity which takes priority over human events. . . . The younger generation [in contrast] experiences a greater degree of freedom from this allegiance. They do not see social occasions as automatically having intrinsic and sovereign validity. Their attitude is more secular—social formality is deferred to only when human concerns are not pressing."[12]

It may be that we have witnessed, not so much a demise of celebration and of liturgy, but a transformation of its forms. The rock concert is a kind of liturgical celebration. It attracts the young en masse and catches them up in ecstasy and enthusiasm. It may be that youth does want to celebrate, but to make the object of its celebration not steadfast tradition, not social amenities, not the pomp and circumstance of power or of privilege—but the capacity to come together spontaneously and authentically, without pretense or external trappings, in a style of immediacy with which it is comfortable.

These factors confront the academy with difficulties in conducting celebrations that will express its reasons for being. Ceremonies to which persons are required to come do not serve well as celebrations, but without required attendance such ceremonies often become peripheral and incidental. An opening matriculation ceremony for entering students is often boycotted by the upper classes and thereby lacks much of the fullness it ought to have. Chapel services once furnished an official channel for celebration on many campuses, but the secularization of life and the pluralism that has become so characteristic of intellectual communities have combined with a disinclination to participate in formally structured events either to make chapel a small group activity or to eliminate it altogether. The fate of the baccalaureate service is more complex. In some instances it has been totally abandoned; in others, it has been preserved by making it religiously syncretistic; in still others, it has been relegated to the status of a small voluntary event for those inclined to attend. Although the fate of the baccalaureate service varies from institution to institution, its fortune is not a simple function of the extent to which any particular institution is avowedly confessional. Some schools that do not otherwise make religion central to their self-definition still preserve a traditional baccalaureate service that involves the whole community, whereas a number of church-related schools have allowed the baccalaureate to become a minor side event or given it up altogether.

The inauguration of presidents probably involves more institutions of higher education with a serious level of celebration than any other single event. In some schools—their number is too small—the installation of deans and even of full professors involves the delivery of a lecture in a special setting. These events can be celebrational. They prompt the academic community to think in a somewhat different way about what it is doing. They engender reflection about aims and purposes, gratitude about heritage and resources, and (especially in the case of inaugurating presidents) enable academic institutions to come together to bear witness to a reality that is broader and more enduring than the life and achievements of any single one of them. While the need to be modest with expenditures on such events warrants due attention, something significant would be lost by abandoning them.

Almost every institution has preserved the commencement and used it as a time of celebration. But it is often an event that takes place after all members of the underclasses have left campus, and thus tends to involve only the senior class even as the matriculation ceremony tends to involve only the entering class. The tendency of the sixties to minimize the place or to denude ceremonial aspects of graduation has waned, but we do well to heed the observations of two quite different observers of these matters. The first was written by a conservative journalist from an older generation, commenting on dislike of wearing gowns and attending commencements that was prevalent in the late sixties.[13]

> I pause to remark about the value—even the necessity—of ritual in a society that is getting a little too shirt-sleeved for its own good. When we deny ceremony we deny memory; we pull up roots. . . .

There is something in the uneasy, apprehensive soul of man that needs an occasional grand occasion. The young people who scoff at commencement exercises put too much stock in being rational. They complain of the academic gowns, the tassels and mortar boards, and they object correctly that these have nothing to do with education. . . .

[But] rationality ought never to be regarded as the be-all and end-all. The apparently meaningless custom has meaning—in the fact that it is a custom. . . .

None of the . . . graduates is likely to recall a commencement address. The words blow away on an evening breeze. But years hence, they may recall the walk across a high school stage, the milk-warm night, the flash bulbs like heat lightning on the steps outside. They will have known a little of pomp and circumstance. And it is no bad thing to know.[14]

The second quotation showing an appreciation of commencement comes from a senior who confesses to having looked ahead to her own commencement as a "time and money-wasting device offered for the enjoyment of parents and alumni," but who, upon attending her commencement found meaning in it:

As the psychological impact of graduating begins to hit me, however, I realize that this, much like weddings and funerals, is a rite-of-passage which I need in order to adjust to my new status as a full-fledged adult alumna. College is a peculiar state of existence to which I have become very attached. To simply pack my bags and walk away at this point would be extremely painful, and anti-climatic, I realize now. This transition from college to the outside world is a big one, and this ceremony is a decisive yet happy step toward making this change. It is a visual, participatory, ceremonial goodbye to people, places, and a stage of life, and I think it is needed.[15]

Although, ideally, celebration should arise spontaneously out of the very joyful maturity that is the essence of a community of endeavor and common discovery, it can be valuable as recollection and reenactment even when it is more of a formalized expectation than a spontaneous one. The communities of which we are a part sometimes serve us well by cajoling us into those ventures that are likely to be appreciated only in retrospect. Persons are not made free only when they are allowed to do as they please; they can also be liberated when they are led to embrace new experiences within an ongoing community of purposive activity. In that relationship they often find themselves pleased to have done what they have had to do, grateful that an initial reluctance did not become the cause of a permanent loss.

Moreover, the test as to whether any one individual should participate in celebrations and ceremonies should not be merely whether that individual gets, or expects to get, a private uplift from doing so. Participation contributes to the possibility that some (or all) of the other participants can experience the benefits of the occasion. If our senior's classmates had not been at her commencement she would not have experienced her uplift. There may be no communal obligation to watch TV, but there are communal obligations to assist at celebrations.

The modern pluralistic campus marked by diversity may have special difficulties deciding about its mode of celebration. Religiously sectarian celebration is suspect in almost all except the most explicitly confessional contexts. Symbolism borrowed from the patriotic motif is marginally appropriate, since much of it celebrates military prowess or national hegemony. The vibrant experiences of community associated with ethnic identity are real enough, but only in rare instances are they likely to catch up an entire campus in their meaning. Yet, these difficulties must not cause the academy to abandon the search for ways to celebrate the central and guiding reasons for its own existence. The community of intellect is no less a potential object of loyalty and achievement of significance than the many lesser groupings that do find ways to affirm, in ceremony and festival, the significance of their own being.

Frolic and celebration are not the end or consummation of the academic experience. They are not even its primary means of self-definition. But neither are they mere addenda or incidental decorations that may, or may not, be worth caring about. They are crucial means of setting the main concern in perspective, of embracing it with festive joyfulness, of keeping it from both superficiality and presumption. They embody tradition, help sustain ethos, and enhance the possibility of self-discovery. They are important in making the main endeavour—the growth of the self through the pursuit of knowledge and learning—less unidimensional, more zestful. And they can contribute to a depth and richness of experience that gives a transformed quality to those intellectual tasks that are the central responsibilities of the academy.

NOTES

1. Harvey Cox, *The Feast of Fools: A Theological Essay on Festivity and Fantasy* (Cambridge: Harvard University Press, 1969), 7.

68   2. Charles Reich, *The Greening of America* (New York: Random House, 1970).

3. David L. Miller, *Gods and Games: Toward a Theology of Play*, (Cleveland: World, 1970), 13.

4. Rubem Alves, "Play, or How to Subvert the Dominant Values," in *Union Seminary Quarterly Review*, (Fall 1970), 55.

5. Ibid.

6. Robert E. Neale, *In Praise of Play: Toward a Psychology of Religion* (New York: Harper and Row, 1969), 97.

7. The modern academic sabbatical seems to fit this pattern, even as to its usual timing.

8. George B. Leonard, *Education and Ecstasy* (New York: Delacorte, 1968), 125.

9. Jacques Barzun, *The House of Intellect* (New York: Harper and Brothers, 1959), 125.

10. Ibid., 254f.

11. Ross Snyder, *Contemporary Celebration* (Nashville: Abingdon, 1971), 17.

12. Slater, *The Pursuit of Loneliness: American Culture at the Breaking Point* (Boston: Beacon Press, 1970), 55.

13. Wearing of gowns is not as traditional as might be supposed, since the use of academic regalia on such occasions came into practice in America only late in the nineteenth century, but that does not necessarily invalidate the point made in the quotation.

14. James J. Kilpatrick, "Commencement: Dying Tradition," *Roanoke Times*, 10 June 1971, 6.

15. Heidi McClellan, "The End of Something Special," *Oberlin Alumni Magazine*, July/August 1973, 6.

CHAPTER SIX

Grading and Growth

THE APPRAISAL OF PERFORMANCE
IN RELATION TO GROWTH

Life in community provides both the hazards and the satisfactions that go with the appraisal of performance. Community is weak where there are no standards of expectation. It can be destroyed where such standards are unfairly imposed or haphazardly enforced. Accidentally formed and loosely amalgamated groups take notice only of extreme deviations and gross misbehavior. We do not tell strangers about their idiosyncrasies, nor stand on the street corner and stop those who pass by to comment on their appearance or mannerisms. The spectators at a public game do not expect to be judged—not very hard at least—by the quality of their cheering. But the players on the team expect to have their skills scrutinized—not always gently—by the coach. Such scrutiny produces not only playing skills, but personal growth.

As groups come to be defined by distinct expectations, as they focus on the achievement of particular purposes, members are increasingly under pressure to behave or to perform in certain ways. Moreover, as communities grow complex the informalities of appraisal—immediate, frequently ruthless, yet surprisingly supportive in certain intimate relationships—give way to more formal procedures for judging behavior and evaluating achievement. Professionals (such as doctors, accountants, engineers, and teachers) have their competency formally tested before they can practice and are continually judged in their performance according to standards that are set up either by the society-at-large or by a professional guild. Professionalism is defunct where there is no scrutiny of performance.

The appraisal of performance has long been a central aspect of the academic experience. While the onus of daily recitations has all

70   but passed, most academic work still entails interim evaluations and final scrutiny. We should not expect otherwise, since learning is a purposive activity, and the learning community is one of deliberate expectations. All the way from primary school through graduate school a student's work is appraised. Under appropriate conditions such appraisal contributes to self-identity and maturation.

THREE KINDS OF APPRAISAL

Robert Paul Wolff has provided us with three terms for thinking about appraisal. The first of these terms is *criticism*, which he defines as the "analysis of a product or performance for the purpose of identifying and correcting its faults or reinforcing its excellences." The second is *evaluation*, which is "the measuring of a product or performance against an independent and objective standard of excellence." The third is *ranking*, which involves "a relative comparison of the performances of a number of students for the purposes of determining a linear order of comparative excellence."[1]

Wolff acknowledges the importance of criticism in the educational process, because without internal and external disciplines energies cannot be focused nor skills and style acquired. But he also believes that evaluation is less educationally meaningful because "once a teacher has shown a student how he can state an argument more cogently, express an insight with greater felicity of phrasing, or muster evidence more persuasively for a conclusion, nothing is gained educationally by adding the words 'good' or 'bad.' "[2] The distinction between criticism and evaluation prompted Wolff to advance the radical suggestion that ranking, by which people are sorted out for the award of scarce privileges—like admission to college on the basis of a high school record or to graduate school on the basis of a college record—is mainly an economic device and should therefore be abandoned. In its place he suggested the use of a lottery system to select from among all those with the requisite minimal qualifications the persons to be admitted to college and graduate school.[3]

Wolff's proposal stems from his belief that it is educationally productive to make appraisal less threatening. By eliminating or submerging the judgmental elements—removing terms like "good" and "bad" from pedagogical interaction and doing away with ranking altogether—more emphasis can be put on criticism, the essential heart of pedagogy.

Instead of drawing the line, as Wolff tended to do, between criticism and judgment, others have drawn a line between judgment and ranking. Thus, the so-called Newman Report, issued in March

1971, accepted the legitimacy of both criticism and evaluation, declaring that "grades recognize and reward academic achievement."[4] However, it criticized ranking, which places the teacher in a difficult (indeed, an illegitimate) role. This report contended that certification is the cause of much pedagogical difficulty because it requires the use of requirements and examinations. "As resentment toward these practices has grown," the report observed, "it has become increasingly difficult to combine the roles of teacher and judge. We have seen many students who have rejected formal teaching and learning altogether because they reject the arbitrary authority which faculty members and administrators hold over their lives."[5]

Proposals to separate criticism from evaluation or to separate criticism and evaluation from ranking were advanced with great urgency in the tumultuous years of student unrest. Such proposals were advocated in the effort to direct attention to learning subject matter instead of earning a grade. It must be admitted that anxiety about evaluation and ranking can introduce extrinsic motivations into the learning experience. It is the case that modes of appraisal that draw comparisons too blatantly are frequently associated with an elitist arrogance that poisons interpersonal relationships. Those with the best scores are often tempted to sneer at or lord it over less—(is the right term "accomplished," or is it "fortunate"?)—associates. On the surface, at least, it is plausible to suppose that something can be gained from eliminating grading as evaluation and ranking from the pedagogical relationship.

While it is tempting to think that much of the anxiety that is dysfunctional to genuine interest in learning might be eliminated by such a strategy, the matter deserves a second look. Consider, for instance, the story told by John Gardner about a military commander during World War II who made it an announced policy to recommend every qualified man in his unit for officer's candidate school. This policy did away with quotas, rankings, and comparisons (except, of course, between the qualified and the unqualified). But the consequences of this policy were to undermine morale. Morale deteriorated because those who were not recommended for promotion no longer had an excuse for their fate. Under the older scheme those left behind "were relatively happy as long as they could say to themselves that they were enlisted men because this is an unjust world, or because the military services do not value ability."[6] Under an announced policy of recommending for advancement every qualified individual (rather than simply the most outstanding) those left behind were shorn of the comforting defense that bad luck or favoritism rather than their own incompetence had prevented their advancement.

72   Another way of addressing the problems raised by ranking—
which is often, particularly when based on personal judgments, an
inexact and uncertain process—is to strive for objective and standardized measurements. Administered on a uniform basis to a wide group
of candidates, standardized tests supposedly eliminate the favoritism
that may creep into relationships between teachers and students. A
high score on a test prepared and administered by an outside agency,
such as the statewide regents examinations in some states, cannot be
explained on a "teacher's pet" theory of rewards.

But the externalization and objectification of testing does not
eliminate anxiety and may create other problems. For instance, many
feel that standardized tests, such as SAT's, favor particular groups.
Such standardized tests have increasingly been charged with being
weighted against minorities and even with being heavily disposed to
favor males. Group distortion can replace the danger of individual
distortion in the awarding of scores.[7] Moreover, the degree of objectivity such tests attain is likely to vary with the extent to which they
measure largely quantifiable achievements. It is far more difficult to
determine creativity and motivation than to assess narrowly defined
information and clearly definable skills. To acknowledge this is to
realize that decisions about individuals should never depend solely
upon the results of such tests even if they are more reliable in measuring some capacities than are personal judgments.

The objectification of appraisal, even if it could be completely
achieved, would not eliminate the anxiety associated with being
ranked. Indeed, if the presumption of objectivity is heightened to
the extent that test results are considered unassailable, the harsh
judgmentalism that is the destructive side of appraisal can seem even
more warranted and thus even more threatening. When allowances
can no longer be made for the possibility of random factors in an
evaluation system, ranking takes on the spector of an immutable
decree.

Appraisals of performance become dysfunctional to the academic
process when they degenerate into a harsh judgmentalism. The "put-
down" that is often characteristic of the academic experience can be a
form of sadism that devastates the spirit of those who are its victims
and corrupts those who are its perpetrators. It carries criticism beyond
the range of helpfulness, of considered and balanced advice. It often
marks an atmosphere of disdain which some academics seem to relish
and others are afraid to challenge. Leonard Kriegel, describing his
graduate school experience, has caught its mood astutely:

Competition was the single law of life that we all acknowledged.
Those who accepted a predatory approach to the world would

have been perfectly at home in Furnald Hall. I cannot remember, even on neighborhood street corners populated with edgy adolescents, individuals who so highly valued the put-down. There were times when I sincerely believed that the sole purpose of intellectualism was to serve as a verbal blade designed to cut the world down to size. . . .

The belligerence was in the air we breathed. What good were you if you could not manipulate language to advance your own reputation? . . . We did not even have the courage to admit our need to dominate.[8]

The tensions between graduate students that Kriegel describes are certainly not present to the same extent in every institution. Whereas in some schools students have even removed library materials so as to deprive others of their availability (thus increasing a competitive advantage), in other schools they may study together and otherwise demonstrate considerable mutuality. The difference between the two environments is not that one institution has appraisals of performance but the other does not, but rather that mutual support has been developed in the ethos of one place but not in the ethos of the other. The development of a supportive ethos is one of the ingredients in community, and one of the necessary elements in maximizing the growth of the self.

What is true of student cultures in some circumstances can be equally true of faculty relationships. Riesman refers to the malicious interaction that has often been generated by faculty since competition for retention and tenure has become particularly strong.[9] Moreover, the current situation, in which the American academy is presented with an oversupply of potential faculty members, has given colleges and universities the power to treat candidates and those on probationary appointment with haughty disregard. The last decade has produced many a horror story about the treatment of those who have not yet been tenured.

BALANCING JUDGMENT WITH ACCEPTANCE

The experience of judgment must be surrounded with nurturing reinforcement. Speaking of the need to balance judgment with mutuality and acceptance in the creation and sustenance of community, Clyde A. Holbrook observed.

Without the full acceptance of the other, we would only have carping criticism; without judgment and discrimination in respect to the other, we would have only sentimental alliance.

The "two" must hold together, accepting and loving in such a way that each knows that he is valued for himself, with all his faults and follies, yet judged in such a manner that he understands that he is not loved either *for* his faults or *in spite of* them, but *in* the faults which at any given moment are part of him.[10]

The simultaneous maximization of judgment and acceptance intensifies community, whereas the heightening of either without the other destroys it. A community anxious to be supportive is flabby without judgment just as a community in which judgment is operative can be harsh without acceptance. That being the case, all strategies for dealing with the problem of appraisal in the academic world that depend upon the elimination of judgment should be just as suspect as efforts to make appraisal overly intense. Even if efforts to soften the impact of appraisal by lowering expectations functioned to reduce anxiety, they would not necessarily promote growth. Actually, judgments of performance are crucial ingredients in providing authentic "buildups," and should not be associated only with "put-downs." They are potential instruments for creating, and not merely threats to the existence of, community.

But for judgments to be helpful, for appraisals to have credibility, for criticisms to be pedagogically productive, they must come from those whose own abilities have survived the test of scrutiny. Bernard Meland has rightly perceived the contrast between being mentored by greatness and merely being intimidated by arrogance. According to Meland, being confronted by greatness can be a transformative experience, but being cowed by threats only breeds resentments.[11] Those who are confronted by greatness know a kind of judgment, but they respond with resolves to strain toward new accomplishments. Those who are badgered by power only wait to strike back.

The symbiotic balance advocated by Holbrook and implied by Meland has to be present in the life of the community; it is not something to be achieved solely by a resolve on the part of the individual. Philip Slater, acknowledging the value and importance of the experience of judgment, points out how difficult it is to deal with on a merely private basis. He suggests that communal structures, even authoritarian communal structures, help to relieve the individual of the burden of moderating her or his responses privately.[12] Institutions of learning should pay attention, therefore, to the communal systems of support and reinforcement that need to accompany systems of appraisal.

The manner in which theologians, particularly those in classical Protestantism, have wrestled with the relationships between virtue and grace may offer a suggestive paradigm for helping to understand the need for a close connection between judgment and acceptance in pedagogical evaluation. A theology of grace emphasizes the importance of acceptance by declaring that persons are not judged on the basis of their merits, but rather are loved by God in a free and unmerited way. On the surface such a declaration of grace seems to undercut the impulse to be morally faithful—why bother to be good if it does nothing to enhance the prospects of being saved? But curiously, it turns out that the very abrogation of the demand to be virtuous as a condition of earning salvation actually enhances the freedom to be virtuous as an act of joyful response. A trusting abandon becomes possible that is more likely to produce fidelity than is an anxious legalism. In making the element of acceptance primary, theologies of grace do not eliminate the element of judgment, but instead transform its consequences for those upon whom it is visited. The repudiation of judgment belongs to antinomianism, not to schemes of grace.

Similar experiential dynamics can operate in the process of balancing acceptance and judgment in pedagogical situations. The stronger the signals of affirmation, the more possible it becomes to render appraisals without producing anxiety and rancor. The sense of acceptance is not dependent upon the evaluating process, nor will it be altogether credible without it. Criticism (which has an element of judgment woven into it) must be conveyed along with affirmation and acceptance before appraisal can be a source of growth. Just as in theology there is no place for "cheap grace," so in learning there is little promise of "easy achievement."

THE SPECIAL PROBLEM OF GRADING

The implications of this general perspective apply widely in the academic experience, particularly to grading. Grading is a formalized and institutionalized procedure that may be involved in all three dimensions of appraisal: criticism, evaluation, and ranking. It can also become an instrument of control and punishment. Because it is potentially so threatening, it has been a much-discussed topic within the educational world.[13] Efforts to achieve a system of grading that will be entirely satisfactory regardless of the conditions under which it is used are probably doomed to failure. That may explain why grading was attacked, and often abandoned, during the upheavals of the sixties. But it also indicates why grading has a place in the academic community and has tended to come back even in those institutions that sought to abandon it or to modify its impact. The important issues

76   concern the manner in which grading is employed, and not whether or not it is used.

A system of grading ought to used as an instrument of growth within a community of support. When a teacher creates and sustains relationships with students that provide assurances of interest and support, the teacher's appraisals will be taken more readily than if an adversarial relationship has developed. The prerogative of the teacher to make evaluations has both a structural legitimation in an office and a more personal root in the manner in which a teacher relates to students. The personal roots depend upon many factors, but one of the most important is the extent to which—by the manner in which grading is done—the students realize the teacher cares about their progress and growth. Wolff is correct in his suggestion that criticism— that is, the making of observations that are designed to be helpful in learning—is particularly valuable and important. But more than mere criticism is needed. The sense of support and encouragement must also be present. The rendering of grades without feedback is pedagogically slipshod and professionally arrogant. But criticism without any indication of evaluation or ranking can send only a truncated signal.

The ability to provide good feedback is a high mark of professional skill and a moral obligation of a mentor. The practice of doing so is not cultivated as profoundly nor used as widely as it should be. The practice of merely placing a grade on a written assignment without taking the pains to indicate the basis on which the grade has been awarded is an appalling instance of professional irresponsibility—no less so because it is so widespread. Even when grades are not used, verbal feedback can consist of ejaculatory condemnations that are far too cryptic and may be as unsatisfactory as numbers or letters that are awarded without attendant comment. Good feedback acknowledges what is commendable about a piece of work, suggests where and why it is deficient, and explains how it could be improved. Institutions owe it to teachers to keep teaching loads (both in terms of class size and number of preparations) low enough to enable the teacher to provide adequate feedback—but teachers in turn need to take the obligation with utmost seriousness. They must realize the need to provide encouragement along with criticism, reinforcement along with ranking.

Feedback may be even more important in Pass/Fail grading systems than in letter or numerical ranking systems. One reason for going to unranked grading is to separate criticism (as helpful and suggestive guidance) from evaluation (as scoring or ranking). But the elimination of the latter does not necessarily increase the extent of the former. A professor inclined to be lazy renders an even greater disservice by putting a "Pass" grade on a paper without the benefit of comments than by putting a letter grade that indicates at least a range of, if not the reasons for, a particular evaluation as to its worth.

Written discursive assessments, such as are required in some institutions where there are no letter grades, would seem to enhance the likelihood that feedback will mark the appraisal of performance. Appraisals made in the discursive mode require thoughtfulness and individually considered evaluations. However, transcripts from institutions where prose evaluations are utilized may be just as devastating to a student's prospects as are numerical averages. Furthermore, they are less easy to appraise by those who have not shared in the interaction from which the comments arose. Perhaps they enable the reader of the transcript to see the person about whom it has been prepared as an individual, and not merely as a statistic, but that result depends upon the care with which they are prepared.

The worst arrangement is to have a "Credit only" scheme without any narrative description or indications of progress and achievement—which, alas, is exactly what some institutions adopted in the sixties and seventies. Granted that a scheme of undifferentiated credits (with no record of a student's failures) may offer release from the competitive pressures associated with ranking, after such release has been "enjoyed" and an individual looks back upon the record, will not an "all-Cr" transcript have something of the character of a mere approving shrug? It may tell little, even to the student whose performance it certifies, about strengths and limitations, about the interplay between effort and achievement. A smile of appreciation (the A), a scowl of dissatisfaction (the C or D), may be far more human than a deadpan face.

If no grade were given except by means of a face-to-face exchange between teacher and student, the experience of appraisal could be transformed. In many cases this kind of encounter is logistically impossible to implement and compromises have to be made. It is probably feasible to adopt a policy in which no student who has kept trying is flunked without a conference, or at least a personal note of explanation that reaches the student before the report from the registrar. Another method of maintaining the interaction between the supportive and the evaluative might be to ask students to give their own informed appraisal of their achievements in a course prior to the determination of the final grade. Where there is a deep difference between the student's perception of accomplishments and the teacher's—something that would probably occur but rarely (at least if there has been adequate feedback throughout the course)—a conference would be in order. Such a conference—or a written exchange of views—would

78   help to keep judgment combined with acceptance, and could be fully
as rewarding to the instructor as to the student.

ON THE EVALUATION OF FACULTY

The focus of the preceding remarks is on the traditional grading of
students by faculty members, but the principle that judgment should
be wedded to acceptance is no less important in considering the evaluation of faculty performance by students. Since this process has
become widespread and has been instituted as a palliative for pedagogical ills, it is important to think about conditions under which it
may contribute to the health and joy of the learning relationship
and the ways it may, as in the misuse of traditional grading, be
counterproductive to the sense of community that all members of
academic institutions should be privileged to enjoy.

Here, for instance, is a statement by one advocate of student
participation in evaluation:

> Student participation should be viewed as an essential element
> in institutional evaluation. If officials of the university are inter-
> ested in the effect their policies are having on the consumers,
> that is, the students, they should be willing to include that group
> in their deliberations. If the students are not happy with the way
> things have been going, their voting behavior will reflect that
> dissatisfaction and will raise some important issues which other-
> wise may never get considered.[14]

In this statement, which is not atypical, commercial metaphors and
power considerations are central. Whatever the faults of traditional
grading practices in which faculty evaluate students, they are premised on a professional model, in which the service of a clientele is
paramount. Those who advocate student evaluations of faculty often
change the premises to that of a power model. Seldom does one
encounter a discussion of the ways that student evaluation of faculty
could enhance the joys and satisfactions of the professor or become
means of helping the students to appreciate some of the factors
involved in making creative criticism. Unsigned evaluations can even
become a means of legitimizing little more than griping.

Moreover, while the effect of ranking and grading on the destin-
ies of students is cited as an occasion of anxiety, it is not always
realized that the effect of student evaluations of professors can also
intensify anxiety whenever they are used as decisive components in
decisions about merit and tenure. There are also rather dubious practices that arise in the attempt to render course evaluations strictly

objective. In one common practice, students are asked to rank professors on several traits on a scale from zero to five—though they are left
entirely on their own to determine the meaning of each step on the
scale. The instruments are then fed into a computer and the average
of the ratings is reported to the third decimal place, even for classes
with fewer that fifteen students! Such a practice is hardly consistent
with any good theory of measurement.

There are ways of evaluating teaching that can be a welcome and
supportive experience for faculty. Master teachers can be used to
facilitate dialogue between other teachers and their students. Skillful
interlocutors can create conditions of candor and openness in which
students will feel free, either individually or in a group, to make
procedural suggestions for the conducting of a course, to register a
sense of disappointment, and to dialogue about what is being accomplished in a particular class.

Moreover, such matters are most useful if they are introduced
into the process in a sufficiently timely manner to result in adjustments
before a course is completed. It is true that the required candor is
difficult to generate, not merely because students may have been
inculcated with a habit of subservience, but also because nothing can
entirely erase the difference between the two sides of the instructional
desk. Preoccupation with constituency-defined power relationships
does little to help combine acceptance with judgment. Course evaluations that are submitted anonymously and used only by deans and
other authorities to judge teaching effectiveness have little role in
enhancing community.

The ideal situation is one in which faculty members proceed with
a full sensitivity to the needs, hopes, and expectations of students—
something students can help the faculty members to develop. At the
same time, students should see in faculty members persons with
needs, hopes, and expectations of their own. The social chemistry
involved is subtle, requires a high degree of trust, and ultimately is
dependent upon the reality of community.

Whatever else may be said of the dynamics involved, the mere
reversal of roles does not overcome the unfairness in hegemony.
Robert Jay Lifton has commented on the dangers in thinking of revolutions merely as role reversals. He cautions against a "generational
totalism" that assumes youth power knows no limits and has a monop-
oly on relevance.[15] Although Paulo Freire, advocate of radical pedagogy and promoter of revolutionary change through education, contends that only the oppressed have the power to effect liberation, he
also argues that the revolutionary process must benefit both parties
and not consist merely of role reversal.[16]

80   The tensions between the one who judges and those who are judged, between the one who evaluates and those who are evaluated, are overcome only by the creation of a new relationship that alters the quality of life for both. That new relationship must entail a balanced synthesis between acceptance and judgment. Productivity and creativity are not cultivated only by the stick of evaluation; they are equally dependent upon the carrot of affirmation.

     The supportiveness appropriate for students has certain essential qualities, while that necessary for faculty has others. Reece McGee has pointed out how necessary supportiveness is to the morale of faculty. Speaking of an institution's responsibility to those who are not outstanding stars, who do not get outside offers to enhance their image at strategic intervals, and who sometimes offer less to the institution than more gifted colleagues, he counsels, "The deliberate strafing of the immobile, or even overlooking them simply because they have no power to force the institutional hand, although it poses no danger to them particularly, offers symbolic threat to faculty who are not in their position. 'If they treat anyone that way,' the musing runs, 'what protection will I have when I am through or old?'".[17]

     Administrators and others who take for granted the value of merit evaluation as a means of ensuring faculty performance—or, negatively stated, of "discouraging the dead wood," need to ponder this admonition seriously. Often, an unsupportive use of merit review—one that never affords encouragement—generally discourages rather than eliminates the mediocre person, and by discouraging performance can even tend to make that person's performance worse. If original selection criteria are sufficiently high and skillfully utilized, then a faculty might better be thought of as cream than as underbrush. An institution needs to worry not only about trimming away the dead wood, but about the danger of putting cream through the separator so many times that it sours.

     We must be concerned about excellence and quality achievement in all members of the academic community. Such excellence is most likely to emerge when discipline is associated with trust in the integrity of the community that imposes it. Creativity and excellence cannot be produced merely by criticism and carping; but neither can they be produced by dissolving expectations. They can only come from the sense that achievement is valued. Grading is one of the important ways of making that evident.

     John Gardner tells of a Marine Corps officer whose success in training recruits was enviable. Speaking of the discipline in Marine Corps training, this officer observed, "It isn't discipline that makes the difference. It's discipline plus morale. When I teach those kids what it means to be a Marine they grow eight inches taller. Without **81** that discipline wouldn't mean a thing. When we finish with these men, they believe in themselves."[18] Needless to say, an officer who says that reinforces the self-esteem in the recruits and engenders their confidence in the possibility of their success. Dare any institution of learning do less in dealing with its constituencies?

NOTES

1. Paul Wolff, *The Ideal of the University* (Boston: Beacon Press, 1969), 59–63.

2. Ibid., 64.

3. Ibid., 143.

4. U.S.Department of Health, Education, and Welfare, *Report on Higher Education and Welfare*, March 1971 (Washington, D.C.: U. S. Government Printing Office, 1971), 41.

5. Ibid., 42.

6. John W. Gardner, *Excellence: Can We Be Equal and Excellent Too?* (New York: Harper and Brothers, 1961), 72f.

7. To point out this possible aspect of standardized testing is not necessarily to suggest that such tests should be abandoned. It may suggest that such tests should be devised with a greater sensitivity to the identities of those who take them and that their results should be interpreted with greater awareness of the dangers in taking raw scores definitively, particularly in a pluralistic society such as the United States.

8. Leonard Kriegel, *Working Through: A Teacher's Journey in the Urban University* (New York: Saturday Review Press, 1972), 51f.

9. David Riesman, *On Higher Education:The Academic enterprise in an Age of Rising Student Consumerism* (San Francisco: Jossey-Bass, 1980), 280.

10. Clyde A. Holbrook, *Faith and Community: A Christian Existentialist Approach* (New York Harper and Brothers, 1959), 130.

11. Meland, *Higher Education and the Human Spirit* (Chicago: University of Chicago Press; rpt, (Seminary Cooperative Bookstore, n.d.), 95.

12. Philip E. Slater, *The Pursuit of Loneliness: American Culture at the Breaking Point* (Boston: Beacon Press, 1979), 22f.

13. For a thumbnail account of the evolution of grading practices, including efforts to make the process increasingly fair, see John S. Brubacher and Willis Rudy, *Higher Education in Transition: A History of American Colleges and Universities 1636–1976* 3rd Edition (New York: Harper and Row, 1968), 94–97.

14. Robert S. Powell, Jr., "Student Power and Educational Goals," in *Power and Authority: Transformation of Campus Governance*, Harold L. Hodgkinson and L. Richard Meeth (eds.) (San Francisco: Jossey-Bass, 1971), 81.

15. See Robert Jay Lifton, *Boundaries: Psychological Man in Revolution* (New York: Random House, Vintage Books, 1967), 107f.

82   **16.** Paulo Freire, *Pedagogy of the Oppressed* (New York: Herder and Herder, 1971), 42.

17. Reece McGee, *Academic Janus: The Private College and Its Faculty* (San Francisco: Jossey-Bass, 1971), 214f.

18. Gardner, *Excellence*, 104.

PART TWO

The Discovery and Dissemination of Knowledge and Culture

CHAPTER SEVEN

The Curriculum: Debates about Boundaries and Methodologies

The central responsibility of the academic community is the discovery, refinement, and transmission of information and insight, the combination of which constitutes knowledge. This responsibility entails the continual reexamination of the origins, development, and foundational premises of the various branches of human understanding. If the stewardship of knowledge is to be pursued faithfully and to good purpose, attention must be given to the nature of knowledge and the interrelationships of its systemic parts, to the premises on which it rests, and to the methods it employs to do its work. No individual scholar can make more than a fragmentary contribution to this overall agenda, but every scholar must aim to make that individual contribution so as to interact with other scholars in a way that gives significant cohesion to the total work of the university.

THE MORPHOLOGY OF KNOWLEDGE

Knowledge as used in this discussion denotes a broad and sweeping complex of those ideas and insights that enable us to understand reality in cognitive terms. Quite understandably, the academy devotes a great deal of attention to the warrantability of those ideas, that is, to whether they are true, and on what premises. Such epistemological concerns are important, and they will be examined in the next chapter. But many issues concerning academic policy and pedagogical strategy depend upon considerations that involve the morphology of knowledge. Thus, the ways knowledge is organized by the academy need to be examined as much as do questions regarding its correctness or adequacy. This chapter will be concerned with the forms and contours knowledge takes. Do its many constituent parts, particularly as embodied in the various disciplines of academic endeavour, interrelate? Is knowledge a structure of coherences meshing into a unitary

86   system of interrelationships or is it a loose collection of incommensurate schema that defy conceptual integration?

Both of these ways of looking at knowledge have advocates in
the educational world. For instance, Allan Bloom, diagnosing the ills
of contemporary education, reveals a preference for the unitary model,
which he sees as threatened.

> The crisis of liberal education is a reflection of a crisis at the peaks
> of learning, an incoherence and incompatibility among the first
> principles with which we interpret the world, an intellectual
> crisis of the greatest magnitude, which constitutes the crisis of
> our civilization. But perhaps it would be true to say that the crisis
> consists not so much in this incoherence but in our incapacity to
> discuss or even recognize it. Liberal education flourished when
> it prepared the way for the discussion of a unified view of nature
> and man's place within it, which the best minds debated on the
> highest level. It decayed when what lay beyond it were only
> specialties, the premises of which do not lead to any such vision.[1]

In contrast to Bloom, Edward J. Bloustein, convinced that knowledge
is important for facing the intricate social, political, and economic
problems of the contemporary world in its unique particularities, had
this to say about its ultimate quality:

> Contemporary knowledge is more a congeries of discrete and
> specialized truths than a unified system; and the congeries keeps
> growing and growing in size and complexity. Moreover, the
> extent of what we know is such that few men can profess to
> anything but a relatively narrow segment of the body of our
> knowledge.[2]

Neither of these views should be identified with any particular
time period or with any particular branch of learning. The unitary
view was especially strong during the Middle Ages, when theology
was considered the "queen" of the sciences and the capstone of a
coherent whole. Both friends and foes of theology have subsequently
assumed that the unified view rests upon belief in an ultimate and
transcendent being, whereas the atomistic view is a product of scientific empiricism and the cultural pluralism that has arisen in its train.
But this account of the matter is overly simplified, if not misleading.
Many theologians have portrayed the will of God as an unpredictable
and situationally perceived factor that functions with respect to fortuitous circumstances that are beyond the reach of structured conceptualization. They have used history rather than nature as the clue for

thinking about the divine, and have contended that conceptualizations of the divine that suggest a freedom to deal at will with historical contingency portray a far profounder ultimacy than do the conceptions that are dependent upon immutability and coherent structure.

Scholars in other disciplines also differ among themselves about the same contrast that religious thinkers debate. Many scientists—as did Albert Einstein—believe that scientific theories must somehow fit into a unitary whole and that to the extent that any of them do not do so, they must be revised. Others, like Niels Bohr, have been content to let incommensurate theories (for example, corpuscle and wave theories of light) stand alongside each other, since they complement each other as explanations of certain natural phenomena. Similarly, students of law have long debated whether there is a general structure of mandates determined by innate necessities for just and orderly human interaction, or whether laws are merely the expedient, even the arbitrary, impositions of those with the power to enforce certain demands upon particular jurisdictions. Many social scientists have cherished, as an ideal, a unified system giving coherence and wholeness to theories about society, while others have stressed the importance of specific empirical data, acknowledged to be valid on the basis of agreed-to procedures for observing a specific range or set of phenomena without a tight commensurability with other sets or ranges of data.

These different presumptions about the nature of knowledge lie at the root of some of the most extensive debates in the contemporary academy. Those debates concern the usefulness and legitimacy of disciplines and specialty fields as the means for parceling knowledge into tractable units for instructional and administrative purposes and, even more frequently, the validity of so-called distribution requirements as the means of forcing students to undertake a course of study that exposes them to a broadly representative range of knowing. If one believes that knowledge is unified and coherent, a heavily required regimen of courses makes sense. But if one believes that knowledge is available to us only in discrete entities that do not necessarily relate to one another, and that it is impossible for any one person to have more than a partial grasp of what is known, then a free elective system may seem more legitimate.

THE DISCIPLINES AS BRANCHES OF KNOWLEDGE: THE SUBSTANTIVE ISSUE

The medieval university divided its curriculum of general learning into the trivium (grammar, rhetoric, and logic/dialectic) and the quadrivium (astronomy, arithmetic, geometry, and music). The relationships between these protodisciplines was such that together they were

88 considered to form a whole and each student was expected to become proficient in all seven branches of learning. Some early American education was organized by classes rather than by disciplines, and at times a single tutor took the same group sequentially though the entire four years of instruction.[3] As the scope and complexity of knowledge has increased, no individual can compass more than a small segment of the known. Each discipline has become increasingly autonomous and less and less inclined toward or capable of relating its body of information and insights to those of other disciplines. As a result, the unity once possible to achieve in education has now been occluded, and disciplinary or field specialization has raised the specter of total fragmentation. Well-honed skill in understanding just one particular part of knowledge has frequently replaced the achievement of a general competence.[4] Is this a condition that must be reversed for the educational enterprise to regain its health, or is it something that can be accepted and even utilized to produce a variety of competencies, each of which is potentially valid and useful?

To explore this question involves a look at the nature of the disciplines. Two rather ordinary illustrations can provide possible analogies (or, perhaps, metaphors) for looking at how the disciplines relate to each other or to a more general structure of knowledge. Consider the difference between being the proprietor of a junkyard and being the curator of a museum. Both are interested in gathering items from the past. The junk dealer is interested in bulk aggregates. Culling and sorting may be used to make the retrieval of materials feasible; basically, however, practicality governs the handling of materials and what is functional in one junkyard may not be in another. In contrast, the curator of the museum is primarily concerned with arrangements that are governed by what a particular display seeks to portray. The way material is identified, classified, cataloged, and displayed determines the message or meaning of the entire undertaking. A chronological scheme might be used, or a topological one, but in either case an identifiable pattern, or scheme of coherence, determines how things are arranged. To be sure, some operational logic may be at work in the junkyard just as individualistic idiosyncrasies may be apparent in the arrangements of some museums. A junk dealer cannot be completely haphazard, nor the museum curator completely coherent. Even so, the purposes that each has in dealing with items from the past makes a difference in the procedures that are used to organize the items on hand.

Consider a different illustration. The books in most libraries are cataloged and shelved according to some classification scheme—Dewey Decimal or Library of Congress are the most prevalent options.

The reigning classification schemes arrange books according to the subject matters about which they are written. (Other arrangement schemes might be employed—a purely alphabetical scheme, for instance, or one based on the color of the dust jackets—but they might be better for bookstores than for libraries.) The classification scheme and the skill with which it is employed are both important in determining the usefulness of a library. What is significant is that, in most cases, the same books end up near each other as long as the classification scheme is based on subject-matter categories. While not every cataloger uses the same classification scheme in the same way—though increasingly clues are taken from master agencies—catalogers come up with generally similar arrangements. There is a logic to the structure of knowledge as embodied in library holdings that reflects a partial coherence. The classification scheme is not a mere accident nor is it used according to mere fancy. But neither is a classification scheme an immutable absolute that provides the only possible basis for a proper arrangement. A book may be placed in one location even though it would be equally significant in one or more other locations. Library classification schemes produce working coherences, not an order based on immutable first principles—yet those working coherences are important.

If we think of the disciplinary specialties within the academy as analogous to the schema that the curator of the museum employs to arrange holdings for display or to the classifications that the cataloger utilizes to place books in a library, these examples may help us to sense why both coherences and incoherences are found in curricular structures. The disciplines do place things of related interest into functional proximities. But, like the classification schemes of libraries, they sometimes create one set of coherences at the expense of possible alternative sets. Just as the classification schemes of libraries are most valid when they take subject matter (rather than something like book size or jacket color) as their controlling factor, so the disciplines are best developed when they interrelate subject matter in meaningful and workable patterns. But just as many books defy classification in a single place, so does much subject matter defy treatment by a single discipline. Therefore the disciplines cannot be considered immutable gestalts.

Some of the most perceptive analysts of the intellectual enterprise have suggested how we find a tension between coherence and incoherence even within various branches of learning. Thomas Kuhn, speaking of the different schools of thinking about natural phenomena present in the early, developmental stages of the sciences, notes the

90   differences that existed between their thought structures. Those differences were not due to the fact that one viewpoint was right and all
the others were wrong, but to "what we shall come to call their
incommensurable ways of seeing the world and practicing science in
it."[5] Kuhn acknowledges the importance of experience in shaping
thought patterns: "Observations and experience can and must drasti-
cally restrict the range of admissible scientific belief, else there would
be no science." But he also notes that "an apparently arbitrary element, compounded of personal and historical accident, is always a
formative ingredient of the beliefs espoused by a given scientific community at a given time."[6]

Michael Polanyi has underscored even more pointedly the element of personal disposition in the formation of knowledge.[7] As used
by Polanyi, the term "personal" does not mean merely individualistic,
but instead signifies fortuitous and unpredictable elements that are
bound up with the odysseys of individuals (or groups of persons) and
that combine to give one rather than another form to the patterns by
which knowledge is understood. Similar suggestions have come from
sociologists of knowledge, who stress the configurations rooted in
cultural variations rather than personal ones.

Noam Chomsky has suggested that there exists in the human
mind a universal and innate generative or transformational grammar
without which it would be impossible to construct languages,[8] but that
different societies have created different languages, thus indicating the
difficulty of translating that generative grammar into a single form.
Thus, differences between languages exist, but they are not so complete as to make it impossible to translate from one language to
another. If any academic discipline becomes so self-contained and
esoteric as to render it incapable of speaking to any of the other
disciplines it needs to be reconstituted.

THE DISCIPLINES IN RELATION TO GOVERNANCE: THE OPERATIONAL ISSUE

The disciplines do much to shape the methodologies considered
appropriate for exploring particular areas and formulating concepts
about them, but no discussion of the disciplinary fields would be
realistic if it regarded them merely as ways of structuring knowledge.
The disciplines exercise a good deal of quasi-official influence on the
certification of scholarly competence. Moreover, they determine dividing lines within the university and exercise resultant power over the
allocation of curricular and pedagogical resources. The relationship
between the two functions of the disciplines, the substantive and the

operational, has become increasingly complex as a result of both the knowledge explosion and the academic revolution. In so far as the disciplinary and specialty fields are substructurings of knowledge, that is, means of dividing knowledge into conceptual schemes of manageable coherences, they provide one set of benefits and create a corresponding set of problems. In so far as they are instruments of control or influence, they provide another set of benefits and create another set of problems.

Just as it is unwise to discount completely the significance of the disciplines for making the organization of knowledge manageable, so it is unwise to undervalue altogether the role of departments in governance and administration. Phrases that refer to the disciplines as "the epitome of selfish professional behavior" or to departmental-ization as "the rationalization of selfish guild interest" are sometimes employed to open the gates to wholesale and uncritical innovations. Such innovations may be useful in forging new conceptual inquiry, but they have to commend themselves on the basis of their capacity to illuminate issues and not merely for their novelty.

Since both subject matter and methodological distinctions are involved in the making of the disciplinary fields, and since both logical relationships and historical contingencies account for the groupings into which the curriculum is divided, how we think of curriculum design will depend to a considerable extent upon how we assess the relative importance of the coherences in substance and methodology in (and between) the disciplines in relation to the incoherences. The analysis of these matters may depend on how particular disciplines are understood and taught in any given institution and how the lines of power and influence have come to be drawn. Clearly, departments that grasp all the power they can muster and require majors to spend most of their academic careers taking courses located entirely within their orbit of influence need to be confronted. Even specialized librar-ies contain books in many classifications, and any librarian who decreed that patrons could read books with only one classification number would be severely castigated.

SOME ILLUSTRATIVE EXAMPLES

It is impossible here to offer an exhaustive analysis of the scope and place of the various disciplines, both as branches of knowledge and as instruments of organizational power. However, some examples will illustrate the issues and problems that often have to be considered in dealing with such matters.

Few disciplines in the traditional structuring of the curriculum appear to have clearer subject matter boundaries and agreements as to working procedures than do the three major natural sciences: physics, chemistry, and biology. But there are coherences and incoherences even in the delineations of the proper subject matter belonging to each of them. Many dictionary definitions of these sciences provide overlapping ideas as to their scope and nature. They reveal the complexities that can arise in attempting to delineate even these well-understood disciplines with clear parameters.

Not one of these disciplines studies substantive reality in its holistic entirety. It is impossible to demonstrate that their contents and structural features are purely logical, incontrovertibly reflective of objectively real divisions in the natural order, and destined to remain just as they now are for all pedagogical eternity. There are borderline subdisciplines like physical chemistry and organic chemistry that concentrate on special areas where a single disciplinary perspective is not adequate. Obviously, an overall knowledge of nature requires work in more than one of the natural sciences. But this is no argument for abolishing the departments that now teach these subjects as currently delineated. Of course, it may well be an argument for requiring students who wish to be proficient in one to study others as well, and also to be sensitized to the differences between them. Few of us would comfortable with a physician who is trained in biology but totally ignorant about the chemistry of the drugs he prescribes. An engineer who knows biology as well as physics and inorganic chemistry will likely be more sensitive to ecological concerns than one who does not. This logic must be carried even further. The physician must know about psychology and morality to be a wise practitioner in today's world since the physician must relate to patients as whole persons. The engineer must also know economics, morality, and aesthetics in order to make decisions than are broadly humane and not narrowly technological.

The complexities in the delineations of the disciplines can be explored further. The natural sciences, for instance, include a group of other disciplines that are associated with them for curricular purposes. Some of these disciplines—such as geology (earth sciences), botany, astronomy—are specialized subject areas closely related in methodology to the more prominent disciplines. These are sometimes grouped with physics, chemistry, and biology as lab sciences. But the disciplines lumped together under the rubric of natural sciences usually includes mathematics and computer science, whether grouped together in single department or separated in different departments.

These particular disciplines may employ far different intellectual methodologies than do the empirical lab sciences. They often pursue highly sophisticated intellectual inquiry that has its own uniqueness. They should not be truncated by treating them merely as service units to other disciplines.

Psychology furnishes a particularly interesting problem. In many schools it is administratively related to the natural sciences, particularly when it has a laboratory component. Many psychologists possibly feel their academic prestige is enhanced by being associated with natural sciences rather than with the social sciences. In other schools psychology is considered a social science. The field itself is marked by ideological divisions. There are psychologists, such as B. F. Skinner, whose view of their work places them close to natural scientists and there are others, such as Jerome Bruner, whose understanding of their discipline places them close to the humanities. In deciding the role that the study of psychology will play in a curriculum the approach taken to the study of psychology in any particular department has to be taken into account in assessing its value in a set of general distribution requirements.

Other disciplines present some of the same problems of scope and context as do the sciences. Many modern European languages, German, French, and Spanish, for example, provide the title both for a discipline and for a department assigned to teach it. But when an institution introduces the study of certain other languages, such as Chinese or Swahili, geographical designations are often employed for administrative purposes: hence, Asian studies, African studies. The different designations often reflect the administrative needs of a particular institution. For good and understandable reasons the study of the major European languages and the country or cultures in which they are spoken has had sufficient attention across the years to attract enough students and require enough teachers to make to make departmental structures workable. But, the introduction of new language fields does not begin with an equivalent interest. The area studies programs, which include language study within the matrix of a fuller program of studies including the history, cultural features, economic/ geographical characteristics, and political systems of particular regions, may make far more sense as broad educational agendas than the traditional classifications. Alas, sometimes they have a very difficult time legitimizing their identity or earning recognition as a component within a set of core requirements.

The study of language can vary greatly from a narrow training in grammar and vocabulary to broad investigations of linguistics,

94   literature, and culture. It may require a reasonably sustained immersion to move from the first to the second level of language learning. These factors bear significantly on the question as to what the inclusion of a language requirement means to a general education. Since the factors vary from department to department and from school to school, they often need to be assessed by particularities in a given department as well by as general considerations as to what the disciplines cover.

The teaching of philosophy can also vary greatly. In some departments philosophy is understood in a broad classical sense as a holistic inquiry into the nature of reality. In other departments it is understood in the more targeted sense of being a study of how knowledge claims are verified. Some departments seek to include both of these, as well as other, approaches. The role played by a philosophy component in a student's learning may depend both on the particular course or courses that the student takes and the perspective from which such courses are taught. Some treatments of logic, for example, have more kinship with mathematics or computer theory than with the humanities. Other courses in philosophy have subject matter and methodological kinships with the study of religious commitments and beliefs.

The relationship between the study of religion and other departments in the institution is particularly complex. Religion is almost always classified with the humanities. To be sure, the study of sacred literature constitutes an important part of the work and may have much in common with literary studies. The study of belief systems and moral ideals often involves subject matters and methodologies long associated with philosophy. Yet, the study of ritual, communal structures, and moral behavior is remarkably similar to what is done in the social sciences. The methodology utilized for the study of religion cannot be jammed without remainder into the humanities, and in many particulars depends for its adequacy on what is found in another group of disciplines. In many institutions the social scientists are interested in the study of religious phenomena, making interaction between them and the religion faculty at least as fruitful as interaction between the latter and the humanists. Such factors demonstrate both the validity and the limitation of the administrative lines that are used to place the disciplines in divisions, but they do not necessarily add up to a clear, unambiguous case for revamping structural relationships in any one particular way.

IMPLICATIONS FOR CURRICULUM DESIGN

If the subject-matter responsibilities of the disciplines and the divisions could be delineated with irrefutable clarity and unambiguous coherences, that might provide a distinct signal suggesting that the curriculum at every institution—at least in the matter of general education—

should very closely replicate that at every other institution. Or, if the present definitions of the disciplines were so obviously political and accidental as to indicate that curriculum design was determined purely by matter of power politics, that would suggest the impossibility of ever finding any commensurable qualities to the structuring of knowledge or the offerings of one institution and those of another. But, the situation with which we work is one in which there are meaningful patterns that each and every institution should feel an obligation to respect, yet in which there is room for variations that make different alternatives possible and even important. Learning would be impoverished if curriculums at all institutions—even those dealing with the same general subjects—were exactly identical. We would be confounded if curriculums had no interrelationships with each other. Therefore, it is necessary to work with the stuff of historical contingency and ambiguity, remembering that those who like these matters oversimplified make better partisans than scholars.

But how can the college or university do curricular planning in a way that is sufficiently alert to such a complex set of factors? An existing institution should always start with an assessment of the strengths and weaknesses of the way it presently handles the material. It can then adjust patterns according to current needs—though it is never easy to obtain agreement even about such a supposedly "neutral" topic as the strengths and weaknesses of the existing curriculum.

If, on the other hand, the institution is a new one, it may start with innovative programs and collegiums that define the relationships between different aspects of learning in unprecedented ways. The chief advantage of such new starts is that they force a rethinking of the many issues that are present with respect to the disciplinary structuring of knowledge and require those who teach to be self-conscious about their intentions. By casting scholars trained in traditional departmental patterns into new learning configurations, such innovative schemes can produce imaginative repatternings—though the work involved requires almost total dedication to this aspect of pedagogy and often seriously reduces the time and attention that teachers in such institutions can devote to scholarship in their disciplinary guild.

Every institution has to face, from time to time, the claim of new materials or new approaches. Consider a problem facing every alert institution. It is being increasingly recognized that the traditional academic disciplines have not done justice to the place and role of women in society nor to the place and role of blacks and other ethnic groups. There is a widespread concern to begin the long process of redressing these oversights by giving increased attention to the roles and contributions of the neglected groups. One pattern for doing this is to pay

96   attention to such concerns within the already established departments, making sure that each teacher includes the appropriate materials in each course. Another way is to create a new department (or program) devoted exclusively to the study of the neglected realms of experience.

The case for dealing with these new concerns within existing departmental structures assumes an inherent cohesion and presumptive validity to the present departmental structuring of higher education along disciplinary lines. It may also rest on a conviction that the neglect of the special concerns of these groups is a deficiency affecting all members of the academy and not merely those whose background and experiences have been neglected. History taught with reference only to the role of whites is not adequate. History taught only with the achievements of males in view deprives everyone of understanding, and not merely affronts the women whose story has been neglected.

The case for setting up special programs or new departments to address new concerns may very well rest largely upon operational considerations. Only if these special concerns are dealt with in special programs is there likely to be a sufficient impetus to pursue them vigorously. The peer pressures and reward schemes of the academic enterprise can fail to reinforce these agendas when they are subsumed under existing structures. Those who are concerned with advancing a deep and fuller treatment of neglected subject matters may need to use one strategy in one set of circumstances and another strategy in another—or even both strategies at once. It is simply impossible to argue that only one of the ways is educationally legitimate.

The growing impulse to teach ethics furnishes another example of the problems that arise in introducing new approaches. The study of ethics has almost never been designated as a discipline. It has most generally been subsumed under philosophy—where it is sometimes zealously explored, other times all but neglected. Ethics has sometimes been a focus of interest within the field of religious studies, where it is often given the designation "social ethics." To become credible in the teaching of social ethics entails doing a good deal of work in disciplines such as political science, sociology, and law—yet never being recognized as being a "true" member of those disciplines (not least because many of them have often eschewed value judgments). To be sure, every discipline can be concerned with ethical issues; therefore, it is sometimes suggested that there is no logical need for having ethics taught in a separate department because the value implications of a subject will be adequately dealt with by existing individual departments. But that is a bit like arguing that since every discipline is (or should be) concerned with its own origins, there is no warrant for having a history department.

If it does indeed turn out to be the case in a particular institution that each department is concerned with ethics and treats the value implications of its subject field with depth and understanding, that provides one pattern that can be fruitfully followed. It then becomes important to prompt departments to give full attention to that concern and translate it into meaningful pedagogy. But if there is no such concern, the situation is different. Then there is warrant for having a special program of ethical studies. Under some circumstances only the latter strategy will elicit interest, attach responsibility, and call attention to the importance of such study. The contemporary academy has yet to come to grips with how to teach ethics, and never will if it demands a perfect rationale as a precondition for doing so.

CROSS-DISCIPLINARY AND INTERDISCIPLINARY STUDIES

One way of increasing the sense of coherence in the handling of knowledge is to utilize cross-disciplinary (or interdisciplinary) instruction. There is potential value in the interchange between highly competent people from different disciplines—each interested in foundational issues—looking at a problem or a set of ideas from different perspectives. But such programs possess no magical power to overcome the inadequacies of individual disciplines. Two clods working across departmental lines can produce twice the lump of either working alone. The interdisciplinary rubric can cover both creative and extremely superficial undertakings. While the very process of coming together to teach in an interdisciplinary way provides a provisional probability that fundamental issues will be faced, that is not an inevitable consequence. The crucial variable is the creativity brought to an interdisciplinary venture by those who undertake it and not the mere fact that the venture is interdisciplinary. Daniel Bell was correct in contending that one of the important aims of general education is to inform people concerning the procedural methods and operational assumptions of the several disciplines.[9] That can be accomplished only by those who have given thought to foundational issues in the making and development of a discipline—and it cannot be taken for granted that all teacher/scholars have thought about these foundational issues or will necessarily come to do so when they are teaching in an interdisciplinary program if they have not done so in their regular assignments.

So-called project-centered learning has an even greater potential than interdisciplinary learning for shifting the focus away from the

98   schema for classifying knowledge according to disciplines to the holistic issues and problems of life itself. Ethnic, gender, and ecology studies—which among other possibilities examine living and vital problems without being chained to the rubrics of academic disciplines as they already exist—can combine material in new and fresh ways and produce new insights. One of the truly compelling arguments for studies of this type is their capacity to examine important issues that interface many of the academic disciplines and even get at material that has fallen into the cracks between them. To do this well, however, requires a clear idea of the substantive issue or problem to be examined. Clarity about the problem to be examined can produce the principle of coherence for such studies that clarity about methodology supposedly provides in the traditional fields.

When interdisciplinary programs were instituted at the University of California great excitement was generated.[10] In the programs in question the course was abolished in favor of a newly conceived pattern of special studies worked out with great care and thoughtful agony to provide a holistic experience. Not without some resemblance to the Great Books approach, though available only to students in the first two years, the aim of the program was to provide a new kind of coherence. The values that came from this approach were often products of the process itself: faculty and students alike read, wrote about, and discussed the same works and their implications. Tussman concluded that clear covenants binding everyone involved to a common effort were required to make such programs work, but noted that the sacrifice of disciplinary specialization and professional autonomy was well rewarded. He also noted that because the process of teaching such courses was so demanding, that faculty members could devote only a few years to their special pedagogical demands, and could not carry on with them indefinitely.[11]

The development of adequate interdisciplinary instruction depends upon how well the positive agenda is articulated and also how completely those who undertake it are willing to devote themselves to it. Approaches that seek to thrive mainly on a rhetoric of disdain for departmentalization easily miscarry. The test of pedagogical health comes not from what is rejected, but from what is achieved.

FRAGMENTATION AND COMPREHENSIVENESS

The desire for unity and coherence is a valid and essential thrust of the scholarly mind, but the inability to achieve that unity in an immutable construct is a persistent, if not inevitable, fact in any curricular arrangement. This seeming paradox means that the impulse to build a comprehensive grasp of the known must be reconciled with an acknowledgment of the limitations and fragmentation in every system by which knowledge is organized—not only within the intellectual understanding of every individual discipline but within the life of the university as a whole. We abandon the yearning for coherence only at the risk of settling prematurely for fragmentation; we claim to achieve wholeness only by ascribing to a limited and partial set of understandings a completeness it does not have.

As long as curricula are deliberately reevaluated from time to time and pedagogical arrangements are never taken for granted, a variety of curricular patterns will produce educational breadth. Where core curricula are used, their rationales should be explained to students so that reasons for doing things become as clearly understood as the requirements that they be done. It is not pedagogically healthy when students (and even their faculty advisers) speak of getting the core requirements "out of the way." Such a way of speaking suggests that such requirements have all too little importance. Even in schools with a core program, in certain individual cases, students might be given the privilege of offering their own construct of basic studies together with legitimizing reasons for pursuing it. If they can convince a committee of the value of putting together a broad and meaningful alternative to the standard fare, why not encourage such a process?

All this having been said, we must remember that much depends upon the depth to which all who teach and all who learn understand the foundation of their own, and other, disciplines and learn how to share their wisdom with others as they do their work. Skillful academic advising can be done only by those who see these issues with the requisite perspective. In general education and in liberal learning even more may depend upon the intellectual curiosity and pedagogical skills brought to the encounter with any discipline or set of disciplines than upon which particular disciplines are studied. But the qualities of intellectual curiosity and pedagogical skills that are required include a thoroughly grounded awareness of what we mean by knowing and how we are to think of intellectual achievement. The discussion must now move to those matters. They are the mind and heart, not merely the skeleton, of knowledge.

NOTES

1. Allan Bloom, *The Closing of the American Mind*, (New York: Simon and Schuster, 1987), 346.

2. Edward J. Bloustein, *The University and the Counter Culture: Inaugural and Other Addresses* (New Brunswick, N.J.: Rutgers University Press, 1972), 37f.

100   **3.** John S. Brubacher and Willis Rudy, *Higher Education in Transition: A History of American Colleges and Universities, 1936–1976* 3rd ed. (New York: Harper and Row, 1968), 84.

4. In a searching examination of the study of economics, Herman E. Daly and John B. Cobb, Jr. have argued that the dominance of the disciplines, which they contend has become the dominant feature of academic life in the last two decades, seriously distorts the study of the problems that confront the contemporary world. The "misplaced-concreteness" which results from the use of categories devised and imposed by the discipline of economics working in isolation from other disciplines precludes the broad inquiry and adequate understanding that is necessary for redirecting economics to the service of human welfare. See Herman E. Daly and John B. Cobb, Jr., *For the Common Good: Redirecting the Economy toward Community, the Environment, and a Sustainable Future*, (Boston: Beacon Press, 1989), especially chapters one to six.

5. Thomas S. Kuhn, *The Structure of Scientific Revolutions*, 2nd ed. (Chicago: University of Chicago Press, 1970), 4.

6. Ibid.

7. Michael Polanyi, *Personal Knowledge: Towards a Post-Critical Philosophy* (London: Routledge and Kegan Paul, 1958).

8. Noam Chomsky, *Language and Mind* (New York: Harcourt Brace and World, 1968).

9. See Daniel Bell, *The Reforming of General Education: The Columbia College Experience in Its National Setting* (New York: Columbia University Press, 1966).

10. Joseph Tussman, *Experiment at Berkeley* (New York: Oxford University Press, 1969).

11. Ibid., 23.

CHAPTER EIGHT

Toward a Post-Enlightenment Epistemology From Certainty About Doubt to Doubt About Certainty

The impulse to provide credibility for one's assertions is an essential thrust of scholarship. A scholar/teacher who treats subject matter frivolously or abandons the obligation to demonstrate its adequacy betrays a trust that is as important to the academy as fidelity is sacred to religion. Even when "games" are used as pedagogical tools, they are legitimate only to the extent that they illuminate matters of substance and import.

But to accept a concern for matters of substance and import, to acknowledge the claim of the truth upon the formulation of ideas, is to raise the problem of knowing and not to solve it. The very mention of these issues presents us with vexing complexities and mind-stretching problems. It demands that we wrestle, not only with the query, On what grounds do we claim validity for the ideas that we profess?, but also with the question, What degree of validity is necessary for the enterprise of teaching and learning to be worthwhile? Debates about these matters are central to the life of the academy.

THE TENSION BETWEEN CRITICISM AND CERTAINTY

The modern university is the intellectual outgrowth of the Enlightenment. The Enlightenment professed to make the critical use of reason the touchstone of knowledge. The Enlightenment had a commendable impulse behind it: it sought to guard against wishful thinking, to compel the scholar to deal with knowledge without regard to whether it conforms to prior tests of orthodoxy and to consider the claim of ideas without asking whether they are acceptable to vested interests.

But the Enlightenment also raised to the fore a special instrument for the exercise of its critical principle—namely, the primacy of experienced facts and the centrality of empirical inquiry.[1] This legacy has led through a series of developments to the triumph of the empirical

102 temper in the contemporary educational scene—a triumph that by its very hegemony has sometimes turned empirical reason into a mode of dominance and changed its critical function into an ideological one.[2]

By thus making the empirical way of knowing dominant, the modern intellectual world has created an inner dialectic between the impulse toward criticism and the impulse toward assured credibility. This was already symbolically evident in Descartes's project, in which the experience of doubting itself became the foundation of certainty. The result has been the development of massive tension between the critical spirit, on the one hand, and drives for certainty on the other. Many suppose that the critical spirit has been the defining characteristic of the university while the drive for certainty has been associated with religion and ideological politics, but a more perceptive reading of the matter would suggest that all intellectual endeavors have been affected by the same tension. The learning enterprise has been anxious to preserve criticism, yet has also manifested drives to make unassailable assertions. One of the most subtle and difficult agendas facing the academy is how to handle this tension so as to avoid the adverse consequences that flow when the dialectic is broken by making either factor absolute.

It is easy to bemoan the loss of a tension between doubt and credulity in many forms of post-Enlightenment religion. Professions of infallibility made for religious authority—whether centered on a leader or ascribed to a text—have been asserted most vigorously at exactly those times when the growth of doubt has threatened the experience of faith. The idea of the infallibility of the pope became a dogma in the later part of the nineteenth century in response to the modernist spirit. Similarly, the ideas of plenary inspiration and scriptural infallibility were given a controlling centrality in several forms of Protestantism early in the twentieth century in response to higher criticism. In both cases the claims of infallibility were part of an attempt to buttress the certainty of faith against the challenges of a critical temper.

The drive for certainty that has caused many religious traditions to locate authority in a single, presumably infallible, source has not lacked its critics in the world of learning. But the thrust for certainty has also been at work in the life of the academy. Positivism, for instance, sought to transform the critical temper of the Enlightenment perspective into a way of declaring certain kinds of knowledge to be positively valid, thus seeking to establish criteria for knowledge that can be asserted beyond a shadow of doubt. Utilizing the concept of verifiability, positivism offered a test for knowledge that depends on clear and definable criteria for determining what may be claimed as being true or factual.[3] The concept of verifiability was generally identified with a scientific perspective and rose to prominence in the intellectual world on the back of a modern propensity to accord special respect to the scientific approach to knowing. In this process, the pragmatic observational empiricism of science has become the basis of a more theoretical epistemology that has been extended to many other subject matter disciplines. It has manifested a yearning for certainty curiously akin in its impulses to the emphasis on infallibility found in many forms of post Enlightenment religion.

THE GROWING SUSPICION OF CERTAINTY

Many of the thrusts for positivistic certainty associated with an ideology of the scientific are currently under suspicion. Deep currents of discontent have formed as a reaction to the narrowing of knowledge to only those intellectual formulations that can satisfy the criteria of verification. Edward Farley has identified three strands of discontent—what he calls "major criticisms or correctives" of the account of reason that stemmed from the Enlightenment and culminated in such a narrow empiricism. According to Farley, this view has been challenged (1) by a thrust to retain the concreteness of experience as against the abstraction required by the empiricist perspective (the romantic corrective), (2) by a realization that tradition can be a bearer of truth (the theological corrective), and (3) by a realization that all schemes of understanding are dependent upon political movements and impulses (the praxis corrective).[4] Farley traces the developments with broad and insightful strokes. The same trends can be described by focusing on the work of selected thinkers and movements.

It is important to observe that attacks on the hegemony of the empiricist view have not stemmed only from a religiously inspired opposition to the thrusts that have been prevalent in intellectual during recent decades. Indeed, many of the people and movements that have been pivotal in forcing a reexamination of the nature of knowing have been associated with the sciences (or with the social sciences) and have focused primarily on the presuppositions of their own disciplines.

Michel Foucault, the French intellectual, seeking to reconceptualize the structuring and foundations of knowledge, has started with presuppositions radically different from those of narrow empiricism. He has used the term "archaeology" to denote a method that undercuts the existing modes of intellectualization in the West in order to get to the roots of knowing. According to one student of his work, Foucault developed a "radically new conception of the role of intellect"

104 which attempted "to undermine the rule of knowledge, to discredit the hegemony of reason, to reveal scientific discourse as a model that repeats itself analogically, that claims objectivity but is diffused with ideology."[5] Foucault has been protesting against positivism and the assumptions that stemmed from it—assumptions which obscured the paradoxical situation of our roles as both knowing subjects and as objects of knowledge. "Foucault's writing . . . problematizes the truths that a Western consciousness has developed around its own representation of itself."[6] His perspective has been associated with structuralism and is not dissimilar to many of the insights suggested in what later came to be identified as the sociology of knowledge approach[7], but it has its own integrity and is not to be jammed without remainder into that movement.

The writings of Herbert Marcuse exemplify a polemic form of the movement against the dominance of the verificationist approach. Marcuse perceived in technological rationality the very elements that enable the creation of social controls that repress rather than liberate human beings. Speaking of operationalist epistemology—his term for the dominant perspective—Marcuse argues that this perspective effectively eliminates many worthwhile ideas simply by "showing that no adequate account of them in terms of operations or behavior can be given." He continues by suggesting that, "The radical empiricist onslaught . . . thus provides the methodological justification for the debunking of the mind by the intellectuals—a positivism which, in its denial of the transcending elements of Reason, forms the academic counterpart of the socially required behavior."[8]

Ernest Becker, in an effort to develop richer theoretical premises for the social sciences, has pleaded for a reversal of those trends that take the physical sciences—in which there is a sharp separation of "fact" from "value," and of the "is" from the "ought"—as the quintessential model for knowing. Such a tendency, he has suggested, leads to the loss of the sense of purpose which was part of the Enlightenment vision—a sense of purpose that was excluded from science in the nineteenth century when the conception of its role was overly narrowed.[9]

Alasdair MacIntyre's book, *Whose Justice? Which Rationality?*[10] provides still another example of a contention that something has gone awry with the Enlightenment heritage. In MacIntyre's book, a long and erudite discussion of Western thought from Homer to Hume precedes the author's argument that contemporary philosophy (and, by implication, much of the contemporary academy) is unable to resolve the differences between various views of justice and various versions of reason that contend with each other for acceptance. Contemporary intellectuals are, he suggests, better able to describe disagreements about fundamental issues than to resolve them. Near the end of his treatment, MacIntyre observes,

> The conclusion to which the argument so far has led is not only that it is out of the debates, conflicts, and enquiry of socially embodied, historically contingent traditions that contentions regarding practical rationality and justice are advanced, modified, abandoned, or replaced, but that there is no other way to engage in the formulation, elaboration, rational justification, and criticism of accounts of practical rationality and justice except from within some one particular tradition in conversation, cooperation, and conflict with those who inhabit the same tradition.[11]

Such conclusions resonate, like Foucault's, with those of the sociology of knowledge approach, but they are developed on other grounds. They radically undercut a view of rationality that presumes it can furnish a controlling critical judgment that is totally and completely valid for everyone, that is, a view of reason that claims positive certainty in knowing.

MacIntyre does not, however, move to dogmatic relativism and sheer perspectivism. Those positions share the same yearning for certainty that is associated with positivism. Dogmatic relativism, recognizing that many formulations of ideas and ideals differ from culture to culture, moves from this realization to its own unqualified assertion about the impossibility of discovering truth. This negative rather than positive form of certainty has had some acceptance in the academy—but it is self-contradictory. Steering adroitly away from that dead end, MacIntyre advocates a concept which he calls "the rationality of tradition-constituted and tradition-constitutive enquiry,"[12] proposing it as a basis for dealing with these vexing questions about the nature and ground of knowledge. He also suggests that some points of contact do exist between different traditions, though they are never sufficiently extensive to enable the resolution of disagreements by critical reason alone.

Probably the most radical undercutting of the claims associated with both traditional metaphysical and radically empiricist knowledge is being provided by the movement known as deconstruction. This movement has affected literary criticism, philosophy, and (to a lesser extent) theological reflection. In its most extreme forms, deconstructionist thinking casts doubt on the ability of linguistic formulations to point to any reality beyond themselves. The deconstructionists are, in

106 a certain sense, the polar opposites of the positivists. Whereas the latter have been seeking to ensure that statements accurately refer to a public verifiable known, the former are contending that there is no certainty concerning the reality of anything beyond the text. They are careful, however, not to make this conclusion into a form of negative certainty, as relativism does. By denying the power of language to be a tool or instrument of thought about a reality that transcends human reflection, the deconstructionists consider language itself to constitute the locus of its own reality and not a means of providing knowledge beyond itself.

Our understanding of the limited nature of knowledge has been further advanced by the ever increasing amount of scholarly work being done today by woman. Many women scholars are pointing out that the formulations of knowledge frequently taken as traditional are male-eyed views that fail to take into account the perspective of women. The use of the male generic as a way of designating universal experience is an indication of the single-eyed perspective, although the difficulty runs far deeper than mere terminology. Many women argue the importance of opening a second eye—not only because a second eye sees new things, but because when working in conjunction with the first eye it provides the possibility of perceiving depth.[13] What is true of formulations that have excluded women—by far the largest excluded group and usually constituting at least half of all other excluded groups—is also true in the case of others whose perceptions have been slighted or ignored by traditional formulations.

The foregoing ways of thinking about knowledge can be characterized (hopefully not too simply) by utilizing metaphors about the roads to the mountain. In Japan it has often been said that "all roads lead to Mount Fuji"—an observation with counterparts in other societies. Dogmatism, whether in religion or in learning, insists that there is only one road, and that unless and until one finds it there is no certainty of getting to the mountain. Dogmatic relativism acknowledges the existence of many roads, none of which is any better than the others, if indeed any of them lead to the mountain at all. Deconstruction suggests that the mountain may not exist, even though the roadways may make interesting exercise paths. But the original use of the metaphor suggests that there can be more than one possible way of reaching a summit. Modesty in knowing counsels us to travel on one road with a sense of direction and expectation, but to remain in conversation with those who are on other roads, so we learn about the mountain from other travelers even as they also learn something about it from us.

A moral perspective on the pursuit of knowledge needs to be concerned about these matters of epistemology not because it has some way to resolve them, but because many possible ways of presuming to resolve the questions are antithetical to the nature of the university. The academic world has to deal with these matters in ways that are consistent with its commitment to open exploration. To do that is more difficult than is often supposed.

A telling illustration of the tension that can arise between different presuppositions about the ground rules for knowing is found in the struggle that rocked the Institute for Advanced Study at Princeton over the proposed appointment of Robert Bellah as a permanent fellow. Bellah is a student of social conditions whose intellectual style is conceptually imaginative, and whose works, such as *The Broken Covenant, Habits of the Heart,* and *The Good Society,* provide paradigmatic concepts for a wide range of creative thinking about the conditions of American society and the ways it can most adequately fulfill its intended destiny. His essays range across the intercultural landscape with brilliant suggestiveness and they often demonstrate the value of collaborative scholarship. When it was proposed that he be invited to join the permanent staff of the Institute, a group of fellows dedicated to hard data and logically self-contained precision became incensed. One of them called Bellah's works "pedestrian and pretentious beyond even the call of journalistic duty." A colleague in the opposite camp rejected this judgment as "preemptory and insulting even beyond the call of polemic passion."[14] The newspaper account of this contentious battle reported that "one of the dissident mathematicians informed the social science colleague who sponsored Professor Bellah that there can no longer be personal relations between them."[15] It is not the fact of this debate, but its tenor and bitterness, that demonstrates the intensity of the potential antagonisms that can develop among those who embrace different approaches to knowledge.

Modesty about our different ways of probing for insight makes it crucial to honor those with different approaches. Often academic departments work to see that everyone climbs the same path to the mountain of knowledge. Individuals who are interested in the value questions associated with a social science discipline, for instance, find it almost impossible to be rewarded in departments dominated by a positivist bent, and vice versa. Similarly, referees for journals do not always respectfully honor methodological pluralism when choosing articles for publication. Schools of thought about the methodological

108   presuppositions of knowing exert sometimes subtle, sometimes blatant, influences on the dynamics of the academic process that bear
functional similarities to prior restraints on journalism. While academics have generally learned to resist external interference with the free
flow of ideas, they have not always demonstrated a corresponding
sensitivity to internal restraints. Lacking proper modesty about their
own way of looking at knowledge in a field, many scholars come to
regard their own particular perspective as more normative than it has
a right to be taken. While this is not the case in all of academe, it is
the case sufficiently often to require a deliberate resolve to avoid it.
At the heart of almost all claims for certainty lies a thrust to find a
single way of determining knowledge to be true. Single measures of
validity provide a seeming certainty because they avoid the possibility
of conflict between methodologies. Claims for the certainty provided
by a particular way of seeking knowledge stand in contrast, therefore,
to a broader approach that is concerned more with the adequacy and
the fruitful suggestiveness of our ways of knowing than it is with
precise and indisputable methods of certifying the correctness of ideas.

There is no way that a pluralistic outlook can be turned into an
ideology without engaging in exclusion—even an exclusion that holds
that those who believe in a more cohesive and singular perspective
are not fit for the academy. As a form of orthognosis, pluralism
becomes self-contradictory. But made into a way of behaving, into an
orthopraxis of openness and of dialogue, modesty about knowing
enhances the essential quality of the academic quest.

Such a broad, or "modest," view of our knowledge can utilize
the contributions of several ways of getting at the known, take each
of them as valid within appropriate parameters, and utilize them in
concert with each other. Such a stance makes it possible to affirm
that several ways of thinking about knowledge have a place in the
academy. For instance, empirical observation can be recognized as a
scholarly tool of great significance, especially in contrast with the
political use of arguments to further causes, or the commercial manipulation of data to produce glowing annual reports or seductive advertising. Empirical observation seeks to be faithful to evidence, to guard
against the warping of data, to avoid the coloring that may creep into
reflection that is distorted by idiosyncratic perspectives. Even though
a pure detachment is impossible, the impulse to read evidence fairly
is a valuable one. Only when the empirical method is regarded as the
sole legitimate source of knowledge does it work mischief.

Within a broader view of knowing there is definitely a place for
reason. Reason, however, does not furnish an "Archimedean point"
from which to judge the validity of all formulations. It has a more

catalytic function—at once generous and nurturing—namely, that of urging clarity and seeking comprehensiveness. Reason helps us to understand ambiguity and paradox as well as simplicity and consistency. To "be reasonable" is not to achieve assured certainty, however promulgated, but to show an open appreciation for the rich and variegated kinds of reflection that can make contributions to our understanding without claiming to preempt all other ways of coming to the truth.

Within a broader view of knowing there is also a place for heritage and for tradition, indeed for many traditions. Traditions are embodied in folklore, in artifacts, in texts, in ethos. The cultivation of skills in the appropriation of heritage and tradition is an indispensable responsibility of learning—present, perhaps, to a greater extent in liberal learning than in technical or vocational instruction—but absent from any intellectual agenda only to its impoverishment. Skill in hermeneutical interpretation is just as valuable a scholarly accomplishment as the capacity to make accurate empirical observations or the penchant for seeking clarity and comprehensive breadth.

There is, finally, yet another source of understanding that is difficult to name. George B. Leonard has used the category "ecstasy" for defining it.[16] The term "vision" might be more accurate. Max Stackhouse has suggested the need of such an additional thrust by observing that, "Rational liberals in the university research a multiplicity of cultural goods, defend the principle of tolerance, and mitigate the pretensions of authoritarians . . . but they give no vision."[17] The imagery of vision is also implicit in the thought of Teilhard de Chardin, who portrayed knowledge as a form of seeing.[18]

The visionary thrust is important in the pursuit of knowledge because it helps to keep alive the sense of wonder and excitement in learning—a sense that is too often missing. A campus clinician, distinguished in counseling, once noted that the freshman year in college is a major shock to the psyche of the adolescent. It forces the personality into a restricted mold at a time when it is ideologically attracted to great ideas, crimping the conceptual style into the cool detachment of precise, yet minute, conceptualization such as marks scholarship dominated by what might be called the verificationist posture. Decrying this phenomenon, he has suggested that "the student can conform if he must, because his previous training has already taught him what the coin of the realm is, but it is not what he wants to do." The student gets the sense that his own ideational products are unworthy, and feels humiliated and inept, wondering how good he is as a thinking person. Thus, to some extent, the colleges themselves produce the "anti-intellectual" they complain about.[19] In the

110   same vein, a college president in an assembly address in the middle
       1950s declared, "The tragedy of American education appears to be that
       the initial sense of wonder and the urge to explore, so characteristic in
       the young child, are lost in his secondary school and are never recov-
       ered during his years in higher education."[20]

           In a provocative analysis charging rationalistic cultural liberalism
       with bankruptcy, William Irwin Thompson details how cultural expe-
       rience is affected by ideological elements used for its interpretation.
       Thompson reminds us of Karl Mannheim's contention that dominant
       perspectives block new insights into knowledge, and examines the
       processes by which academic outlooks based upon the empiricist
       premise have enforced conformity to particular ways of thinking.
       Thompson claims that the most visionary thinkers of our time are
       those who have moved off the campus altogether, or those who have
       set up special enclaves on the campus in which they are free to do
       their own thinking without interference from the guardians of episte-
       mological narrowness. Speaking of the disillusionment among young
       people with the staid carefulness of the scholarly enterprise, and
       their realization that the intellectual action lies elsewhere, Thompson
       suggests that "the young feel intuitively what is happening, and that
       is why we are witnessing the forms of revolt and withdrawal around
       us. When rationality is not possible because the institution of reason,
       the university, overloads the mind with data without meaning, the
       institution perishes in its own excremental productivity. Once the
       individual is without the institution, he can ascend to suprarational
       levels of imagination, intuition, and creativity or descend to the levels
       of subrational panic."[21] This premature obituary for the educational
       institution is obviously overdrawn both in its reports of what has been
       happening and in its suggestion as to what can happen if only the
       academic enterprise is laid aside. Its value lies not in suggesting imagi-
       nation to be a self-sustaining approach to knowledge but in suggesting
       its importance as a corrective. Thompson points us to a complemen-
       tary modality of knowing that can supplement and complement other
       emphases in the academy.

           The term "vision" surfaces in the literature with ever-increasing
       frequency to describe this element in a gestalt—suggesting what may
       be a ground swell of interest in a broader understanding of what the
       intellectual enterprise is about. The objective calculus of rationality
       is not necessarily repudiated, but neither is it accepted as the only
       legitimate basis for the university's intellectual venture. For instance,
       historian Van Austin Harvey, describing two approaches to the writ-
       ing of history, and drawing on materials taken from the writing of one

of his colleagues, suggests a way of learning in which love, communion, and authenticity are the central dynamics.

> Whereas the old historiography employed the model of the disinterested scientist getting at the facts, the new historiography claims that unless the historian is "open himself to encounter other human beings," that is unless he permits his self understanding to be called into question by the past, he cannot really apprehend or understand that past. The old positivistic historiography absolutized bloodless detachment. The new historiography insists that "one should be *engage*, with one's whole selfhood at stake, in the 'world' in which one moves." This new attitude does not invalidate painstaking research, to be sure, but it does mean that this research is only a preliminary step in understanding history. The culmination of historical understanding comes when one grasps the possibilities of existence which have come to expression in the past and which are repeatable in the present and in the future.[22]

Every one of us has probably heard a statement such as the following made about some idea advanced by a colleague: "My, that's a brilliant suggestion, but who would put any stock in it without hard data to back it up?" This statement is biased toward certainty rather than creativity. Surely, those who originate brilliant suggestions are just as important for the advancement of learning as those who gather corroborating data. Often it is those with the imaginative and creative capacity to originate the suggestions that others put to the test who contribute most to the advancement of knowledge in every field of learning. Observations and empirical data do not yield a richly meaningful body of insight and learning apart from theoretical concepts. Moreover, it is not even possible to search for and use data intelligently without an hypothesis with which to work.

THE MORAL MEANING OF A MODEST UNDERSTANDING

There is an ethical dimension to the concern that knowledge be faithful to the nature of reality. There is a corresponding ethical impulse discernible in the visionary perspective, a concern for human fullness and for the appreciation and enjoyment of meaning and significance. In the first, facticity is given highest value, and concern for precision and correctness is the consequent obligation. In the second, imagination and inspiration are highly valued, and concern for wholeness of understanding and depth of insight makes the moral claim.

112   Bernard Meland who used the term "appreciative consciousness" to denote an adequate scholarly perception, insisted that reality
is perceived in depth through patterns and relationships rather than
by facts alone: "Precision, analysis, comprehension, and form are not
alien to the appreciative consciousness; but these are but means to an
end. And as such they are tentative and subject to revision before the
great on-going mystery in which our lives are cast—a drama in which
wonder, inquiry, and the appreciative mind play the creative roles."[23]

More recently, Parker Palmer pleading for a richer, more inclusive epistemology than that which is currently dominant in the academy, has underscored the moral requirement of modesty in knowing
in this way:

Many of us live one-eyed lives. We rely largely on the eye
of the mind to form our imagery of reality. But today more and
more of us are opening the other eye, the eye of the heart,
looking for realities to which the mind's eye is blind. Either eye
alone is not enough. We need "wholesight," a vision of the
world in which mind and heart unite "as my two eyes make one
in sight." Our seeing shapes our being. Only as we see whole
can we and our world be whole.

With the mind's eye we see a world of fact and reason. It
is a cold and mechanical place, but we have built our lives there
because it seemed predictable and safe. Today, in the age of
nuclear science, our mind-made world has been found flawed
and dangerous, even lethal. So we open the eye of the heart and
see another sight: a world warmed and transformed by the power
of love, a vision of community beyond the mind's capacity to
see. We cannot forsake our hearts and yet we cannot abandon
our minds. How shall we bring together these two lines of sight?
How shall we use both eyes to create not a blurry double image
but one world, in all its dimensions, healed and made whole?[24]

This account could go on to report how thinkers as diverse as
Jacques Barzun, Alfred North Whitehead, Ortega y Gassett, H. Richard Niebuhr, and others of similar stature have envisioned the intellectual life with a fullness and a richness that combines the value inherent
in care about detail with the value that attends conceptual expansive-
ness. A passion for exactness must be combined with an intellectual
generosity if the climate for learning is to have rich balance. In learning, as in religion, balance is a better measure of maturity than certainty. Balance may not offer us certainty, either the factual certainty
of verified detail or the assertive certainty of some visionary mysticism,
but it can offer a rich satisfaction with the scholarly quest.

To live with uncertainty as regards our grasp of the truth requires a stance that is similar to that proposed for dealing with moral obligation under a theological scheme of the free forgiveness of sins. Justification by faith acknowledges the full and complete demands of the moral law yet forces every person to realize that these demands are never completely met—even that they cannot be fully met. Luther used the phrase "sin bravely" to portray the enigmatic obligation to take as ultimately demanding a moral law that one knows it is impossible to fulfill totally. In this manner the tension between obligation and impossibility is rendered acceptable without being dissolved. Analogously, in the realm of intellectual achievement the requirement to deal correctly with reality remains an ultimate claim, but the realization that all efforts to do this are imperfect remains an existential inevitability. Liberation from the demand to be absolutely certain means that we can face the prospects of "understanding partially" without treating questions of knowing with casual disregard and also without having to claim absolute status for our formulations. To do that opens the necessity of using touchstones such as elegance and maturity, and not correctness, as measures of scholarly achievement.

NOTES

1. See Edward Farley, *The Fragility of Knowledge: Theological Education in the Church and the University* (Philadelphia: Fortress Press, 1988), 4f.

2. This has been termed "academic fundamentalism" by Page Smith; see *Killing the Spirit: Higher Education in America* (New York: Viking Press, 1990), especially 5 and 297.

3. Two kinds of knowing were held to be verifiable. The first consists of axioms—formal propositions, often expressible in mathematical form, that are true by definition or on the basis of logical elaboration: for instance, if by definition X equals Y, then 2X equals 2Y, and so forth. Other verifiable statements are true by virtue of their correspondence with observable reality: for instance, five major bodies of water, all but one of which have shores bordering both the United States and Canada, form the Great Lakes. Statements of the second sort can be verified by observation—although such observation need not take the form of direct, that is, firsthand scrutiny. Highly sophisticated inquiries can be employed for the gathering, sorting, and arranging of data, provided these are specifiable and theoretically available to the same extent to anyone wishing to follow the procedures for setting them up.

4. Farley, *Fragility of Knowledge*, 6–9.

5. Karlis Racevskis, *Michel Foucault and the Subversion of Intellect* (Ithaca: Cornell University Press, 1983), 23.

114   6. Ibid., 38.

7. This term covers many outlooks that emphasize the role that social location—that is, the position one has in cultural, political, or economic systems—plays in the way one reads experience, formulates ideas, and considers what constitutes the truth. Ironically, this claim is sometimes asserted as though it is a general and universal insight itself exempt from social location.

8. Herbert Marcuse, *One-Dimensional Man: Studies in the Ideology of Advanced Industrial Society* (Boston: Beacon Press, 1964), 13.

9. Ernest Becker, *The Structure of Evil: An Essay on the Unification of the Science of Man* (New York: Braziller, 1968); see especially 384ff.

10. Alasdair MacIntyre, *Whose Justice? Which Rationality?* (Notre Dame: University of Notre Dame Press, 1988).

11. Ibid., 350.

12. Ibid., 354.

13. See Patricia Altenbernd Johnson and Janet Kalvern, eds. *With Both Eyes Open: Seeing Beyond Gender* (New York: Pilgrim Press, 1988), especially chapter 9.

14. "Dispute Splits Advanced Study Institute," *New York Times*, Late City Edition, 2 March 1973, 43.

15. "Foes of Institute Dig in for a Fight," *New York Times*, Late City Edition, 4 March 1973, 26.

16. George B. Leonard, *Education and Ecstasy* (New York: Delacorte, 1968), 80f.

17. Max L. Stackhouse, *Ethics and the Urban Ethos: An Essay in Social Theory and Theological Reconstruction* (Boston: Beacon Press, 1972), 135.

18. Pierre Teilhard de Chardin, *The Phenomenon of Man* (New York: Harper and Brothers, 1959), 32.

19. Joseph Katz and Associates, *No Time for Youth: Growth and Constraint in College Students* (San Francisco: Jossey-Bass, 1968), 434.

20. Samuel B. Gould, Address at a College Assembly 2 June 1955, in *Knowledge Is Not Enough*, (Yellow Springs, Ohio: Antioch, 1959), 18. Title of address is not given.

21. William Irwin Thompson, *At the Edge of History* (New York: Harper and Row, 1972), 98.

22. Van Austin Harvey, *The Historian and the Believer: The Morality of Historical Knowledge and Christian Belief* (New York: Macmillan, 1966), 171.

23. Bernard E. Meland, *Higher Education and the Human Spirit* (Chicago: University of Chicago Press, 1953); rpt, (Chicago: Seminary Cooperative Bookstore, n.d.), 77.

24. Parker J. Palmer, *To Know as We Are Known: A Spirituality of Higher Education* (San Francisco: Harper and Row, 1983), xi.

CHAPTER NINE

Elegance and Maturity: Measures of Scholarly Style

Scholarship involves the acquisition, testing, classifying, and transmission of information and ideas. But those functions alone do not adequately portray the rich and subtle dimensions of scholarly accomplishment. A telephone book is remarkably accurate and replete as a source of information and is organized with remarkable cogency, but it hardly qualifies as literature. By analogy, a scholar is not simply a custodian of data or an arranger of details, but a living human being whose manner of working with ideas is as crucial as the correctness or the range of those ideas.

THE SIGNIFICANCE OF SCHOLARLY STYLE

So much that we do in the academy must of necessity be concerned with factual data and procedural skills that we do not give sufficient attention to what it means to acquire intellectual luster. Teachers may even feel they have accomplished something significant if their students grasp a small portion of the materials that they have read and manage to express themselves in minimally correct modes of discourse. To pay attention to the niceties of learned inquiry and the subtleties of a polished manner for dealing with ideas has become almost beyond our ken.

Yet we forget these things at great cost to our aspirations. Aesthetics and morality involve a person's whole being, and so does the most satisfying pursuit of learning. Scholarly achievement needs to be touched with grandeur and informed by wisdom if it is to reach its highest levels. The divorce between epistemology (which concerns the accuracy of ideas) and ontology (which concerns the quality of being) that has come to characterize much modern consciousness has tended to limit our conception of what it means to be competent as a scholar. To focus on the content and validity of ideas rather than upon

116   the whole measure of the way in which ideas are set forth is to leave scholarly achievement only half portrayed. The value of what we profess is dependent upon the manner in which we profess it as well as upon its content. Knowing cannot be divorced from presentation.

When scholarly competence is examined valuationally rather than merely epistemologically the realization of what it means to be a scholar must be enlarged. Such an enlargement of the way to think about scholarship may be especially needed in the modern academic scene, not merely because a cognition-dominated ethos has become almost overpowering, but because the protests against this dominance often take the form of mere repudiation rather than the constructive articulation of an alternative vision. It is not sufficient to condemn the intellectual technician: it is also necessary to grasp what it means to be a conceptual artist. While the critique of an inadequate academic consciousness must not be blunted, a negative polemic that demonstrates many of the same shortcomings it castigates hardly provides a cure.

We must search, then, for terms that can recast the academic consciousness without hurling aspersions upon it, for rubrics with which to describe accomplishment in learning that neither discount the significance of epistemological adequacy nor settle for it alone as a measure of scholarly attainment.

ELEGANCE AS A TOUCHSTONE OF SCHOLARLY ACHIEVEMENT

One such term is found in both the physical sciences and the fine arts. When physicists speak of their theories they frequently refer to them as "elegant." This term implies several things; internal consistency, a comprehensive power to explain, a striking coherence with a wide range of experience combined with expressibility in a single (even a simple) formulation, and the capacity to elicit a certain respect, perhaps even wonder and awe. While batteries of data may be helpful for realizing the range of information that must be covered by a science, one would never apply the term "elegant" to a stack of computer printouts, to undigested observations of details, or to voluminous files of unsorted information. However, the means for gathering and arranging data—especially if remarkably probing—might well be termed elegant (as would, for example, a marvelous filing system or a uniquely conceived software program).

There has to be a bit of inspiration behind the elegant formulation, a sense in which it catches the imagination and even engenders appreciation for the orderliness and remarkable functionality of the natural world, and (equally) for the agility of the human mind's capacity to make abstractions about reality. Speaking of personal knowledge, Michael Polanyi notes three things that we can appropriate for thinking about elegance as a rubric for intellectual endeavor: "the power of intellectual beauty to reveal truth about nature; the vital importance of distinguishing this beauty from merely formal attractiveness; and the delicacy of the test between them, so difficult it may baffle the most penetrating scientific minds."[1]

When artists speak of elegance they point to form in harmony with function, to emotive power, to aesthetic integration, to the appropriateness of the medium to the created form. The elegant piece of art is compelling, it thrusts out in the fullness of its aesthetic integrity to grip the imagination and to invite a response from the viewer or the hearer. It invites response, not merely because of the shape, medium, color, mass, tone, or setting alone, but (most usually) because of the uniqueness and authenticity of the way or ways it weaves these into a totality. Elegant art cannot be measured merely by tests for its accurate reproduction of external features in some object—passport photos do that. Rather, elegant art must be recognized by a capacity to point beyond itself, even beyond the means of its execution, to something profound about reality. Elegant art engulfs something of the observer into itself, and makes that observer a participant, not merely a detached perceiver. Such art captivates and inspires, takes hold of a viewer and draws that viewer into participatory ecstasy. The artist who conceives and executes an elegant piece of work has something of the same thrill in accomplishment as does the scientist who arrives at (by discovery or invention, who knows exactly which?) a "break through" theory for the enriched perception and understanding of a natural phenomenon.

Physicists and artists can easily be conceived as standing at opposite ends of the curricular spectrum—if not, indeed, to be participants in utterly different cultures. But they are surprisingly alike in the way they use the term elegance when they speak about high attainment in their work. Those who practice the disciplines between—if one can rightly think of a spectrum with the theoretical sciences at one end and the fine arts at the other—can learn something from the congruence of terminology for judging accomplishments in such diverse branches of learning. The disciplines in the middle of the spectrum do not as often speak of elegance as do the sciences and the fine arts. Some of them, particularly those that deal with historical contingencies and human foibles and yet want to be scientific, tend to amass complex data grounded in a detailed empiricism. When this tendency comes to dominance, the image of the "hard nose" takes precedence over that

118   of the "clear eye" until scholars in the disciplines between the sciences and fine arts sometimes become vendors of information and merchants of self-consciously complex generalizations rather than artistic creators of intellectual beauty.

The intellectual disciplines that appear most to appreciate the quality of elegance seem to be those in which the formulations transcend verbal categories. The theories of the physical scientists that thrill them most are often expressible in the symbols of mathematics, and the creations of artists are embodied in pictorial, graphic, or auditory representations. So we must ask, Are words dysfunctional to elegance? Does reliance upon discursive communication condemn a scholar to something less attractive or compelling? Jacques Barzun does not think so.[2] By relating conversation to manners he brings the use of words under the tests of elegance. True conversation is marked by a sifting and winnowing process for the pursuit of inquiry rather than a mere exchange of fixed ideas in a crude trade off. Elegance in conversation, therefore, relates to manners—it "excludes pedantry on the one side and arrogance on the other, while retaining a pleasurable echo of both conflict and learning."[3]

Barzun admires high finesse in the use of words. He has harsh judgments to render on those who would undercut it. Speaking of the fortunes suffered by scholars at the hands of publishers, he complains that "intellectuals submit without protest to the devices by which democratic collaboration destroys an [elegant style]—from unnecessary lunching and pathological conferring to following house rules of English and yielding to the alterations that remake the finished work as in a clothing shop, to fit the arbitrary customer."[4]

Barzun's view seems to set elegance in intellectual achievement against popular expectations and commercial interest. This may sound like a convergence of elegance and elitism. But elegance need not exclude the common person. The opposite of the elegant is not the common touch—as Abraham Lincoln demonstrated with the Gettysburg address—but the pedantic mind-set that confuses detail mongering with thoroughness and that overlooks the importance of attractiveness and beauty in the design and execution of intellectual achievement.

To be sure, elegance may be little cherished by those concerned with the conquest and manipulation of crude vitalities for the sake merely of attaining mastery over others or gain for themselves. A concern for bottom lines—whether in terms of power or in terms of money—may work at cross-purposes to a concern for intellectual beauty. Nor does a penchant for the tawdry evaporate from a community merely because that community is officially designated a seat of learning. Even in the academy, action heroes made visible by the media may be more in demand as assembly speakers than reflective scholars who have made distinctive contributions to learning. The elegant replaces the tawdry only when a vision of good form and distinctive insight is coupled with attention to care and polish—the appreciation of which it is the duty of the academy to burnish to a high luster.

We can take a lesson on these matters from the black community. As it has come to define its own self-consciousness more adequately it has adopted the phrase, "Black is beautiful." This idea draws attention to aspects of being that are richer than merely correct cognition and more attractive than merely operational power. Phrases such as "Black is correct," or "Black is powerful," while not without some potential for establishing identity, do not have the same significance.

Elegance is an elusive quality. It may help to portray it by contrast with its alternatives. Elegance is something of an opposite to sloppiness or grubbiness. It cherishes orderliness and form, not so much by making a virtue out of conforming to prescriptive patterns—the figures crammed on the income tax return could never qualify—but in the conviction that orderliness and beauty are functional to truth. It is entirely possible to see elegance in a well-arranged report or laboratory write-up, in a neatly prepared term paper or dissertation, in a skillfully nuanced grant proposal. The format in which a poem is arranged—even the manner it which it is printed—is part of its quality. Such materials catch attention by pleasing the consciousness rather than by jarring it. No subject matter in the curriculum can fail to be enhanced by learning to deal with it elegantly.

Elegance is the opposite of the pedantic. It is not concerned with detail for its own sake, but with detail that has been combed for importance, assessed for significance, selected for pertinence, and arranged according to design and purpose. Teachers should not demand attention to minutiae merely to demonstrate they are sticklers for details. A careful scholar discriminates, judging the difference between junk and valued specimens. Scavenging does not the elegant scholar make.

Elegance also stands in contrast to the artificially pretentious or flamboyant. Neophytes reading papers at professional societies often betray themselves by the contrived complexity of their verbiage. When older, and perhaps wiser, hopefully they will speak more plainly, from a true and indigenous grasp of complexity that comes naturally and without affectation. In less charitable moments we quip about "graduate-school mouth," the expression of a yen for elegance than does not yet have the skill to give it substance. Better, perhaps, that

120   error, than the resort to four-letter words for emphasis and shock—
the inelegance of the back alley or locker room. Nor are the carping
crescendoes that so easily infect our expressions in the effort to be
emphatic as valuable as the cautious understatements that dispose of
inadequacies with impeccable reserve.

Erasmus of Rotterdam, himself not always free of invective,
knew in his most sober moments what we must come to know—that
complexity is of itself no adequate test of truth. Indeed, great ideas
have something of a simplicity about them:

> The first thing that strikes anyone who comes to know
> Erasmus even slightly is his enormous respect for learning, for
> good scholarship, for sheer intellectual grasp. All his life he felt
> he was fighting the monster of ignorance. He was persuaded
> that truth is strong and compelling and seductive, in spite of
> the attempts of the "barbarians" to obscure it. Furthermore, he
> would say, you can know the truth when you see it because it
> is always simple and clear. If you come upon complexity and
> contradiction, you have found a human perversion of the truth,
> not the truth itself.[5]

A sophisticated understanding often has to take into account
ambiguity and be aware of the polarities in existence that cannot be
neatly dissolved. But valid complexities that reflect the kaleidoscopic
nature of reality are different matters from contrived complexities and
sham sophistication. The finely tuned mind will not hesitate to cherish
the truly simple (that is, the single-minded and fully integrated formulation). Such simplicity gives a Shaker chair its beauty or a New
England meeting house its authenticity. But the same mind will know
there may be other beauty as well, such as the beauty of a cathedral
adorned with much intricate detail. To understand what is good in
all forms of beauty requires breadth of understanding. Similarly, to
understand what is insightful in various forms of truth requires richness of insight. A capacity for elegance does not spring into fullness
merely through the massive acquisition of information, but emerges
slowly through an almost unconscious osmosis of the very culture of
a community in which beauty is functional to truth.

A SECOND TOUCHSTONE: MATURITY

If the term "elegance" helps us to understand how to craft ideas, the
term "maturity" helps us to understand how we are to be responsible
members of the commonwealth of learning. The vocation of the

scholar involves dealing with ideas with a breadth, richness, and beauty that comes from long experience, and also involves learning how to relate to others with a civility that should be the identifying characteristic of a special kind of community. To be knowledgeable in a moral manner means to work with truth profoundly and to work with other people sensitively. Maturity in the doing of truth in company with others is as crucial as elegance in asserting it. Grace and wisdom should be as functional to scholarship as the mastery of data and critical acumen.

Maturity depends upon stabilized identity, self-acceptance, and self-understanding. It is expressed as a capacity to empathize with others and to engage in debates and controversy with fairness and poise. A prime ingredient in maturity is discernment, a capacity to separate what is valuable from what is worthless and what is important from what is trivial. Discernment, as James Gustafson has suggested, is a crucial ingredient in moral awareness. Commenting on its importance, he has shown how the idea of discernment raises the level of moral competence above the debates between the defenders of rules or principles—who are looking for certainty in moral choice, and the advocates of deciding according to circumstances—who achieve a resolution of the problems by contextualizing choice without trivializing decisions. Gustafson applies the term discernment to describe the capacity of "persons who seem to be more perceptive, wise, more discriminating than others are in judging, whether the object judged is a performance of a symphony, a person and his behavior, a political situation, or a novel."[6]

Gustafson weaves several strands into his view of moral discernment. He mentions the capacity to grasp the essential quality in an object or in another personality in such a way as to describe that quality succinctly and fairly. He indicates the importance of observing or appreciating literary or artistic accomplishment with a set of instructive values that are used imaginatively rather than imposed mechanically. Discernment includes insight as to potential consequences, a capacity to move from the universal to the particular and back again, the ability to take account of all relevant information, the openness to feel deeply and responsibly without losing a reflective perspective instructed by critical distance, and the ability to be as firm or as flexible as conditions require. All of these capacities are related, according to Gustafson, to a person's odyssey as well as to that person's set of beliefs and principles. In short, the ability to be discerning involves perception, discrimination, accuracy, sensitivity, empathy, and modesty. The last term, perhaps the most important one of all, is for Gustafson a quality of spirit related to a person's standing in humble

122 submissiveness to God, but it is also the key perspective I have used to develop an acceptable epistemology.

The idea of discernment can transvaluate a conception of intellectual ability from the sharp, brittle, and hypercritical to the wise, resilient, and empathetic. Without in any way denigrating competence, these rubrics add the ingredient of compassion to what it means to be an academician. Compassion prompts us to care deeply and thus permits us to pursue goals while guarding against a trampling down of others. Compassion has more kinship with honest doubt than with cocksure assertiveness, more interest in service than in unilaterally achieved success. It is authenticated in experience more richly than verified discursively. It is available irrespective of status. It is elicited by example, bestowed through sacrifice, and accepted as though a gift. It cherishes mellowness without condoning softheadedness and recognizes that elements of failure are compounded into every historical success. It replaces the raucous with the resilient and the quest for quick and total victory over others with gratitude for modest, even shared, gains. It is so conserving-minded as to be pained by the destruction of any existing value, yet so radical as to expose every achievement to criticism and potential recasting.

Compassion, which is a central ingredient in maturity, stands in contrast with both conformity and confrontation. Conformity is a condition of sickly serenity in which dull personalities do not differ or the uncommitted live for no causes. Conformity benumbs the spirit into believing that peace reigns when there is only a sullen silence, that contentment may be had only in a life immunized from problems, that harmony is possible without differences, and that mutuality can be so perfect as to eliminate tension. Confrontation, on the other hand, means obsession with differences in which hardened antagonists oppose each other with vengeful bitterness and in which advocacy becomes the occasion of intransigence. In conforming people are subhumanized because they render themselves incapable of differences; in confrontation they are dehumanized because they turn differences into tools of rancor and reason into an instrument of aggression. Unless the spirit is transformed, an intellect is a potentially destructive tool.

Polarizations destroy communication because in them people play to the galleries, appeal for attention, and seek to score points until every relationship is poisoned by covert agendas and all interaction is rendered divisive by the perpetuation and intensification of rivalry. Compassion can transform conflict without eliminating it. It can foster conditions in which encounter becomes communicative and thinking becomes an instrument of mutuality. Shouting matches using epithets give way to exploratory conversation. Compassionate individuals will, for instance, steer away from arguments directed at other selves rather than at issues, at personalities rather than at policies. They will avoid that too easy trap of blaming widespread ills on devil figures, of employing castigation and invective rather than pinpointing difficulties, and they will seek therapeutic solutions for social difficulties. Compassion, as an ingredient in maturity, prompts the solution of difficulties with the least necessary fuss—remembering that some situations do call for serious encounter and firm stands. If situations can be corrected by patient work behind the scenes, what is the warrant for attention-getting heroics? Compassion helps to ameliorate antagonism because it transforms the will—engendering cooperation rather than coercing submission.

In maturity, then, we find a union of discernment, a capacity to make discriminating judgments, with compassion, which seeks to make such discriminating judgments the means for building community between persons. Maturity involves capacities to empathize with others and to dialogue with them in ways not dissimilar to those that Barzun identified as qualities of elegance in conversation. Real conversation is not mere chitchat such as one so often hears at a cocktail party. Conversation is the interchange between those seeking to probe issues and examine problems more deeply than can any individual alone. The competency to point out error, inadequacy, and foolishness are needed for one side of conversation in the academic process, while the grace to admit mistakes, to profit from criticism, and to be open to growth are needed for the other side. Maturity is needed both in those who play the critic and those who are criticized. It ensures that criticism will be made with sensitivity and empathy and thus redeems the process from what otherwise might be mere polemic or invective.

The concept of intellectual maturity may be best appreciated by considering the meaning of the phrase "a reasonable person." This phrase as ordinarily used does not indicate that someone has mastered the intricacies of logic, or that all of that person's thinking is factually accurate. The term "reasonable" denotes a quality of resilience, a capacity to discuss matters fairly, a perspective that sees the complex implications of issues without losing sight of fundamentals, and (perhaps above all else) an ability to put others at ease in the exploration of misunderstandings. Truth emerges from dialogue more as a consequence of candor and gracefulness in the very being of the persons involved than from the use of critical harshness in the nailing of mistakes or from punching holes in the formulations of an opponent.

124   In thinking about maturity as a touchstone of achievement we must recognize knowledge as a corporate rather than merely an individual accomplishment. Maturity acknowledges, at least to some extent, a coming-to-flower of ideas based not merely upon individual effort (however important this may be), but upon perceptions vicariously assimilated from a heritage. If knowledge is pursued with total oblivion to and contempt for covenants, communities, and consensus of the scholarly guild, it can easily become too self-styled. If knowledge is pursued in a slavish dependence on the prior accomplishments of others considered authoritative, it can easily become formalistic. A mature intellect does relate to the past and is concerned with the exegesis of the intellectual heritage, but it also knows the importance of inspiration, of seeing beyond the safety of rootage in authority. Conversely, a mature intellect does respond to the inspiring event of the present, even to the inspiration uniquely experienced by an individual self, while at the same time guarding against the dangers that are inherent in the undisciplined fantasy of the private imagination.

TOWARD A SYMBIOSIS BETWEEN ELEGANCE AND MATURITY

In addition to the ways elegance and maturity provide important rubrics for thinking about scholarly achievement, the possible symbiosis between them provides a still richer sense of the balances that give depth and richness to the intellectual enterprise. Elegance yearns for genuine simplicity and guards against contrived or affected confusion; maturity warns against oversimplification and the portraying of difficult matters with formulations that ignore complexity. Elegance fights against the confusion that comes when too much material is handled without the categories to give it meaningful relatedness; maturity guards against illegitimate simplification that obscures the enormous ranges of experience. Elegance points to symmetry and design, which are discoverable in many aspects of reality; maturity provides perspective upon the absurdities and incoherences that are also tough and persistent aspects of experience. Elegance helps us to appreciate the relationship between knowledge and beauty, maturity helps us to appreciate the interrelationship of knowledge and wisdom. Elegance is most at home with clarity, maturity with charity. Elegance prompts the fine crafting of ideas and rejoices in finesse; maturity leads to procedural graciousness and respects poise.

    Perhaps the order of nature is more amenable to elegant portrayal than the order of history. Politics and culture contain surds that are not readily glossed by interpolation into overarching generalizations. Politics and history do not manifest the marvelously patterned coherences often found in the phenomena contemplated by the natural scientist. It is, therefore, the task of a conceptually imaginative education to produce a capacity to judge the materials with which one works, to know also the conditions of the times in which one lives, and to turn to the relevant and illuminating rubrics and paradigms that are most adequate for making sense of the plethora of considerations that must be taken into account in constructing a perception of reality. Both elegance and maturity in intellectual attainment can help to do this: elegance, by focusing on the value and importance of patterns and forms; maturity, by keeping us aware of the exceptions and absurdities that confound neat answers.

There was a time when being an academician implied a certain quality of personhood referred to in the phrase "a gentleman and a scholar." The association of these two ideas in a familiar figure of speech, while unfortunately stated with the male generic, bears witness to an important conjunction of qualities that is enhanced by saying "a gentleperson and a scholar." The quality of gentleness is appropriate for a person of learning. Gentleness involves loyalty to truth above concern for selfish gain; it implies commitment to candor in dialogue in contrast to bombast in rhetoric designed to advance a political cause; it insists that the exploration of issues, development of critical insight, and sharing of ideas are more important than forcing others to accept one's own point of view.

Scholarly attainment may find itself positioned defensively against cruder measures of human success, though hopefully not to the point of having to drink hemlock. Those who are devoted to the scholarly style should be ready to demonstrate that elegance and maturity are no less important in the world of concrete decision making than in the so-called ivory tower. Those scientific theories that embody elegance have remade a world and given new power, new productivity, and new means to many people with which to cope with life. Maturity and wisdom do not ruin politics on those rare occasions when they appear in the world of organizational interaction. Nations have been destroyed from without and rotted from within, not because the gentler and grander qualities have been overly evident, but because crass shrewdness and political opportunism have been the dominant stances and have invited hostility and distrust from others.

Former Cornell president Andrew White, whose academic specialty was history and whose methodological assumptions were scientific, called for the teaching of history by a method that would make it applicable to the immediate needs of society. White, perhaps as

126 much as any well-known American college president, represented a reaction against educational luxury confined to "elegant learned investigations of mere scholarly interest."[7] But White was no anti-intellectual vocationalist searching for the crudest version of "know-how" training. He was especially critical of education designed only to enhance the ability to make profit. While he was critical of scholarly types who became entailed in minutiae he was also critical of those who valued education only as a means of making money. "He rejected the first because they would substitute 'dates for history, gerund-grinding for literature, and formulas for science.' And he wished equally to guard higher education from the second group, to whom 'Gain is God, and Gunny-bags his Prophet.' "[8]

The scholarly world should hold high the torch of learning and both explain and exemplify the vision of elegance and maturity as measures of accomplishment. The worth of the latter qualities, even in affairs of commerce and politics, should not be contemptuously dismissed. But these traits may be commended best not by oral defense in abstract essays, but by being made operable in the work of those who profess their value. True, a rhetorical defense of these ideals must be reiterated constantly, because—like all great virtues—people easily forget to exemplify them adequately. The validity of elegance and maturity as touchstones of scholarly style cannot be made altogether dependent upon the extent to which the academic guild embodies them. They are the rubrics for a morality of knowledge and pedagogy, not categories for a sociological description of the academy. They point to goals and ideals rather than describe attainments. Many practicing academicians fall considerably short of these measures; indeed, even the most careful scholar falls short at some time or another. Such inadequacy is to be expected. It is not the presence of such inadequacy that violates the integrity of our calling but the willingness of so many to settle for something less demanding. Often, pedantry takes over as a measure of scholarship because under its demands accomplishment can be more easily measured. It is easier to be correct about factual data than wise about life (and easier to measure). It is less demanding to accumulate a battery of detailed achievements than to envision goals and be perceptive as to meanings (and less subject to controversy in evaluations). This being so, the fortunes of elegance and maturity as the ultimate measures of scholarly achievement can thrive only under conditions in which grace and acceptance are more functional in an institution's life than judgmental competitiveness. The steward-ship of knowledge thus requires a search for clues as to how to create the right conditions for scholarly *praxis*. That exploration is the task of the following chapter.

1. Michael Polanyi, *Personal Knowledge: Towards a Post-Critical Philosophy* (London: Routledge and Kegan Paul, 1958), 149.

2. See Jacques Barzun, *The House of Intellect* (New York: Harper and Brothers, 1959), 60ff.

3. Ibid., 69.

4. Ibid., 37.

5. E. Harris Harbison, *The Christian Scholar in the Age of the Reformation* (New York: Scribner's, 1956), 90.

6. James M. Gustafson, "Moral Discernment in the Christian Life," in *Norm and Context in Christian Ethics*, Gene H. Outka and Paul Ramsey (eds.) (New York: Scribner's, 1968), 18.

7. Cited in John S. Brubacher and Willis Rudy, *Higher Education in Transition: A History of American Colleges and Universities 1636–1976*. Third Edition (New York: Harper and Row, 1968), 163.

8. Ibid., 162.

CHAPTER TEN

Doing Truth:
On Sustaining a Scholarly Ethos

The responsibility of the academy for the discovery and enrichment of knowledge and culture entails more than giving form and content to knowledge: the academy also has an obligation to maintain and inculcate fidelity to certain distinctive attitudes and procedures that give scholarship a professional identity. Scholarship is a guild achievement. Membership in the guild carries with it obligations to work according to a highly cultivated understanding as to what is appropriate in a very special kind of community. A few obvious implications of this understanding can be codified in rules; the more subtle ones must be internalized—"felt in the bones," so-to-speak, or made "habits of the heart."

Skilled professional practice cannot be regarded as something that follows automatically from the possession of an advanced degree. Academic malpractice is often stumbled into—as, for instance, by students who have never been carefully instructed about the nature of plagiarism, or by faculty members who have not paused long enough to consider the difference between academic freedom as the protection of highly responsible professionalism and scholarly license as a carte blanche for freewheeling.

Members of the scholarly community have no automatic immunity from the temptations to greed and irresponsibility that are growing at such at alarming rate in contemporary culture. It may be too strong to assert that "virtually any undergraduate or graduate student can relate harrowing stories about tribulations suffered at the hands of irresponsible instructors,"[1] but there is no question that the actualities of academic life fall short of the ideals by which it is supposedly defined. Graduate school training has become increasingly less reliable as an introduction to good practice even as the demands made on the profession of teaching have become more intense. The requisite sensibilities and commitments that sustain academic morality cannot be absorbed by casual osmosis even if the ethos of the academic guild can help to shape the values and commitments of those who immerse themselves in its milieu. These matters call for deliberate attention, explicit articulation, and intentional commitment. More attention should be given, both in the preparation of teachers and in the practice of the profession, to those aspects of professional behavior discussed in books such as *The Academic Ethic*[2] by Edward Shils and *Saints and Scamps: Ethics in Academia*[3] by Steven M. Cahn. Moreover, people are likely to embody the right impulses only to the extent that they can experience professional integrity in a community of committed practice.

HONESTY AS AUTHENTIC TRANSPARENCY

No obligation of scholarship is more central than the obligation to convey to others completely and correctly the content and contours of the ideas with which one works as well as the ground (or premises) from which one has arrived at particular conclusions. This is more than a responsibility to tell the truth (as does a witness under oath). It is an obligation to be so authentically transparent as, in a certain meaning of the term, to "do truth." Hence, the impressions created as well as the details enunciated are involved. The message and the medium must be congruent. The stance of a professor must differ from that of a salesperson or an advertiser, whose apparent enthusiasm for some product need not necessarily be accompanied by an entirely genuine inner conviction (as long, at least, as the gloss can be obscured) that the product is all it is presented as being.

Highly publicized violations of academic honesty have been relatively few in number, but this does not mean than such practices are rare. Cases of academic dishonesty are not normally tried in public, and institutions are not anxious for the adverse publicity that would come from making them known. When an unusual set of circumstances brings academic dishonesty to public attention people may even be surprised. For instance, in the mid 1970s the academic world was shocked when it was discovered that a senior student at one of the most prestigious universities in America had forged letters of recommendation in order to assure admission to the graduate schools he was anxious to attend. These forgeries were uncovered when a new public law was enacted, requiring confidential material in files to be made available to students. Rather than do that the institution returned letters to the senders—in this case to senders who had never written them. What made this episode so tragic was the fact that the student, with an enviable record in studies and a reputation for "near

130   genius ability," would almost surely have been admitted to the school of his choice on the basis of what professors would gladly have written on his behalf. In the 1980s the academic world was equally shocked when it was discovered that the publications of the dean of a distinguished medical school were largely taken without acknowledgement from the works of others.

It is impossible to know how widespread are such instances of academic dishonesty. The volume of published materials is enormous and constantly growing. Many doubt whether the external scrutiny (or "policing") of materials is even possible.[4] The effort needed to uncover either fraud or slipshod work is time consuming and not something to which many persons wish to devote their major attention. Those individuals who do bring instances of fraud to light are not always appreciated.[5] The integrity of scholarship depends to a very large measure on the inner sense that there is something very special about being truthful in the academic sense.

Surely, one of the most important educational responsibilities of an institution of higher education is to teach all who enter its halls a habitual integrity in the handling of subject matter. Learning what constitutes academic honesty is too important to leave to chance. Moreover, the foundations for such honesty are less and less likely to be brought into the academy by habits inculcated by the culture at large. Many distinguished institutions underscore the importance of academic honesty through an honor system, requiring each student to pledge that work submitted for a given assignment has been done without illegitimate assistance or unauthorized appropriation. Honor codes are important systemic devices for emphasizing a central obligation of scholarship. They affirm the community's responsibility for integrity. But strange as it may seem, many schools do not have honor codes. In such institutions honesty in academic exercises is enforced by a proctoring process that all too often involves a cat-and-mouse game between students and instructors. Such game play tends to create an impression that cheating is less a contradiction of the scholar's most fundamental premise for being than behavior that, if discovered, brings extrinsic punishment. The externally coercive enforcement of academic honesty may even imply that cleverness and intrigue are acceptable means for trying to beat the system—a premise more appropriate for training to serve in an espionage unit than for membership in the scholarly community.

The scholarly guild will have little integrity if its members do not understand themselves as functioning on their honor. Scholars cannot be directly proctored and monitored as are classes taking quizzes under hawk-eyed instructors. Fraudulent or careless work can possibly be revealed for what it is, since published results of research can be scrutinized for both originality and warrant—but where would scholarship be if every published article had to be treated as suspect? The time required to enforce academic integrity by external monitoring—even if necessary—is time forfeited to an alien necessity, whether in undergraduate classrooms or professional publications.

It is not the flagrant falsification or misappropriation of materials that presents the greatest temptation. An investigator who becomes known as one who slights details or extrapolates without warrant will probably be stigmatized—in the long, if not the short, run. More complex temptations arise in those situations where extrinsic considerations misshape scholarly work without necessarily falsifying it. Sponsored research, for instance, introduces partisan or commercial factors into the dynamics. The dangers posed by such factors were discussed in a session of the American Association for the Advancement of Science held in February 1975, as the problems in reporting research results were canvassed. The temptations to slant research to favor particular points of view were frankly faced, and pressures upon universities to obtain research grants geared to particular concerns or resulting in particular findings were acknowledged.[6] Political power or commercial interest can create pressures even when the most scrupulous effort is made to avoid flagrant violations of scholarly integrity. The problem of doing the truth under such conditions becomes not merely the simplistic one of avoiding fraud, but the complex task of deliberately guarding against the subtle temptations to render truth subservient to other claims. Moreover, it involves not merely the conscience of the individual researcher, but the stances taken by the institution as a whole in its relationships with the sponsors of research and even with its benefactors.

Tensions also arise between the obligation to share the truth and the desire for personal credit. Even exciting and distinguished intellectual achievements can be affected by this tension. For example, the process of discovering the fundamental genetic material, DNA, which won a Nobel Prize in 1961, was marked by great rivalry. One of the principal investigators in this dramatic achievement has written an autobiographical account of the emotional problems that arose throughout the investigative process. Tension arose between the principal investigators, finally reaching a point where one of them lost interest in the project, and others became furious with each other because they felt their contributions had been appropriated without due recognition. The account of the discovery of DNA suggests that the process was marked by misunderstanding between a mentor and

132   his student, and was compounded by the normal concern of the originator of the idea to receive the credit for its development. The account also explores the effects on the dynamics of the search in England of the realization that Linus Pauling, working at the California Institute of Technology, might obtain the result in America before the team did in England.[7] The lesson to be garnered from this account is not that the ideal of sharing all scholarly discovery openly is a mistaken one, but that the problems of living up to that ideal in concrete historical circumstances may be tremendous. Teachers who supervise research, for instance, must be especially careful not to appropriate the work of students as though it were their own.

If the processes of scientific discovery, surrounded as they are by acknowledged canons of procedural respect for the work of others, can become matters of such emotional tensions, how much more can the handling of campus relationships test the mettle of openness? The obligation to do the truth encompasses how one analyzes issues and also what one says about colleagues and other matters of institutional life. There should not be two standards of truth at work in the academy: one for use in the output of self-conscious scholarship and the other for use in the cloakrooms of the faculty club or the deliberations of committees.

Another threat to academic integrity comes from the need to market educational wares in a period of shrinking clienteles. Educational institutions increasingly resort to merchandizing techniques to attract potential students. This prompts them to put forth the best face, to publish brochures and catalogs that list their resources in ways that overpromise what they can realistically deliver. For instance, there is a rather widespread practice among college admissions offices of treating certain S.A.T. scores as NIP's—not in the profile. The scores of those admitted on athletic scholarships, with learning disabilities, under minority quotas, or from overseas, are set aside when computing the averages. In reporting on these practices the *New York Times* ironically headlined the story "College SAT Lists Can Be Creative Works."[8] At a time when students may be deciding for or against a particular institution on the basis of the caliber of students it enrolls, administrative obfuscation prompted by merchandizing pressures should be zealously guarded against. Nor is distortion of the truth by means of selective use of facts a temptation only for publicity oriented administrators. In situations where departmental fortunes hang on the number of students they attract, does not everyone make the most persuasive case for majoring in their own field—perhaps even to the point of downplaying the limitations and disadvantages?

To do the truth involves more than merely being correct about   133
what one *does* say; it also involves having integrity in making choices
about what *one ought* to say. Truth becomes a function not merely
of what is verifiable, but of what is required to achieve intellectual
wholeness. Truth in the political sphere and in the economic order is
not measured as rigorously. Spying, for instance, could hardly be
possible if the giving of full and complete impressions were a cardinal
duty. Nor are entrepreneurs necessarily obligated to publish trade
secrets or advertise the shortcomings of their product. Publishers (of
trade books, at least) need not create advertising blurbs that offer a
balanced selection of both the favorable and the unfavorable comments from reviewers. But the academy must expect its members to
govern their fidelity to truth by a very high level of expectation. To
gossip on the basis of hearsay may be as pernicious as fraudulent
reporting of research findings; exaggeration may be as wrong within
the academy as false witness is in litigation; the selection of what is
opened to public view may be as crucial as what is said in detail.

Such a measure of the obligation is a statement of an ideal. No
one stands perfect as measured by the ideal. Since scholarship is a
human achievement, and since scholarly communication is carried on
by persons afflicted with the infirmities of the flesh and the frailties of
human willfulness, shortcomings are functionally unavoidable though
probably not theoretically inevitable. The proper response to this discrepancy is to acknowledge shortcomings and to respond to them
with new resolves, not to redefine the obligation in ways that make it
attainable with ordinary effort or on terms consistent with integrity as
measured by other communities of endeavour.

PURITY OF MIND AS INTRINSIC RESPONSIVENESS

A second ingredient in sound scholarly praxis defies description by a
single extant term. The phrase "freedom of inquiry" points toward it,
but is also misleading. The scholar whose imagination has been fired
by the vision of a great idea is enthralled by a great passion rather
than cut loose from obligations. The term "self-motivation" also points
toward this ingredient in scholarly praxis, but is inadequate because
it assumes that the scholar drives herself or himself whereas in a
profounder sense the scholar responds to the call of the truth. The term
"idle curiosity," which Thorstein Veblen used to indicate detachment
from any ulterior motives,[9] is also unsatisfactory, for it seems to suggest a listlessness or lack of purpose that is utterly foreign to the
quality that needs to be described.

134   In the absence of better terminology, the phrase "intrinsic responsiveness" may best point to the quality in a scholar's dedication that gives it a unique place in the various callings to which people are beckoned. The scholar says "Yes" to the claim of knowledge as something to be cherished because knowledge has its own intrinsic value.

The scholar is not merely an autonomous individual doing what casual inclination or temporary whim may dictate. Nor is the scholar someone else's individual, doing only what an heteronomous agent orders. The scholar is "truth's servant" who works within a context of fidelity to knowledge, both its nurture and its application. Under that covenant the scholar may have many kinds of secondary interests to pursue, ends to serve, and duties to honor. The knowledge of the scholar may be useful and may be put to use, but in relationship to ideas the scholar is "detached" from every extrinsic impulse to shape pursuits, tailor opinions, tamper with data, or subordinate methodological independence to the requirements of any secondary agenda.[10]

Strange as it may seem to many scholars, the best paradigm for this role is drawn from a religious model: not from priests, who as protectors of institutional prerogatives often prove themselves incapable of tolerating a radically vertical covenant with truth, but from prophets, who fear God so much that they fear no earthly rulers. Prophets exemplify the qualities of intrinsic responsiveness in the doing of truth far better than can those in commerce or politics. Some pastors of confessing churches in Germany during the days of Nazi tyranny proved to be better resisters than tenured professors on the payroll of the state. In Vietnam, it was Buddhist priests and monks who often witnessed most persistently against the corruption in official circles. Socrates, who was committed to his process of soliciting truth without regard for conventional hesitations, may also be cited as a model, for in this regard he is often thought of as having a kind of religious quality to his life. Civil servants and bureaucrats perform valuable service within the body politic, and entrepreneurs provide important goods for people's welfare, but theirs is a horizontally rather than a vertically defined kind of loyalty, and therefore only infrequently achieves the quality so important to the scholarly doing of truth.

Academicians like to believe that the most dangerous—perhaps even the main—threats to academic integrity come from outside the institutional walls of the academy. They are on guard against a public that is suspicious of strange ideas, against ecclesiastical bodies that try to enforce orthodoxy by fiat, and against politicians who would make loyalty oaths or safe opinions prerequisite to the right to teach. Against such threats constant vigilance is necessary. But there are also pressures within the academy that work against the definition of a scholar's responsibility in intrinsic terms.

The possibility of academic freedom depends not only upon the protection of teachers from external pressures and dictates, but upon the way in which teachers treat each other in the give-and-take of pedagogy and governance. Departments that choose only colleagues who agree with their approach to a subject may actually endanger that openness and breadth of perspective that is essential to academic inquiry. Teachers who give high grades only to students who agree with their interpretations and accept their perspectives threaten academic freedom and openness perhaps even more than external vigilantes. This is the consequence not only if such a practice is actually the case, but even if it is alleged by students to be the case. It is often necessary to bend over backward to ensure that one is perceived as being fair.

Academicians can betray their own ideals without intending to do so. For instance, for good and proper reasons it is important to provide excluded groups and excluded points of view a place in the scheme of things. In this way a desireable breadth is nourished in the institutional ethos. But, alas, if previously excluded groups brought in through such affirmative action seek to reverse the power balance, and hence themselves try to control the situation so as to favor only their perspectives, little has been gained. Affirmative action must strive to guard many points of view so as to enrich the composition of the community, not merely change which groups dominate.

The dynamics of intrinsic responsiveness can be threatened by the use of fear to elicit performance. To be sure, it is impossible to completely eliminate the sense of anxiety from educational pursuits. But artificially induced anxiety runs counter to the cultivation of an intrinsic responsiveness to ideas. The use of the caning rod in preparatory and parochial schools, recounted so frequently in literary accounts of teaching[11] has largely died out. But psychically debilitative competition may be little better, whether experienced by students or by faculty. Peter Cohen, in an analysis of professional education at the Harvard Law School, recounts the story of a suicide that occurred near the end of one academic year. He blames the tragedy upon the institution's internalization and intensification of society's competitiveness, upon the use of ratings and the thrust to elicit performance by fear. Cohen asks, "Why competition here, where everybody is after the same basic information? Where it oughtn't to make the least bit of difference how and when you get the facts, just as long as you do? And yet, even in high schools and especially in the colleges dog eats

136   dog. The fast, the slow; the privileged, the underprivileged. In a manner that doesn't come anywhere near the battles of equals which supposedly characterizes clean competition; it can't even be called a fight—it is a slaughter."[12]

Students encounter these problems on one level; faculty, particularly junior faculty, encounter them on another. Tenure decisions have become so momentous as to fill the first years of teaching with more anxiety than joy, with more concern about professional destiny than about achieving mastery of subject matter. These consequences can be mitigated by sensitivity on the part of colleagues and administrators, but that requires imaginative vision and deliberate resolves. Instead of acquiescing to the economic factors that are making the early odysseys of scholars so traumatic, the academic world should be massively concerned with setting in motion countervailing dynamics that can reinstate the sense of intrinsic satisfaction to the pursuit of scholarship. We all need to help each other in seeking to create that set of conditions that make possible freedom and joy in professional achievement.

MAINTAINING THE ZEST IN BOTH RESEARCH AND TEACHING

Those familiar with campuses and their controversies know that one of the most prevalent ongoing debates in the academy concerns the relative attention that should be devoted to teaching on the one hand and to research on the other. Even strangers to the inner conflicts of the academy have heard the slogan "Publish or perish." As popularly understood, this contrast implies that professors who spend time and energy teaching students cannot possibly also find time to push back the frontiers of knowledge, and conversely, that those who hole up in the laboratory or library are unlikely to be interested in the classroom or to be inspiring from the teaching podium.

The issue of teaching versus research is more than a discussion of how the scholar should allocate time. It is a matter upon which bread-and-butter decisions affecting promotion and tenure are often based as well as the more elusive factors of scholarly visibility and professional prestige. These matters become intensely controversial and deeply felt because the reward system of many institutions is determined by how they are treated. Where a professor's money (or fame) lie, there scholarly priorities are apt to be also. Moreover, more than the individual professor's commitments are involved; the institution as a whole is also subject to pressures as it eyes the plums awarded by industry and government—even by foundations—for activities that "push back the frontiers of knowledge," or otherwise promise to be innovative.

This debate about the relative importance of teaching and research in the pursuit of scholarship must be addressed by examining the guild's fundamental responsibility to truth. Teaching and research are both aspects of the stewardship of knowledge and should not be evaluated except in terms of that stewardship. Research is essential to the discovery, extension, and refinement of knowledge. Teaching is essential to its promulgation and often to the training of those who will be future members of the vocational group most concerned with knowledge. Both tasks must be adequately cared for by the academy considered as a generic aggregate—though not necessarily to the same extent by each particular institution or by each particular faculty member. Varieties of gifts and diversities of vocation are possible in the vineyard of learning. It is legitimate to protest an emphasis on research that is based on infatuation with novelty for its own sake, or a tendency to homogenize the measure of scholarly achievement by this single test.

But it is hard to imagine a lively scholar who is not concerned, to some extent, with both the joy of discovery/interpretation and the challenge of nurturing/mentoring. This is not to expect that every faculty member will be equally adept at both roles. An institution can afford to have on its staff some individuals who naturally do best in the classroom. They should be rewarded for such gifts, both with the calculable rewards of salary increments and with the more subtle reward of approval and appreciation. An institution can also afford to have on its staff those who do better in the laboratory or at the writing desk. They also should be rewarded and appreciated. Even within institutions where it is more appropriate to emphasize one of these functions over the other, there is a proper place for both. In no institution should the reward scheme be so radically slanted as to make it impossible to respect individual variations. A British report on higher education produced in 1961–63 was on target in its observations, which expressed "total disagreement" with the view that emphasis on research takes away the value of faculty service to students. It declared that research is a possible inspiration to them. "One ounce of example is worth a pound of exhortation." Conversely, Thorstein Veblen sounded a warning against engaging in research without also teaching.

> Only in the most exceptional, not to say erratic, cases will good consistent, sane, and alert scientific work be carried forward through a course of years by any scientist without students,

138   without loss or blunting of that intellectual initiative that makes
             the creative scientist. The work that can be done well in the
             absence of that stimulus and safeguarding that comes of the give
             and take between teacher and student is commonly such only as
             can without deterioration be reduced to a mechanically system-
             atized task-work,—that is to say, such as can, without loss or
             gain, be carried on under the auspices of a business-like academic
             government.[13]

     Similarly, Jacques Barzun, surely no example of a clogged schol-
arly pen, expressed the uneasiness about a breed of scholar whose
orientation is primarily toward research.

          Somehow, the scholar [whose orientation is primarily toward
          research] adapts himself to the demands of lecturing, examining,
          keeping office hours, serving on committees, reading disserta-
          tions and fellowship applications, writing letters of recommenda-
          tion, and identifying at sight a few useful members of the central
          administration. For the rest, he toils in the library or laboratory
          under the mantle of his discipline, meaning not the medieval
          hair-shirt but the silk-lined cloak of professionalism.
             In that guise he and his peers constitute the chief asset and
          heaviest burden of the new university, the prevailing belief being
          that research is the great justification of the whole enterprise.
          The analogies at work here are with science and industry. Only
          research make science progress; only research and development
          keep the nation (economy, industry, culture, consumer market)
          thriving. *New* is the keynote. New products, ideas, ways of doing
          the same thing, on the chance they will be better, *newer*.[14]

     In criticizing the demand for excessive research Veblen made a
commercial model the villain of the piece. Similarly, Barzun made
technology and the consumer model of new products the villain of
the piece. Even though written two generations apart their observations are instructive. The individual scholar's involvement in either
teaching or research should be motivated by intrinsic interest in the
subject matter and the advancement of learning. Creativity in scholarship is threatened neither by attention to teaching nor by preoccupation with research, but by making either activity the hostage of purposes foreign to the academy. A concern with marketing teaching in
order to compete for scarce students may become in one period as
dysfunctional to pedagogical health as the use of research to bolster
prestige can be in another.
     The factor that tends to be overlooked in this misplaced debate
is the obligation of the academician to stay intellectually alive. The

formulations of knowledge are in constant flux, so that no scholar/ teacher can rely only upon what was learned in graduate school as the basis for adequate performance. It is often presumed that an ongoing program of research keeps the investigator abreast of subject matter—that it puts a scholar on the "cutting edge of the discipline." But proper attention to teaching may do the same—indeed, a teacher who reads widely and thinks continuously about what is required to stay abreast of a discipline, and of the understandings required to know how a chosen discipline relates to larger intellectual issues, can remain even more alive than the researcher whose pursuits lead only to an ever-narrowing specialization.

Perhaps the usual way in which the relative importance of teaching and research are discussed can be improved by developing more adequate conceptions of what is meant by each. If teaching, for instance, is considered merely to be a classroom encounter in which a transfer of routinely known information from a knowledgeable mind to a blank receptacle takes place, particularly if that transfer is presumed to depend upon compulsion, then obviously teaching by itself does not provide an adequate expression of scholarly commitments. If, however, teaching is conceptualized as a series of dynamic encounters in which two or more persons explore a subject through a common excitement with the issues it raises and the implications it entails, then teaching will be seen to involve some of the attributes associated with research. Conversely, if by research is meant an individualistically pursued, atomistic, linear, and simplistically progressive quest for detailed facts by the single experimenter working alone, then it may typically compete for the attention of the faculty member to the detriment of a relationship with students. If, however, research is understood as involvement with a whole guild in the search for a greater detailed and more insightful understanding of a field, it will put the investigator on the frontiers of knowledge and most likely provide a source of excitement that cannot but improve the quality of pedagogy.

There are various kinds of research. That most typically sponsored by the university is investigative: it involves the discovery of some new information or the creation of an original concept. Parker Palmer has suggested another model of research, which involves interaction between teacher and students in a mutual quest.[15] In this kind of exploration the scholar enters a situation and solicits hypotheses from the persons or the groups being studied. Such hypotheses may first be suggested in confused and even contradictory forms. In such research the examination of the hypotheses is done by the group that has proposed them and about which they may be formed. This kind of research stimulates the subjects of an investigation to engage in

140   dialogue, to be participants in the process of discovery, and to learn about themselves as much as they may be learned about. It is often particularistic rather than universalistic or generalizable in focus. It takes a mature and sophisticated individual to engage in this kind of research, which is so much a form of teaching that it creates a learning situation for both the researcher and the subjects of the research.

To these models of investigative and dialogical research I would add a third kind of productive scholarship worthy of recognition by the university. This kind of research, rather than "pushing back the frontiers of knowledge," refines existing frontiers and polishes extant information into more useful and elegant formulations. It might well be called interpretative research—and may well be refolding or circular rather than linear in format. It is more likely to be reflective than investigative, holistic rather than atomistic. The synthesizer, whose mind ranges across the wide landscape of the known and finds new configurations and new ways of stating truth, has much to contribute. Interpretative research usually culminates in writing—in "think pieces" that illuminate even existing information. Writing is an important discipline and challenge. Doing it well ensures the continued growth of the scholar, both because it involves digging deeper down into the wells of information and because it involves reviewing and refining factors already known into an enriched perspective. Such work of interpretation is potentially as broadening to the grasp of a field and to the development of scholarly stature as is the investigative type of research. Doing this kind of research helps the scholar to stay alive and vital just as much as does the doing of the kind of research that discovers some new item of information.

> The man who has never written history cannot comprehend the difficulty of the task. Properly the style emerges in the midst of the process in which the mind is engaged, but unless the subject is to some extent dictated by a sense of involvement the product will be the tasteless fruit of the syllabus merchant. Even though the choice of a subject is often the result of accident, man, matter, and manner are inseparable. If they are not, the art of history is smothered. The facts may be amended, even replaced, but what makes the historian is the play of his mind over the subject, and of that the only evidence is his style, wherein lies the proof of his understanding, the proof of coherence. Always allowing that facts are beautiful, nothing is so easy—or so barren—as their recital, just as nothing is so difficult—or so fruitful—as the fusion of mind and matter that produces a joy forever.[16]

As long as the beauty of which this quotation speaks is forthcoming
from the effort to write it, secondary history is as valuable as primary
history, interpretative scholarship as much to be honored as the investigative. The consequences of doing research of this kind are bound to
contribute to the quality of the teaching of those who do it. But
teaching is a complex art that needs further examination. This art will
be the special focus of the discussion in the next chapter.

NOTES

1. Steven M. Cahn, *Saints and Scamps: Ethics in Academia* (Totowa, N.J.:
Rowman and Littlefield, 1986), xi.

2. Edward Shils, *The Academic Ethic* (Chicago: University of Chicago
Press, 1983).

3. See note 1.

4. See "Science Can't Keep Up with Flood of New Journals," *New York
Times*, 16 February 1988, C1, C11.

5. See "Two Critics of Science Revel in the Role," in *New York Times*,
19 April 1988, C1, C7.

6. For an account of this meeting see "Scientists Find Public Often
Misled by Faulty Research Data," *New York Times*, 2 February 1975, 32.

7. James D. Watson, *The Double Helix: A Personal Account of the Discovery
of the Structure of DNA* (New York: Atheneum, 1968), see especially 57f.

8. See "Colleges' SAT Lists Can be Creative Works," *New York Times*,
25 November 1987, Late Edition, B10.

9. Thorstein Veblen, *The Higher Learning in America* (New York:
Huebsch, 1918), 273.

10. This does not cancel the realization, which I suggested in chapter
8, that our knowledge is always partial and our perceptions always colored
to some extent by the standing grounds from which we look at things. It
only suggests that scholars, as they try to be intentionally conscious of their
standing grounds, will seek to avoid deliberate subservience to pressures that
would cause them to tailor their findings according to factors extrinsic to the
claim of the subject they are examining.

11. For a collection of accounts of teaching that suggest the frequency
and even the sadism of such practices, see Claude M. Fuess and Emory
Basford, *Unseen Harvests: A Treasury of Teaching* (New York: Macmillan, 1947).

12. Peter Cohen, *The Gospel According to the Harvard Business School*
(Garden City, N.Y.: Doubleday 1953), 168.

13. Veblen, *The Higher Learning*, 273.

14. Jacques Barzun, *The American University: How It Runs, Where It Is
Going* (New York: Harper and Brothers, 1959), 20.

142   15. See Parker J. Palmer, *To Know as We Are Known: A Spirituality of Higher Education* (San Francisco: Harper and Row, 1983), 62f, 98ff.

16. Charles F. Mullett, "There Mark What Ills the Scholar's Life Assail," *Drew Gateway*, Winter 1973, 106.

CHAPTER ELEVEN

Pilgrimage and Professionalism in Pedagogical Interaction

ON THE NATURE OF TEACHING

An academic institution brings students and teachers together for edifying interaction. Such interaction involves far more than the transfer of information or the inculcation of habits. It nourishes ways of thinking and acting that identify members of a guild—a guild in which freedom and individuality rather than conformity are the most cherished values. Learning is an odyssey, a journey into frameworks of understanding and perceptions of meaning that are shared in a special way by those who seek to be openly committed to dialogue and inquiry. Teaching is the art of guiding that odyssey.

There is something very special about the dynamics involved in teaching, for the sharing of knowledge and culture increases the well-being of those who give of themselves in the process even as it benefits those who receive from the interchange. In many kinds of human interaction goods must be hoarded in order to be possessed. A piece of pie given to another person cannot be eaten by oneself. Money that is spent on one's own needs cannot be spent for the sake of another. But an idea shared with someone else remains as full and rich for the original possessor as it becomes for the recipient—and may even be expanded by the act of sharing. In a similar way, some forms of power must be guarded and clutched for the self in order to be controlled. Politics and commerce often deal with "zero-sum" circumstances in which gain for one person (or group) results in another's loss. Under such circumstances power is preserved defensively for the self and bartered for strategic purposes. But in teaching power takes the form of enabling, so whatever the giver shares with a receiver makes both stronger.

Pedagogical interaction is a unique experience. Søren Kierkegaard saw this truth and applied it to the relationship between God and human beings.

When God becomes a Teacher, his love cannot be merely second-ing and assisting, but is creative, giving new being to the learner, or as we have called him, the man born anew; by which designation we signify the transition from non-being to being. The truth is that the learner owes the Teacher everything. But this is what makes it so difficult to effect an understanding; that the learner becomes as nothing and yet is not destroyed; that he comes to owe everything to the Teacher, and yet retains his confidence; that he understands the truth and yet that the Truth makes him free; that he apprehends that guilt of his Error and yet that his confidence rises victorious in the truth.[1]

The dynamics that Kierkegaard described in terms of an interaction between a transcendent deity and the believer have counterparts in the pedagogical relationship between teacher and student. The learner does owe the teacher much, but instead of putting the learner in the jeopardy that attends being a debtor, it puts the learner in the companionship that attends being a partner. When learning takes place, truth is not so much "handed down" from one side as it is "opened up" for all sides. When shortcomings are discovered and acknowledged, the consequences may be corrective growth and not the destruction of hope. Since pedagogy involves the sharing of ideas, those who teach grow in the fullness of their own attainments as they help others to acquire enlarged visions and competencies.

We teachers run a constant risk of destroying the authenticity and freedom of those over whom we exercise pedagogical supervision. Teaching has fewer structural restraints imposed upon it than almost any other professional relationship. The teacher can "play God"—less by conscious intention than by failing to be sensitive to the feelings of those who are the victims of pedagogical hegemony. It is no accident that writers such as Ivan Illich and Michael Rossman—sometimes thinking more of public secondary education than of university teaching—would "de-school" society. They see schools, and more particularly the special guild that staffs them, perpetuating unfreedom through the exercise of specialized professional prerogatives. But even those fully committed to institutionalized forms of the educational enterprise, such as Steven Cahn[2] and Philip Rieff[3], are no less insistent about the need to avoid the misuse of pedagogical authority.

The interaction between the teacher as a professional and the student as a pilgrim depends upon the creation of a fragile balance that is in constant danger of being destroyed. There should be no teacher who does not also study since good and lively teaching involves continual effort to remain abreast of a field and excited about it. Moreover, there is no student who does not teach, since membership in a learning group has consequences for all its members, and one's very presence in such a group affects its dynamics.

But the fact that both teachers and students share in a common process does not mean their roles can be completely equated. The fragile balance involved in good learning can be destroyed as easily by denying differences in maturity and function as it can by turning those differences into legitimations for an arbitrary exercise of power. A truly healthy interaction can be achieved only by those who know how to embrace a tension between the common obligations and the functional differentiations that provide the pedagogical equation with its creativity.

A MONARCHICAL APPROACH

One way of thinking about the relationship between the teacher and the student looks upon the teacher as someone who says, "Here are the ideas that you must learn and the procedures that you must follow to do so." This "monarchial" model conveys an image of the teacher as the expert whose grasp of subject matter legitimizes control from the blackboard side of the desk. In this model, learning is understood as taking place from "the top down" (or from the front of the room to the back) and is considered basically unidirectional. While the teacher who approaches pedagogy monarchially often bases his or her demands upon a sense and mastery of a field, thus giving those demands a presumption of special validity, the student may hear only grim commands.

To be sure, only the most arrogant faculty member presumes upon the teacher's standing as a professional to get away with condescension toward students. But the treatment of students with disdain is not unknown in education—even at the highest levels of graduate study. Condescension may show up directly in attitudes that make it clear to students that the professor has little truck for halting first steps and less patience with slowness. It may show up in behavior that parades erudition as a form of show. It may be evident in a double standard of expectation regarding such matters as promptness in getting work done, thoroughness in making criticisms, and responsibility with schedules and obligations. Teachers do not always hold themselves to the same standards they impose on students. Failure in these matters may even border on malpractice.

Condescension may also be present in those attitudes that regard the teacher's interpretation of problematic and controversial matters as unassailable. Many Ph.D. candidates can tell horror stories of the

146   callousness shown by some committee member during the supervision of a dissertation. Delay in getting back comments on drafts is not uncommon; the thrust of criticisms is sometimes switched in midstream; and lack of openness toward the perspectives of candidates on matters over which there is a legitimate possibility of different interpretations of the subject have been known to make the completion of a dissertation slow and even impossible.

Such problems, perhaps exceptions rather than the rule, do give the profession a reputation that is less than universally salutary. It is possible, faced with the pressures of academic schedules and possessing an authority that can render decisions unilaterally, for faculty members to fall into instances of instructional hegemony. While not many teachers cavalierly neglect appointments, they often assume their convenience has a far more weighty claim than that of students'; some refuse to be bound contractually by their syllabi, and add extra assignments near the end of a semester, or advance deadlines without due notice. Others fail to indicate clearly and in advance the arrangements that will determine grades, the rules that govern written work, or what absences will mean. Still fewer consult with their classes before working out assignment deadlines. There is a tendency for all teachers to think of themselves as singularly in control of the regimen—not only with respect to those matters of substance where guidance of the process is rendered plausible by professional knowledge of the subject matter—but also in matters of procedure, where the teacher's attitude may be little more than a rationalization of self-serving convenience. Submitting grades on schedule, for instance, is a problem in many institutions. Some instructors, usually the same few, lack the most elementary sense of responsibility about this matter. Clearly, they operate with a presumption of privilege rather than with a sense of obligation to communal expectations. Why should not the timely submission of grade reports be as rigid an expectation as paying tuition bills on time and why should it not be enforced by analogous monetary strictures?[4]

A monarchial pedagogical posture not only engenders procedural irresponsibility but often affects the handling of subject matter. Paulo Freire has characterized a certain kind of pedagogy as a "banking" concept of education. In such a way of teaching the professor issues communiques and makes deposits of information for students to receive, memorize, and repeat.

> Narration (with the teacher as narrator) leads the students to memorize mechanically the narrated content. Worse yet, it turns them into "containers," into "receptacles" to be "filled" by the teacher. The more completely he fills the receptacles, the

better . . . a teacher . . . is. The more meekly the receptacles permit themselves to be filled, the better students they are. . . .

In the banking concept of education, knowledge is a gift bestowed on those who consider themselves knowledgeable upon those whom they consider to know nothing.[5]

The banking model as Freire describes it, whatever its appeal in the past has been, is increasingly unacceptable. Moreover, it is not practiced only by conservatives in political power who would perpetuate their control through oppression of the poor and powerless. It can appear just as insidiously in the training methods of crusaders, reformers, and revolutionaries whose intention is to produce cadres of "true believers."

AN INTEREST MODEL APPROACH

Sometimes, however, instead of saying, "Here are the ideas that you must learn," the teacher asks, "What are your ideas?" Assuming that true learning must be self-motivated (which is the case) the interest (or "consumer") model transfers choices and initiatives to the student side of the desk in order to create learner autonomy (which is deemed necessary for self-motivation). This model is the authoritarian model in reverse, equally unidirectional in its premises. Now, the learner is in charge in place of the teacher.[6]

As a means of advancing the contention that the learner's initiative has a valid place in the pedagogical process the interest model of education points to certain dynamics that are vital to good learning. Students are not likely to learn unless their curiosity has been aroused and their enthusiasm cultivated. Instead, they use their imaginative creativity to figure out ways to avoid the learning process or beat the system. To the extent they do this they cannot benefit intellectually to any great degree from being in college.

In the sixties, the interest model was used as a polemic against traditional patterns of learning. Claims that a guild of trained professionals have guidance to offer those who are entering into the intellectual life were dismissed as a "Big Daddy complex."[7] Efforts to define standards of accomplishment were caricatured as the exercise of "the cop's (i.e. policeman's) role in the classroom."[8] The learning situation was conceived as a hassle in which the possession of power is the central issue. In order for student autonomy to be respected, it was argued, grades should be abolished, since grading allows the teacher

148   to exercise control over the student; requirements have to be abandoned, since requirements are extensions of faculty authority; students must be given roles (significantly operative if not indeed decisive) in the hiring of teachers because they alone are able to judge how well their needs can be served by particular candidates. "The goal of higher education," writes one proponent of student directed learning, "should be to free people, by teaching them how to do their own learning. That means that higher education should move toward student-centered learning, a process whose primary purpose is to teach people how they learn best."[9]

That interest is a crucial ingredient in learning cannot be gainsaid, but interest can be aroused and cultivated and does not necessarily stem only from the inclinations of individuals following their own bents. The teacher who sits on the desk and starts a class with, "What shall we talk about, today, folks?" provides no better model than the autocrat who declares, "Learn it this way, or else!" A unidirectionalism defined entirely from below is no better than a unidirectionalism imposed from above.

TOWARD BALANCED INTERACTION

If the monarchial model, according to which the teacher says to the learner, "Here are the ideas you must learn," leads to a loss of interest or the oppression of individuals, and if the interest model, in which the teacher says only to the student "What are your ideas?" leads to a consumerism that can endanger the substantive content of the curriculum and even politicize the pedagogical relationship, is there a viable alternative? If the monarchial model can be faulted as the exercise of a "cop's role," and the interest consumer model may be thought of as a "cop out" from the inevitable responsibility of professional guidance, can teachers and students find a modus vivendi for common endeavor?

Imagine the teacher, who by both articulation and by demeanor, phrases the question in this way. "What ideas must be explored as we work together to learn about this matter?" That question should be linked with another: "In what ways do you believe we can best explore together the question at hand?" Inquiries couched in these terms shift the focus away from "Who is in charge?" to "What must be known and understood to belong to the community of scholars?" They can make wisdom and maturity, rather than control and certification, the measures of teaching.[10] They should be answered through a conversation between professors and students—that conversation being the long extended process of working together in a learning encounter.

It may be the case that educational institutions are not always adept at facilitating that conversation. Many explanations of their failures in this respect are offered. Three of these will suffice to illustrate the pervasiveness of the problem and the difficulty of overcoming it. Some lay the blame on the pressures of accreditation.[11] Others describe the difficulty to the power possessed by faculty members.[12] Still others lay the blame on the failure of graduate schools to teach the arts of pedagogy.[13]

Whatever the explanation for the inadequacy of teaching or whatever be the contemporary condition of the art, teaching will come to the fulfillment of its high vocation only when its importance is affirmed and its connection with scholarly achievement is understood. The effort to understand the dynamics of learning and teaching should be a concern of everyone in the academy throughout their entire educational odyssey.

A teacher must maintain intellectual integrity and procedural fairness in the exercise of office. John Milton looked upon this obligation as the first duty of the scholar, and expressed it with quaint and memorable power:

> When a man hath bin labouring the hardest labour in the deep mines of knowledge, hath furnisht out his findings in all their equipage, drawn forth his reasons as it were a battell raung'd, scatter'd and defeated all objections in his way, called out his adversary into the plain, offers him the advantage of wind and sun, if he please; only that he may try the matter by dint of argument, for his opponents then to sulk, to lay ambushments, to keep a narrow bridge of licencing where the challenger should passe, though it be valour enough in shouldiership, is but weakness and cowardice in the wars of Truth.[14]

In teaching, Milton's contention that open fairness is the only legitimate posture of the scholar requires the teacher to grasp and present the range of options for the treatment of a given topic or issue. There are limitations, of course, upon the capacity of any one individual to grasp with equal appreciation all the ways in which a particular matter is understood. But scholarly fairness is an ideal that stands over and against every limited presentation of a topic and that judges every slighting of evidence or misinterpretation of a point in question. The teacher need not pose an unattainable neutralism; the teacher has a right to opinions and a duty to defend them by the tools of inquiry and argument. But unlike the defense of positions as commonly practiced on the political stump, the

150   defense of positions within the academic classroom depends for integrity upon the acknowledgment that other positions are advocated and a careful scrutiny of the cases that can be made on their behalf as well as the justifications for the contentions of the teacher. It is impossible to cultivate the intellectually liberated disposition without exposure to individuals who exemplify the art of being reasonable in this high sense. We dare not forget Philip Rieff's contention that the scholar "can only interpret an authority which is not reducible to power."[15]

Indeed, lecturing can have a place in a balanced pedagogy. A skillfully delivered lecture—too few are—offers one paradigm for excellence in the handling of ideas. A person can observe, from hearing a lecture skillfully done, not only subject matter content, but also what it means to communicate powerfully, what is entailed in being clear and cogent, when the light touch and the leavening of humor are appropriate, and how ideas are crafted. Any student who has avoided or been deprived of the experience of watching a master lecturer using presentational powers in the grand manner has been denied one of the valuable experiences of learning. Moreover, a lecture in which a variety of opinions are fairly presented and alternative points of view are judiciously explored is at least as capable of being liberating as a rap session among like-minded persons who reinforce each other in simplistic commitments to but a narrow set of prejudices.

.   Moreover, every good lecturer knows that even the lecture method can be something of a dialogical experience. The faces of the hearers speak: blank looks signal the need to cover a point in a different way; excited eyes reveal awakening to some new insight; scowls indicate disagreements that should be honored and addressed with thoughtfulness. Teachers who lecture well are sensitive to their hearers and can read the expressions on their faces. They tailor their presentation accordingly. Moreover, the good teacher can also teach classes how to listen with an active zest.[16]

Similarly, discussions differ greatly in the extent to which they foster inquiry. There are great differences between an unguided free-for-all and a focused group inquiry. There is also a difference between a focused group inquiry and a manipulated process. Discussion per se does not automatically qualify as an adequate pedagogical device. To guide it well requires the same sensitivity to the delicate balance between inquiry and resourcing that is true of every other pedagogical method.

FAIRNESS AS THE CARDINAL QUALITY OF THE TEACHER

Pedagogical interaction, therefore, is not a simple function of the philosophy of education one espouses. Neither pedagogical traditionalists nor pedagogical innovators have a singular custody of the traits that enrich the teacher/scholar's capacity to open the minds of others to the majesty of truth. Arrogance is the cardinal sin of pedagogy, but it is not confined to people with particular points of view about education or any other matters, nor does it appear only within certain age spans.

A sharp distinction should be made between a liberal mind and a mind that espouses liberal positions. The former is flexible and has a high tolerance for ambiguity, understands the partiality of every stance toward issues, and is flexible and open to new considerations. The latter is likely to be rigid, to cast issues in terms of clearly defined contrasts, and will not entertain the possibility of alternatives. It can become a willing tool of agenda advocacy and ideological commitment. Similarly, a distinction can be drawn between a conservative mind and a mind that espouses conservative positions. The former is cautious and deeply appreciative of the values to be preserved by the continuation of existing order. It also is tolerant of ambiguity, understands the partiality of every stance of advocacy, and may not necessarily be closed to considerations leading to the shift of its commitments. The latter is often rigid, postulates issues as matters of life or death, and is willing to be a tool of vested interest or the perpetuation of the status quo. Mature and liberated liberals can live and work with mature and responsible conservatives—especially in the guild of scholarship. Those who are simply committed to liberal causes can only confront those committed to conservative positions—producing a match of wits or a stand-off of wills that belies much of what liberal learning is supposed to be about.

Fairness in the presentation of issues and a treatment of others that seeks their empowerment as learners cannot be commended without being professed—professed not only as a proposition but exemplified in the very marrow of behavior. Great teaching thus presupposes character; it relies upon a process in which integrity and fidelity become contagious. Stunts may attract interest, and conniving in campus intrigue may produce apparent professional advancement, but neither creates the respect that is the precondition of great teaching. Teaching depends upon credibility, resting on stature and fidelity to truthfulness and fairness, resulting in candor and credibility. Manipulative intrigue, gimmickry in the transmission of ideas, scheming calculation in the pursuit of professional goals—all eat at the vitals of the scholar's being.

A teacher's covenant with fairness in the presentation of ideas extends naturally into a responsibility for the enrichment of the self-hood of students. The guiding touchstone in this aspect of the scholar's covenant is defined no less professionally than that which governs

152 the handling of subject matter. It hinges on respect for the wholeness
of the student's selfhood in the uniqueness of its given individuality.
A teacher is never justified in showing disdain or contempt for students—a stricture, alas, not always honored in the academy. Nor
should students hold teachers in such a fearsome awe that mutuality
becomes impossible.

It is not easy to measure people's capacities to respect each
other's selfhoods. It cannot, for instance, be identified merely by an
easygoing style that puts a premium on chumminess. In no way does
it demand a leveling of all participants to a single plane and common
pattern. In describing the personalities and pedagogical attributes of
three distinguished Harvard professors of his acquaintance, Adam
Ulam observed,

> Those three were certainly not young, could not (with the excep-
> tion of Schumpeter) be described as dynamic as the term is
> currently understood; the difference of age and background
> interposed a barrier to that close communication and frequent
> contact which is supposed to be of such great importance in
> education. They were certainly courteous, easily approachable
> and helpful, but would have been devoid of that impulse that has
> of late prompted many an elderly and sometimes a distinguished
> professor to embrace vociferously what he conceives to be the
> cause of youth. A certain degree of distance does not imply lack
> of sympathy, often quite the contrary; respect for accomplish-
> ment and age is not a sign of repression but of maturity and a
> civilized mind.[17]

A healthy pedagogical interaction requires that candor and
respect be practiced in relationships between members of a group. We
may not know how limited is our capacity to respect others until those
with whom we must relate have backgrounds and foregrounds other
than our own. To the extent that students, for instance, are already
molded or are willing to conform themselves to the teachers's image,
they do not force teachers to reckon with differences that test the
mettle of community. Teaching in institutions with monolithic clienteles may, therefore, be less demanding of true competence than
teaching in institutions dealing with special groups and having more
diverse constituencies.

In his autobiography about his struggles with conditions in an
urban university Leonard Kriegel has shown how important it is to
appreciate the needs of special groups.[18] Assigned to teach in both
honors classes and special educational programs connected with open
admission, he came to see that both learning conditions required

attention to the subrational feelings that prove so decisive in determining responses in the classroom. Teaching is more than the intellectualized communication of propositions from one mind to another: it is an encounter between selves that is influenced and determined by the totality of the interactional equation. Kriegel was successful not least because he was unsure of his capacities and wrestled painfully to respond to the factors that make community possible—especially a classroom filled with those of different backgrounds and expectations. He felt the drain that malaise within a student body can put on the classroom encounter, a drain he discovered to be greater (at the time he wrote) in the case of the honors class than with those in the special program. Deeply perceptive of the conditions he wrestled with in the late sixties—conditions that surely can differ from class to class and generation to generation—Kriegel observed the following about his efforts.

> My students were not looking for the kind of purpose that is distinctly political or even for advice on how to live their lives. What they wanted, strangely enough, was a missionary in the wilderness, a figure who would fill them with reverence and dread. I felt my own energies at a distance now. I did not want to convert anyone. Nor did I want to entertain. I could not give them what I thought they needed: a clear idea of the centrality of literature to their lives and even, if you will, a reason why their studies might offer alternatives to the pettiness around them. They were consumed with the questions of life styles, with the unspontaneous worship of the new and spontaneous, with the breakdown of intellectual and personal discipline, with the difficult thought that the mind, as much as the body, demanded expression.[19]

What Kriegel realized to be especially true of the groups with which he worked is true to some extent in all teaching relationships. A teacher must be sensitive to students at the level of their deepest yearnings. Great teaching springs not from having preconceived notions of "where students are at," but from the capacity to form a fresh and perceptive reading of this as it varies from course to course, from group to group, and from time to time. The capacity to make such a reading is surely as much the skill of an expert as it is an attribute of a companion. It never springs simply from giving to students the whole task of specifying what they would like to explore or the terms on which they would like to shape the nature of the encounter.

Martin Buber, in a discussion of teaching, stressed the necessity of mutuality in the interchange between the teacher and the student

154   and the need to balance individual growth with communal experiences:

> An education based only on the training of the instinct of origination would prepare a new human solitariness which would be most painful of all.
> The child, in putting things together, learns much that he can learn in no other way. In making some thing he gets to know its possibility, its origin and structure and connexions, in a way he cannot learn by observation. But there is something else that is not learned in this way, and that is the viaticum of life. The being of the world as an object is learned from within, but not its being as a subject, its saying of *I* and *Thou*. What teaches us the saying of *Thou* is not the originative instinct but the instinct for communion.[20]

Speaking also of the importance of cultivating "reverence for the form" in the educational experience, Buber remarked, "Modern education theory, which is characterized by tendencies to freedom, misunderstands this other half, just as the old theory, which was characterized by the habit of authority, misunderstood the meaning of the first half."[21]

The teacher's effort to enrich the selfhood of the student is essentially and ultimately supportive, but it may well include a temporary and provisional over-and-againstness that may seem to make the teacher a quasi adversary of the student. It is the teacher's responsibility to set demands before the student, demands that ought to be greater than will be lapped up by the student with enthusiasm. If those demands are set too high, the result will be despair; but if they are set too low, the result will be a failure of students to regard the intellectual life as a serious challenge. The complex and demanding task of the teacher is to create a situation in which just the right amount of anxiety is counteracted with just the right amount of confidence.

Ortega y Gasset has given a conceptual foundation for the dynamic involved by emphasizing the distinction between wishing and willing.

> It is the virtue of the child to think in terms of wishes, it is the child's role to make believe. But the virtue of the grown man is to will, and his role is to do and achieve. Now we achieve things only by concentrating our energy; by limiting ourselves. And in this limiting of ourselves lies the truth and the authenticity of our life. Indeed, all life is destiny: if our existence were unlimited in duration and in terms of the forms it could assume,

there would be no "destiny." The authentic life, young people, consists in cheerfully accepting an inexorable destiny—a limitation we cannot alter. It is this state of mind which the mystics, following a profound intuition, used to call "the state of grace."[22]

The curiosity of the child—often cast in terms of wishes—does open inquiry. But inquiry cannot be satisfied by wishful thinking alone. Similarly, the interest model of the student does provide an entry into learning, but it cannot by itself lead to a sufficiently disciplined experience of learning. Until and unless a person comes against limits and thus discovers it is impossible to dodge difficulties by shifting agendas, that person will not become mature. The supportive role of a teacher is to help students cross the threshold between childhood and maturity by creating a demand that they put away the childhood of mere interest for the adulthood of destiny.

This requires a judicious blending of encouragement and goading. The good teacher does not set standards that require no strain, nor does the good teacher permit the fledgling to quit at times of disillusionment or discouraging exhaustion. Though enthusiasm burns out, the teacher's support must not. A good teacher sets up high hurdles and then helps the student learn to jump them. A good teacher should probably look tough to students and easygoing to "macho" colleagues who think only monarchical rigidity upholds standards. This means that popularity with students should not be used as the main measure of teaching success. But it also means that the approval of colleagues is an insufficient measure of good teaching unless accompanied by clear evidence of student appreciation.

It is no small achievement to strike the healthy balance in which pedagogical interaction holds together an equality of obligation and a differentiation of achievement, an openness to interest and a demand for discipline, a deference for seniority and full standing for the junior partner. But it is precisely such a rare combination that provides a possibility of uniqueness to the pedagogical enterprise and that makes it a high calling toward which to aspire.

NOTES

1. Søren Kierkegaard, *Philosophical Fragments of a Fragment of Philosophy* (Princeton: Princeton University Press, 1962), 38.

2. Steven M. Cahn, *Saints and Scamps: Ethics in Academia* (Totowa, N.J.: Rowman and Littlefield, 1986).

3. Philip Rieff, *Fellow Teachers* (New York: Harper and Row, 1973).

156   4. Anyone familiar with the academic world will realize the highly controversial implications of that seemingly innocuous suggestion!

5. Paulo Freire, *Pedagogy of the Oppressed* (New York: Herder and Herder, 1970), 58.

6. For a defense of the interest model see Michael Rossman, *On Learning and Social Change* (New York: Random House, 1972), 49f.

7. Michael Rossman, *The Wedding Within the War* (Garden City, N.Y.: Doubleday, 1971), 155.

8. Ibid., 156.

9. Robert S. Powell, Jr. "Student Power and Educational Goals," in *Power and Authority: Transformation of Campus Governance* Harold L. Hodgkinson and L. Richard Meeth (eds.) (San Francisco: Jossey-Bass, Inc., 1971), 66.

10. See John Smith, "From Tension to Community—a Fresh Approach to the Teaching-Learning Situation," in *Faculty Forum*, Nos. 58 and 59, Winter and Spring, 1972, 1–2, 5.

11. Robert Powell, an advocate of interest learning, makes accreditation and vocationalism the villain of the piece. As he puts it:

Currently in higher education, the dominant goal appears to be, not self-development, but rather job accreditation. Tests, grades, honors, degrees—these tangible signs of approval and success form the basis for what takes places in the classroom, and the students are taught that securing and achieving them indicate that one is "accredited" and ready to leave the campus and take a job reserved for those with such credentials. And, of course, the way one secures those credentials is to listen carefully in class to what the professors are saying, take rapid and complete notes, and then, using the best memory techniques possible, return to the professor on the exam in a form as undigested as possible the facts and theories he lent the students during the term. ("Student Power and Educational Goals," *Power and Authority*, Hodgkinson and Meeth, (eds.) 67).

The process Powell is describing is referred to by students on one campus as the "Binge and Purge Model."

12. William Arrowsmith ascribes the difficulty to the power possessed by the faculty, a power that enables faculties to ignore their obligations to be interactional. "Scholars," he writes,". . . are unprecedentedly powerful, but their power is professional and technocratic; as educators they have been eagerly disqualifying themselves for more than a century, and their disqualification is now nearly total." ("The Future of Teaching," reprinted in *Campus 1980: The Shape of the Future in American Higher Education*, Alvin C. Eurich (ed.) [New York: Dell, 1968], 118.)

13. Jacques Barzun suggests:

[The graduate school] knows and wants to know nothing of the verified facts about learning, memory, and habit; about temperamental differences in verbal and visual powers; about anything that might prepare its graduates for the age-old difficulties in imparting knowledge. It sends out "masters" and "doctors" in the humanities—the academic study of literature, music, and the plastic arts—who have not an inkling **157** of the psychology of perception, just as if Helmholtz and William James had never lived. And these cripples, many of whom have never taught undergraduates while earning a license to teach, are seldom enabled to correct their own patent deficiencies as speakers, writers, and judges of work. Though it is upon them as inspirers of the next generation in college that the continuity of scholarship depends, no opportunity exists to tell them of such elementary faults as mumbling, disjointed utterance, and unorganized thought. In short, the graduate school reproduces on a lofty plane the errors of omission chargeable at every stage since the fifth grade. (*The House of Intellect* [New York: Harper and Brothers, 1959], 131).

14. John Milton, *Areopagitica: A Speech of Mr. John Milton for the Liberty of Unlicenc'd Printing* (New York: Dayson and Clarke, Ltd., 1927), 36.

15. Philip Rieff, *Fellow Teachers* (New York: Harper and Row, 1972), 19.

16. Lectures that are pretaped and presented by mechanical devices, or lectures electronically "piped" to multiple sections, do not qualify under the foregoing observations. They should be used only as emergency measures— if at all.

17. Adam Ulam, *The Fall of the American University* (LaSalle, Ill.: Library Press, 1973), 39f.

18. Leonard Kriegel, *Working Through: A Teacher's Journey in the Urban University* (New York: Saturday Review Press, 1972).

19. Ibid., 185.

20. Martin Buber, *Between Man and Man*, trans. by Ronald Gregor Smith (New York: Macmillan, 1948), 87f.

21. Ibid., 89.

22. Jose Ortega y Gasset, *Mission of the University* (London: Kegan Paul, Trench, Trubner), 77.

PART THREE

For the Well-Being of Society

CHAPTER TWELVE

Learning and Social Responsibility: Prolegomena to the Discussion

THE DEBATE ABOUT VIETNAM

The bitter controversy occasioned by America's involvement in the Vietnam War gave a pointed intensity to the debate about the relationship that should exist between scholarship and society and between educational institutions and public policies. Campus concern about the war expressed itself on escalating levels of intensity. At first there were "teach-ins" that engaged in policy analysis and that questioned the premises on which the country had made military commitments in southeast Asia. These were followed by expressions of uneasiness by members of academic communities over cooperation with military programs. On some campuses the presence of ROTC programs was challenged as being incompatible with the purposes for which knowledge should be pursued. Research contracts related to war activities were criticized, often because they included provisions for keeping the findings secret. Recruiters for the armed services and for the CIA were picketed in some instances and in others were asked to relinquish the privilege of setting up displays in prominent places on campus—something other potential employers generally are not permitted to do. Sometimes, overt physical interference—in the form of sit-ins and blockages—was used to thwart institutional activities that were deemed to advance the conduct of the war.

Often the opponents of the war and of cooperation with the agencies conducting it were pitted against administrations striving to preserve the "open campus." A significant number of faculty members, many of whom had previously accepted the neutrality of scholarship as an important premise and who had shied away from public stances, issued declarations condemning the war as politically and morally wrong, and even participated in protest movements designed to call attention to the futility and immorality of American policy. In

162 contrast, other faculty members perceived political activism as a threat to the institutional neutrality associated with academic freedom. A large body of literature emerged, often more tractlike than deeply philosophical, arguing whether it is appropriate for institutions of higher education to involve themselves in efforts to shape public policies. The resulting controversy was often heated and ideologically polarized. For instance, Theodore Roszak declared that the claimed neutrality of the university, coupled with a willingness to provide instruction in any matter desired by the wider culture on terms congenial to that culture, was a form of "academic delinquency."[1] On the other hand, Robert Nisbet decried the corrosive effects of all the pressures that were leading the university away from devoted adherence to the "academic dogma" that knowledge should be pursued solely as it own end.[2]

Since the end of the Vietnam War the debate about the social responsibilities of universities has focused more specifically on investment policies in countries with repressive systems, such as South Africa.[3] Universities holding stock in corporations that do business in South Africa have been faced with demands either that they sell their stock holdings in such countries (divestment) or use their proxy power to exert pressure that would force the companies to withdraw (disinvestment). Both of these demands pose issues regarding the relationship of the university to the outside world.

At first glance these debates about the social responsibilities of the academy may seem to be like the older debate between the advocates of pure learning and those committed to an education that serves practical social needs.[4] But the new debate has a different dimension. It has not questioned whether institutions of higher learning should make service to society a guide for determining their curricular purposes, but rather whether they should seek to influence the society to adopt particular social agendas and goals. Not contributions to society—the need for which has been well conceded in theory if not universally advanced in practice—but actual involvement in political affairs has been the subject of this new controversy.

Debates of this order—one might at times be tempted to call them "epithet volleys"—raise momentous issues. Although the problems involved in defining the responsibility of the academy in social and political matters have occupied a great deal of time and attention, dealing with them has not yet produced a common understanding. We will be sorting out these issues for years to come. This, and the subsequent chapters in this section, will try to discern lines along which they can be addressed.

EDUCATION FOR SOCIAL RESPONSIBILITY IN HISTORICAL CONTEXT

The feeling that education equips persons to benefit society has a long and persistent history. Plato gave expression to such a conviction in a memorable passage in the fifth book of *The Republic*, when he wrote:

> Until philosophers are kings, or the kings and princes of this world have the spirit and power of philosophy, and political greatness and wisdom meet in one, and those commoner natures who pursue either to the exclusion of the other are compelled to stand aside, cities will never have rest from their evils—no, nor the human race, as I believe—and then only will this our state have a possibility of life and behold the light of day.[5]

Many centuries later Francis Bacon was similarly convinced that knowledge finds its most important end in the service of human well-being. Writing about the errors into which the use of knowledge can fall, he emphasized the importance of directing knowledge to the service of the public good and expressed dismay concerning how infrequently this goal is achieved:

> The greatest error of all the rest is the mistaking or misplacing of the last or furthest end of knowledge; for men have entered into a desire of learning and knowledge, sometimes upon natural curiosity and inquisitive appetite; sometimes to entertain their minds with variety and delight; sometimes for ornament and reputation; and sometimes for victory of wit and contradiction; and most times for lucre and profession; and seldom to give a true account of their gift of reason to the benefit and use of men.[6]

Plato's confidence in the value of philosophy for affairs of state, as well as Bacon's belief that knowledge is best used "as a rich store-house for the glory of the Creator and the relief of man's estate," have been utilized on the premise that the educational institution trains individuals who assume, usually after graduation, roles as concerned and productive citizens. The contribution of the college or university in this pattern remains essentially indirect. What graduates do with their learning is left to be determined by their individual consciences. Educational institutions do not assume a direct burden for guiding graduates into particular callings or for taking particular stands regarding public policy. Whether that is what Plato envisioned as the role of philosopher-kings, it has become the way in which educational institutions have generally made their peace with the tension between

164   intellectual inquiry and public obligation. Alas, the result is that graduates of most institutions leave with a some sense of social decency but
no consuming concern to make a more just and humane world.

The most fully developed and extensive symbol of the conjunction of the service-claim with that of the presumed neutrality of the
academic enterprise was articulated by Clark Kerr.[7] The multiversity
Kerr advocated serves society both by training individuals who are
better informed, more perceptive, and presumably wiser as potential
leaders in society, and by providing research services on a contractual
basis. The multiversity as Kerr defended it is not merely engaged in
pedagogy, but in the production of knowledge and techniques that
are useful for outside groups. This new way of understanding higher
education's mission has shifted the premises of the discussion in an
important respect. It makes the university a direct participant in social
and economic processes.

Purists, like Adam Ulam, who adhere to the tradition of learning
for its own sake, have argued that this transformation has undercut
the essential vocation of the university. Knowledge should be pursued
for purposes intrinsic to its possession, and should not be made hostage to social or economic agendas. Social concern, in any matrix, only
weakens and confuses the educational agenda. Democracies, which
are political realities, should respond to social feeling and social needs;
but educational institutions, dedicated to work on rational principles
alone, must resist all outside pressures. Because they have failed to
do this, "They have allowed themselves to becomes seats of obscuran-
tism, of political and philosophical partisanship rather than of learning, sources of national weakness and cultural and scientific backward-
ness rather than of strength."[8]

Writing in the same vein as Ulam, Robert Nisbet has advanced
the thesis that the controlling premise of the university—it's "academic dogma"—should be that knowledge is valuable when pursued
for its own sake, without reference to practical applications, political
objectives, or social benefits. He has complained that a new type of
academic figure—often associated with the multiversity—appeared
on the campus after World War II and blurred the focus of the educational agenda. This type of academician, building a reputation on
marketable research, acquires power, teaches (if at all) only as an
incidental function, is tied to industrial and defense establishments,
and helps to hasten the politicalization of the university. Thus, according to Nisbet, the university, tempted by the world of external involvements, gave up the premise that knowledge alone and for its own sake,
is good. The belief that the university could and should significantly
influence and perhaps even seek some measure of control over the

fortunes of society tempted the academy to search for new glories, and infected it with the overweening pride that the Greeks called hubris. Feeling itself successful, the university succumbed to the temptation to be powerful as well: "Why could it not be, at one and the same time, philosopher-king, philosopher Croesus, philosopher-soldier, philosopher-statesman, philosopher-healer, philosopher-humanitarian, even philosopher-revolutionary? So might Faust have dreamed."[9]

Ironically, Kerr's multiversity was attacked from two sides. The defenders of neutrality argued that it did not keep knowledge sufficiently detached from society; socially concerned activists argued that it only serviced the injustices and advanced the prevalent wrongs of its time. Unlike those anxious to detach the university from policy controversies in order to explore knowledge in its own integrity, such activists wished knowledge to be an instrument for advancing particular social purposes. They were critical of the multiversity because it seemed unable (or unwilling) to become a center of opposition to the Vietnam War and of other destructive policies, such as ecological callousness. Activists wanted knowledge to relate to social purposes—but in a critical and judgmental way rather than a subservient way. Thus, while both traditionalists and activists have been critical of the multiversity, the grounds for their antagonism have been strangely opposite. One objected to the university's service-oriented involvement with the social/political/economic establishment; the other objected to the university's failure to become a critic of dominant social policy. When both poles attacked the center, even for contrasting reasons, pressures built up and foundations shook, but the issue was not resolved.

THE SOCIAL CONSEQUENCES OF KNOWLEDGE

Daniel Bell has made the bold projection that the university will come into its own as the dominant institution of a postmodern society. This will happen because the university is the place where theoretical knowledge, which Bell regards as the clue to the future, is pursued: "Perhaps it is not too much to say that if the business firm was the key institution of the past hundred years, because of its role in organizing production for the mass creation of products, the university will become the central institution of the next hundred years because of its role as the source of innovation and knowledge."[10] Bell contends that the university's concern for knowledge gives it a peculiar position from which to influence society. In its new, expanding, and challenging forms it will become a source of power and of social direction

166   largely because of its theoretical acumen. Along the same lines, Peter
      Drucker has contended that knowledge will come to replace money
      as the form in which capital resoutces are created in a new order.[11]

          If Bell and Drucker are right, the university must prepare itself
      for an ever-expanding social role. The ivory tower will be a pivotal
      guide in shaping the society of the future, not a retreat in which to
      reflect on truth in splendid isolation from social responsibilities. This
      role will demand a resolution of the issue at stake between those who
      advocate neutrality as a means of preserving the academy's freedom
      and those who press for social involvement as a means of implement-
      ing the academy's relevance. If the academy acquires the pivotal role
      Bell and Drucker project for it, scholars will no longer be able to rely
      upon neutralism to preserve the privilege of the intellectual to sift and
      analyze the claims of all parties and agendas in a detached way. What
      they think and say will draw them into controversy. Yet neither will
      scholars do well if they forget the canons of fairness and evenhanded-
      ness that distinguish academic life from crass partisanship. Those who
      wish to be active in social controversies will have to understand the
      special restraints and transcending commitments to truth that pre-
      serve socially concerned scholarship from becoming mere propagan-
      dizing. The social implications of teaching and research will have to
      be dealt with. Socrates's admonition, "The unexamined life is not
      worth living," will become a new awareness that the unexamined
      pursuit of learning is not worth embracing.

          We will have to develop a reasoned ground from which to face
      challenges like the one so forcefully articulated by Noam Chomsky.
      He was aware, as was Kerr, that the affairs and accomplishments
      of academic institutions are intermeshed with social processes, but
      Chomsky condemned "The New Mandarins" who are willing to ser-
      vice society without questioning its requests or scrutinizing its
      demands. He also criticized those academicians who pose as experts
      for the shaping of policy without asking questions about the moral
      consequences of policies they have a role in molding. Speaking of an
      intellectual and scholarly legislator whose views on foreign affairs he
      abhorred, Chomsky declared, "He is not a breast-beating superpatriot
      who wants America to rule the world, but is rather an American
      intellectual in the best sense, a scholarly and reasonable man—the
      kind of man who is the terror of our age."[12]

          Chomsky criticized the experts, particularly as found in think
      tanks and as exemplified by academicians who serve as advisers to
      policy makers. They are often, he contends, "self-serving" and benefit
      so much from the system as to make it impossible for them to criticize
      it.[13] Chomsky offers his vision of what the university can be:

We can conceive the possibility that the schools, or the intellectu- **167** als, might pay serious attention to questions that have been posed for centuries, that they might ask whether society must, indeed, be a Hobbesian *bellum omnium contra omnes*, and might inquire into Rousseau's protest that it is contrary to natural right that "a handful of men be glutted with superfluities while the starving multitude lacks necessities." They might raise the moral issue faced, or avoided, by one who enjoys his wealth and privi- lege undisturbed by the knowledge that half the children born in Nicaragua will not reach five years of age, or that only a few miles away there is unspeakable poverty, brutal suppression of human rights, and almost no hope for the future; and they might raise the intellectual issue of how this can be changed. They might ask, with Keynes, how long we must continue to "exalt some of the most distasteful of human qualities into the position of highest virtues," setting up "avarice and usury and precaution . . . as . . . our gods," and pretending to ourselves that "fair is foul and foul is fair, for foul is useful and fair is not." If American intellectuals will be preoccupied with such questions as these, they can have an invaluable civilizing influence on society and on the schools. If, as is more likely, they regard them with disdain as mere sentimental nonsense, then our children will have to look elsewhere for enlightenment and guidance.[14]

Chomsky's vision offers an alternative to the situation in higher learning in which individuals are prepared to serve society but not to challenge social injustice. His call raises issues concerning the ends to which knowledge is put, or will be put, if moral questions about its use are taken seriously rather than bracketed. It should not have taken an unpopular and unproductive war to catalyze debates about these matters. Such considerations should be at the very heart of educational policy, they should be the touchstone for determining education's role in society. Plato's philosophers were not envisioned as mere operational experts facilitating the achievement of purposes defined by other parties, but rather as the shapers of policy and the persistent guardians of the public trust. Similarly, educated citizens of a free society cannot be trained merely to offer society technical expertise— whether in the form of scientific know-how or operational skills— while not being imbued with the imaginative capacity to push persis- tently for justice and community in human affairs.

Lewis Mayhew, who is an astute student of higher educational aims and practices rather than a social activist, has also decried the distortion and misuse of academic privileges. He criticizes colleges and universities for being unresponsive to social needs. "The needs," he points out, "are all plain to see: education of the disadvantaged,

168   repair of urban blight, scholarly and effective criticism of society, and educational based service to many different groups. But instead of providing for these needs, institutions and their professors have become narrowly preoccupied with graduate training and research, leaving the larger task unattended."[15]

Mayhew's judgment was confirmed by a study done by the Carnegie Foundation for the Advancement of Teaching on the state of higher education in the early eighties. This study reached discouraging conclusions about the prospects for expecting commitment to public service from those being currently educated. It found that today's students are parochial and uninformed about global issues; they have highly developed competencies but few corresponding commitments. The report blamed the colleges for this condition: "As we talked with teachers and students, we often had the uncomfortable feeling that the most vital issues of life—the nature of society, the roots of social injustice, indeed the very prospects for human survival—are the ones with which the undergraduate college is least equipped to deal."[16]

It is undoubtedly easier to suggest that universities ought to bear public responsibilities than to create working instances of the socially prophetic, yet academically open, university. It is easier to hurl criticisms at the failures of the academy than to achieve an adequate pedagogical embodiment of social concern. So many counter pressures are at work—individual selfishness and lethargy, group vested interest, and national idolatry; the crunch of time and the shrinking of resources; a natural inclination to avoid the controversial; unexamined mind-sets and professional stances that have made peace with the surrounding social world—that to transform the agenda of the academy can only be an uphill battle all the way. Even some of the most ardent advocates of social concern can be obstacles to the transformations that are needed because they make the pursuit of agendas more important than the cultivation of process, give more loyalty to causes than to the pedagogical encounter, and set formal learning and social witness at odds with one another.

THE SOCIAL IMPORTANCE OF CRITICAL ANALYSIS

The first thing that educational institutions owe to society is to provide perceptive analyses of how public policies are shaped, and more particularly, to define the role of the educational enterprise in relation to that process. Louis Kampf, considering literary studies, set down an agenda that can be applicable to the entire university. "What role, we must ask, does higher education play in America's social and economic system? To my knowledge, no such analysis exists. Without it we are reduced to making unsystematic criticism of curricular and educational techniques. To move beyond such trivia requires a determination of how developments in the academy relate to developments in society, what relevance educational ideology has to social fact."[17]

To answer the question posed by Kampf could take not one, but many major investigative inquiries. The inquiries should be undertaken as fairly and as probingly as possible, though each would have qualities dependent upon the commitments of the investigator. Value concerns are interwoven with all empirical analyses, particularly of social behavior and institutional procedures. Neutrality in the strict sense is impossible in dealing with such complexities, but fairness is possible. Studies done from one perspective have to take stock of their premises through interaction with studies done from other perspectives. The value and dependability of such studies is not a simplistic function of an objectivity presumed to be the sole possession of some one particular investigator who eschews value commitments, but stems from the public interplay that brings out the contrasts between various findings, and bids all to compare them with care and perspicacity. Single descriptive studies do not in themselves give the one and only true picture of what is taking place, particularly when those studies describe factors with which the investigator is closely aligned. But they do shed light upon practice, they do discover possible patterns, and they often do help to demonstrate the complexities involved.

If the first need in relating scholarship to social concerns is to gain and to delineate an accurate sense of how policies are publicly shaped, and how educational endeavors relate to those dynamics, the second need is to bring values and commitments into the open— abandoning a misleading confusion between neutrality and objectivity. The thrust for fairness in scholarly endeavor is a moral value of crucial importance, but scholarly fairness does not depend upon a simplistic neutrality and even less does it depend upon a refusal to deal with value questions. Objectivity is made possible not by the absence of commitments and values, but from the ability to take them into account in collecting data and thinking about problems. In science the position of the observer must be known and specified in order for its effects on the data to be taken into account by calculation—thus producing an objective observation. This is even more the case in the social sciences and the humanities, for in them the prejudgments and assumptions of the investigator are more complex and subtle and therefore probably even more consequential for results. Indeed, the scholar who can indicate the values that guide an inquiry being undertaken is far more likely to be fair and open than the scholar who

170   pretends to work without any particular perspective or to be entirely
free from any presumptions and controlling outlooks.

Writing about these matters, Conor Cruise O'Brien has commented on the way in which American scholars can wax eloquent
in condemning the prostitutions of scholarship under revolutionary
regimes, yet fail to realize that their own perspectives are often uncon-
sciously subservient to the counterrevolutionary politics pursued by
their own country.[18] Ideological servitude as demanded from totalitarian regimes is inimicable to scholarship, but ideological befuddlement
born of naive confidence in one's neutral standing ground is not much
better.

Derek Bok, in a long and detailed examination of the public
responsibilities of higher education, has suggested the limits of neutrality—even as an institutional stance. He declares that individual
investigators have an obligation to deal with values as they do their
work, and even finds some place for institutional clarity about commitment.

> How valid is the concept of institutional neutrality in an era
> when universities have grown so deeply involved in the life and
> affairs of the society? In my opinion, the term does retain a
> limited value. It still helps remind us that official orthodoxies may
> inhibit free expression and collective efforts to induce political
> change will invite retaliation from the outside world. On balance,
> however, the concept of neutrality has brought more confusion
> than clarity because it is so easily taken to mean that universities
> should seek to carry on with no institutional values or moral
> commitments. . . . In reality, universities must constantly
> address moral issues and ethical responsibilities in all their rela-
> tions with the outside world.[19]

Northrop Frye also helps us to think about the limitation of
neutrality, which he calls detachment, in yet another way. He finds
detachment an acceptable, even a necessary virtue for the pursuit of
learning, but argues it betrays us when applied to the scholar's stance
in the social context. "[Detachment] turns into the vice of indifference
as soon as its context becomes social instead of intellectual."[20]

In order to avoid indifference the scholar must be concerned
about society and about the uses to which knowledge is put in that
society. Nor can that concern be adequately addressed merely on an
individual basis. It requires the input that comes from the combined
concern of an entire profession as controversial issues are examined
in an open community.

The question about the academy's role with respect to society is frequently phrased, "Should colleges or universities take stands on social and political matters?" Some answer that question with a "No," others with a "Yes." Still others hold that institutional involvement in such matters should be confined to those instances when the well-being of a particular university or the well-being of the academic enterprise as a whole is at stake.[21] A negative answer to this question presumes that it is possible for the academy to remain entirely aloof from all involvement with the society in which it is located. Such a condition seldom exists. Moreover, the appeal to neutralism can even be used to destroy the possibility of meeting a moral challenge and may even be prompted by a desire to prevent an institution from becoming involved with controversial matters in ways that are disapproved by those arguing for neutrality.

Those who give a positive answer to the question, "Should institutions take stands?," are all too likely to suppose that all that comes in the way of social change is reluctance and hesitation to act—as if the mere repudiation of neutrality with a "Yes" answer is a sufficient expression of social concern. That simplistic premise, central in some forms of activism, is unworthy of an institution that should make the exploration of social complexities one of its central tasks. Finally, if institutions of higher learning abandon their neutral detachment only with respect to those social concerns that directly and specifically affect their own fortunes, does that not lead to little more than self-serving behavior?

The question needs to be posed in this manner. How can institutions of higher learning render the most appropriate and constructive contribution to achieving greater social justice and a more enriched public life? Phrasing the question this way invites thoughtful inquiry and may lead to a deeper analysis, which is the stuff of academic life. The academy has a stake in social and communal well-being that it neglects at peril to itself and to the impoverishment of the public weal. It dare not turn its back on social obligations, for so to do is to be morally derelict. But unless it develops the skill to be socially concerned in ways that are indigenous to its own nature and compatible with its mandate, it will not only harm itself but will find that its efforts turn counterproductive and self-defeating. The discussions that follow examine both the opportunities that are present in the work of the academy for placing social concern among its other responsibilities, and also the restraints that the college or university must recognize as it goes about that task.

172 NOTES

1. Theodore Roszak, "On Academic Delinquency," in *The Dissenting Academy*, Theodore Roszak (ed.), (New York: Pantheon Books, 1967), 3–42.

2. Robert Nisbet, *The Degradation of the Academic Dogma: The University in America 1945–1970* (New York: Basic Books, 1971).

3. There have also been arguments about the involvement of universities with companies making nuclear weapons or with companies whose activities threaten the environment, but these issues have not been as strongly pursued nor as fervently debated as those related to the issue of South Africa.

4. See Chapter 1.

5. B. Jowett, trans., *The Dialogues of Plato*, 2 vols. (New York: Random House, 1937), 1: 737.

6. Francis Bacon, *The Advancement of Learning*, First Book. The passage is located at what in several editions is numbered as V.11. In the fifth edition edited by William Addis Wright (Oxford: The Clarendon Press, 1900) it is found on page 42.

7. Clark Kerr, *The Uses of the University*, (Cambridge: Harvard University Press, 1963).

8. Adam Ulam, *The Fall of the American University* (LaSalle, Ill.: The Library Press, 1973), vi.

9. Nisbet, *Degradation of the Academic Dogma*, 240.

10. Daniel Bell, "Notes on the Post-Industrial Society," in *The Public Interest*, No. 6 (Winter, 1967): 30.

11. See Peter F. Drucker, *The Age of Discontinuity* (New York: Harper and Row, 1968).

12. Noam Chomsky, *American Power and the New Mandarins: Historical and Political Essays* (New York: Pantheon Books, 1967), 371.

13. Ibid., 342.

14. Ibid., 319f.

15. Lewis B. Mayhew, *Arrogance on Campus* (San Francisco: Jossey-Bass, 1970), 110.

16. Ernest L. Boyer, *College: The Undergraduate Experience in America* (New York: Harper and Row, 1987), 283.

17. Louis Kampf, "The Scandal of Literary Scholarship," in *The Dissenting Academy*, Roszak (ed.), 56.

18. See Conor Cruise O'Brien "Politics and the Morality of Scholarship," in *The Morality of Scholarship*, Max Black (ed.) (Ithaca: Cornell University Press, 1967), 59–74.

19. Derek Bok, *Beyond the Ivory Tower: Social Responsibilities of the Modern University* (Cambridge: Harvard University Press, 1982), 299.

20. Northrop Frye, "The Knowledge of Good and Evil," in *The Morality of Scholarship*, Black (ed.), 9.

21. See Edward Shils, *The Academic Ethic: The Report of a Study Group of the International Council on the Future of the University*, (Chicago: University of Chicago Press, 1983), 89.

CHAPTER THIRTEEN

Power and Credibility: Contrasting Modes of Social Influence

A satisfactory understanding of a proper social role for the university may well depend upon drawing a distinction between two different ways of seeking to affect social conditions. These can be differentiated by using the shorthand designations "power" and "credibility." Power signifies a capacity to bring about changes by forcing people to do certain things, even at times against their will. Credibility signifies a capacity to achieve results by use of persuasion. Power works through fear; credibility works through trust.[1]

UNDERSTANDING SOCIAL DYNAMICS IN TERMS OF POWER

Power as used in this discussion connotes a form of social control in which consequences are obtained by making others submissive. Armies and, to a lesser extent, police departments do much of their work by exercising this kind of power. To be sure, such power (which might be called clout) can be employed on behalf of moral agendas, but power coerces people against their will rather than transforming that will into an instrument of voluntary cooperation. This way of thinking about power can easily slip into a reductionism in which the concept of power is equated with mere force and divorced from moral legitimation. A. Bartlett Giamatti attributes the start of this reductionism to an essay by Emerson, who portrayed politics as an open contest for control.[2] But the movement has been fed by many other streams. The admonition to "take power seriously" has been common in both political and theological realism. Reinhold Niebuhr, for instance, observed that "the fact is, Christianity or any other religion, or for that matter any rational or educational force, has never developed a sufficient number of individuals with so perfect a passion for love as to change the main facts of history."[3] Admonished by such observations,

174   realists have concentrated on the role that power plays in the social
order, looking upon power as the capacity to get things done—to
change the main facts of history—by coercion. Those who ignore
questions of power, or who prefer to depend upon other modes of
influence, have even been accused of being naive and sentimental, of
misreading the nature of the "real world."

Deterrence, which has served so long as the operative dynamic
in the diplomacy of the major powers, is grounded on the premise
that the threat to annihilate is the only way to keep others from doing
what you do not want them to do. In an ironic contrast, terrorism,
which is the working tool of groups on the periphery of things, is
grounded on the premise that the threat to use force is the only way
to get others to do what you do want them to do. Moreover, covert
operations, which have escalated in scope and frequency in the last
three decades, are premised on the contention that reasonableness
and respect for international due process are not very effective as a
way of dealing with conflict. Clout and/or intrigue alone count.

Totalitarian regimes often scorn the idea that human affairs can
be shaped by open discussion and mere persuasion. Lately, the behavior of public officials in democratic countries has shown the extent to
which power may be unjustly grasped and used to protect or further
the purposes that some group in office feels to be important. Ruling
groups in both the Watergate and the "Irangate" scandals, to cite
blatant instances, resorted to manipulative means to further policies
they believed to be necessary to national survival even when those
policies were rejected by duly elected representatives of the public.

To think about power as the only way to deal with the social
order is to conclude that social changes and institutional transformation must stem largely, if not entirely, from overt pressures created
by economic, political, and military means. The mastery of clout is
deemed all-important. Fears—fear of deprivation, fear of shame, fear
of injury, fear of disaster, fear of death—become the coinage of social
interchange. Perhaps this is why we use the metaphor of conflict
even to speak about social programs designed to ameliorate human
deprivation—as for example, when we speak of a "war" on poverty
or a "war" on drugs.

Those who think that relationships between nations and between
groups within nations are wholly determined by power rather than
facilitated by morality and reason often look upon the academy as a
place for the creation and development of ever new technologically
and ideologically sophisticated means to destroy or subvert opponents. Such people think of the university as the provider of resources
for developing more and larger instruments of deterrence with which

to threaten adversaries. Persons who see clout as the rule of life are also likely to see the function of education as the preparation of persons to accept the harsh necessities of living by these realities, deliberately minimizing the place of moral concern so that people are prepared to employ crude force with the fewests qualms.

Such a reductionistic realism is usually applied to the world outside the college fence. Few academics have as yet embraced it as the guiding principle of the educational enterprise. But if this point of view were to dominate the academy, the very foundational premises of the academic enterprise would be brought into question. Alas, the life of academic institutions—presumably citadels of persuasion—has not been immune from the effects of thinking that power alone determines how things are decided. The Port Huron Statement of the Students for a Democratic Society called students and faculty to join in the radical reconstruction of educational institutions, declaring in part: "[Students and faculty] must wrest control of the educational process from the administrative bureaucracy. . . . They must consciously build a base for their assault upon the loci of power."[4] Direct actions designed to embarrass or coerce administrations into making particular decisions rely more upon power than on credibility as a working premise. At the same time, many persons (some serving on boards of trustees) are increasingly tempted to think that educational institutions should be controlled by powerful presidents who exercise unilateral powers of decision making much as do the chief executive officers of corporations or the commanders of military units. Meanwhile, many faculty members think that only to the extent that the teachers determine all policies will the academy be wisely run. The slogans "student power," "administrative power," and "faculty power" each evidence the erosion of confidence in the possibility of maintaining community by persuasion.[5]

CREDIBILITY AS AN ALTERNATIVE MODEL

But if there are many institutions in our culture in which the operation of power is central and increasingly hegemonic, there are other institutions in our society that continue to be effective without any significant mastery of clout. Voluntary associations live because they elicit allegiance. Our society includes—this is a factor of unique significance for its health—many organizations and groups that thrive on their abilities at persuasion. Members stay in such organizations not because their obedience is demanded and enforced, but because they are genuinely in agreement with the purposes of such organizations

176   and willingly support them. The capacity to elicit allegiance as demonstrated by the voluntary association is based upon credibility: voluntary associations flourish because people believe in them.

It would be foolish to ignore the impact that voluntary associations can have upon society—an impact more dependent upon their witness to commendable values than upon their use of political threats. Consider the achievements of the American Friends Service Committee, which not only engages in much social service of a beneficial sort, but also seeks to influence public policies. Over the years the credibility of this group has stemmed from its dedicated service of human needs, from its high moral idealism translated into practice, and even from its refusal to become flagrantly involved in power politics. The work of humanitarian groups like the American Friends Service Committee may well provide a clue to the way in which social witness and concern can be combined with the premises of the scholarly enterprise.

To be sure, the ordinary educational institution is not a purely voluntary association. Educational institutions might be better compared to courts of law. Courts of law, at least as conceived in Western democracies, function as much or more by virtue of their credibility as by virtue of their power. Granted, courts are backed by coercive power and can directly call upon the coercive power of other agencies to preserve their procedural integrity, but the influence of courts depends mainly on procedural credibility. The Supreme Court of the United States can overrule even the president who controls the military apparatus of the entire nation. It does so by utilizing precedent and spelling out reasoned opinions. Operationally speaking, its decrees carry the credibility of the pen—but when informed by legal scholarship and protected by constitutional arrangements the pen is a mighty instrument of influence.[6]

While the political realist will contend that the will of courts would be useless without the coercive power of the state, to emphasize the latter at the expense of the former is to lose sight of something very important to a free society. If punitive sanctions are the only basis by which the edicts of the courts are rendered effective, if power alone is decisive, what would keep a chief executive who controls the military from flaunting the orders of the Supreme Court? If everything is reducible to clout, the decisions of courts would be nullifed by those with strong arms and ruthless wills.

The health of a free society is highly correlated with the extent to which courts are effective without the use of naked coercion. Trusting acceptance of their judgments, however inarticulate the base of such a response, is a crucially important element in the maintenance of a democratic order. The trust and confidence that courts enjoy stem, to no small extent, from the realization that their aim is to achieve fairness in the administration of justice. Judicial bodies weigh the claims of precedent and tradition against the claims of immediate need and popular will. Courts have credibility to the extent that people see them as seeking to make judgments according to premises of equity and fairness. If courts become, or even are perceived as having become, merely the extension of the state's power (and not as instruments that give legitimacy to that power) then their contribution to the covenantal basis of democratic society will lose much of its credibility. Likewise, if the courts become mere instruments for taking the public's pulse, or for imposing the will of the most vocal or the largest or the most powerful segment of society upon those who transgress a popular agenda, they will similarly lose their credibility. If the Supreme Court hired pollsters in place of law clerks and merely reflected the popular will in reaching decisions, it would compromise its judicial role beyond recognition—though a Court that allowed strict constructionalism to block out the compelling implications of changing human needs and social values could prove equally inadequate in the exercise of its judicial vocation.

While no analogies are directly applicable, the qualities that make a good scholar seem more like the qualities that make a good judge than like the qualities that make a good political operator, a good entrepreneur, a good sheriff, or a good military commander. The role played by the courts in our system of government—a role with significant social impact—is a better paradigm for the academy than the role played by the organized pressure group, the political caucus, the law enforcement agency, or the revolutionary cadre. When functioning well, courts bring fairness and nonpartisanship to the arena of social interaction. They have often effectively influenced the development of public policy, as instanced in the abrogation of the separate but equal doctrine upon which segregation existed, and more recently in rulings regarding the care of the environment. This way of influencing policy is slower and more circumspect than the method which might be exercised by legislatures, less spectacular or disruptive than that of revolutionary cadres—but it can be at least as influential and far more enduring. The credibility of the voluntary association is achieved through service; the credibility of the law courts is earned by deliberations linked to the concern for precedent and equity. Academic institutions will sometimes find it possible to establish credibility in ways analogous to the ways service oriented associations commend themselves, and sometimes in ways that emulate the courts. In either instance, the institution of higher education will base its influence on

178 credibility rather than on clout, and those who exercise roles within the life of such institutions will be governed by the procedural constraints that distinguish a civil order from a brawl.

AN INEVITABLE TENSION WITH POWER

Peregrine Worsthorne, a columnist for the *London Daily Telegraph*, has recognized the tensions between the premises of academic life and those of the political world. He suggests, however, that the political world is becoming increasing dependent upon the knowledge possessed by the scholar/expert, and that consequently academics are becoming increasingly influential in the power struggles of the world. But, according to Worsthorne, "They do not feel at home in it. Theirs is the world of theory, of concepts, of ideals, or talking rather than doing."[7]

We can hope that scholars will never come to feel entirely at home in the world of power. If the main purpose for the pursuit of knowledge is transformed so as to make the achievement of clout more controlling than the pursuit of the truth, something deeply vital to the academic enterprise will be eclipsed—perhaps even lost. If knowledge is seen only as an instrument of power, then knowledge will no longer be treated as a public trust. The possession of knowledge will be looked upon only as an instrument of private strategy. If knowledge is seen only as an instrument of power, instead of seeking to achieve insight to satisfy curiosity and to enlarge intellectual vision, scholars might then be expected to amass data mainly in order to gain control of logistical know-how and to seek the dominance of political causes.

The tension between our usual understanding of action and our usual understanding of inquiry must be admitted, understood, and kept forever in the forefront of consciousness—but it is not a tension stemming from a pure dichotomy between social involvement and detached irrelevance. It is a tension between two ways of doing things: between attempting to achieve civic stability by manipulating forces and attempting to enhance civil well-being by shedding light upon the civic condition; between operational logistics that drive only toward the achievement of particular agendas and an openness in the pursuit of truth that cares for the good of all; between attempting to control destiny by willful fiat and seeking to shape destiny by imaginative intelligence. Information and learning considered only as instrumentalist tools with which to extend power do not liberate. Only when knowledge is allowed to point us to something that can be shared with others who live beyond the boundaries of the interest

groups with which we are identified does knowledge acquire the   **179**
capacity to set us free.

This is not to argue for making knowledge an end in itself in contrast to turning knowledge into the tool of a political or social agenda. Jack Boozer has observed the dangers that lurk in making reason and freedom ends in themselves, rather than pursuing them as means to the service of human goals. The result can be rootless and even meaningless, as dangerous as partisan and politicized learning. "The great deception of higher education," he suggests, "is to involve one in the glamourous pursuit of truth, wherever that pursuit may lead as if the whole process were intellectual, determined completely by the weight of data upon a receptive mind."[8] The pursuit of truth must be related to the service of something beyond itself, yet it must not be so subordinated to the demands of such a relationship as to eclipse its own integrity.

THE POSSIBLE RAPPROCHEMENT WITH CREDIBILITY

At one time in the cultural odyssey of Western society much credibility rested on a common set of beliefs about the nature of human existence and the purposes of human community. What was often called "Hebrew-Christian" morality (a term that slights both the Greek and Roman components of Western history) enjoyed a tacit, if not explicit, credibility. There were standards "to which all would repair"—truths that were taken as "self-evident." But as Robert Bellah has argued, the covenant that made this foundation for social order credible has been "broken."[9] A technical utilitarian ideology has replaced moral reason as the dominant outlook of the society.

The transformation of social expectation that Bellah describes may mean that the academy can no longer influence society. Clearly it no longer has, nor can it hope to have, a creedal or philosophical unity that gives it a warrant for issuing binding moral directives. But it may have a stance, a quality it can achieve in its own life, that gives it a fulcrum for witness.

Surely it is clear that colleges and universities, for all the carping about their irrelevance that went on in the sixties, enjoy considerable public support. Perhaps that support is only a practical concession to the fact that they have control of the most effective accrediting power in contemporary culture: the "power" to confer degrees that can facilitate entrance to advanced employment. But that factor, while hardly to be denied, is not the only source of the deference accorded to education by society. However erstwhile their hopes, however tentative their confidence, however tinged with suspicion and alloyed with

180   contempt their feelings, most people see education as providing a
liberating perspective, a possibly elevating vision, and a concern about
truth, that can serve the public weal from a standing ground that
transcends mere greed, blind partisanship, and the crass pursuit of
private advantage. Education as ideally practiced provides an alternative foundation for human interaction. In contrast to the realities of
power and intrigue, it provides a vision of civility and compassion. In
contrast to the realities of propaganda and distrust it upholds the
value of an openly shared pursuit of knowledge. In contrast to a
thoughtless rush for affluence, it extols the significance of beauty
and reflection. Society is better whenever these things are sustained,
however inadequately. Moreover, when those dimensions of experience are given embodiment the human enterprise is beckoned to a
more worthy level of well-being.

The greatest contribution that education can make to social and
communal well-being is to extend the skills that make it possible for
people to live together with civil grace and to enhance the conviction
that such an effort is worth making. A key question about any social
involvement by academics, in so far as that involvement is identified
as academic in quality, should be, "What do they do more than others—that is, more than others who also seek to influence society?"

One thing that educational institutions must do more than others
is to be arenas in which all possible implications of a problem can be
canvassed. John F. A. Taylor, who has struggled to understand how
social concern can be compatible with academic fairness, has pointed
to the social dimensions of scholarly reflection:

> We confuse neutrality with privacy, detachment with indiffer-
> ence, the objectivity of the impartial observer with the vacant
> merit of having no opinion on public questions. We have been
> so solicitous to preserve the freedom of the individual inquirer,
> to tolerate nonconformity, to license the unpopular dissent with
> which a new initiative may lie, that we have forgotten our equal
> interest in the community to which dissent is addressed, to
> which it must be addressed and in which it must be heard, if it
> is to be in any measure effective. We have forgotten, in the crowd
> of soliloquies, the significance of the public debate. Of that debate
> the university is the silent and neutral guardian. A guardian is
> essential, for it is the debate, not the soliloquy, the public and
> orderly exchange of opinions where we are divided, not the
> private holding of opinions where we are agreed, that needs
> protection.[1]

Taylor continues, arguing that controversial matters of public policy
must be debated within the university and that the chief contribution

that the university offers is the "civilization of argument." In "civilizing argument," universities, like law courts, must possess the skills
to identify the issues over which there is contention and provide the
conditions under which they can be examined on their merits.

Inquiry is the defining premise of the academic institution. This
is one of the chief things that the academy does (or ought to do) more
than others. Inquiry is compatible with academic freedom but does
not necessarily abrogate social concern. Academic freedom should
safeguard not merely the protection of the odd soliloquy of somebody
on an intellectual tangent, but the full integrity of policy debates.
It commits the university to protect, not merely the accidental or
idiosyncratic views of individuals, but an entire process of investigation and discussion in which all points of view have equal access to the
discussion. Above all else, academic freedom should protect, indeed
deliberately cultivate, open consideration of the question, "What is
knowledge for?" Institutions that pursue their agendas without ever
asking that question often sell their intellectual wares to the highest
bidder—developing curricula without reference to social needs and
engaging in intramural controversy about internal matters while the
world about them grows progressively more precarious for lack of
responsible guidance.

A credible attention to the social consequences of learning will
thread the narrow path between two contrasting stances. It will avoid,
on the one hand, training individuals who are content merely to
service society on the terms dictated by the surrounding culture,
persons who fit unobtrusively into conventional patterns. It will avoid,
on the other hand, creating simplistic partisans whose disgust with
the status quo prompts them to embrace uncritically some new order—
having little or no awareness of the possible difficulties such a new
order will bring. Painstaking, thorough, in-depth analysis is the seedbed of credibility. If, as Samuel Gould once suggested, the university
is especially equipped to reform American society,[11] it will demonstrate such qualifications only when its thinking is done with vigor,
with attention to the implications of every possibility advocated, and
with a deliberate openness to objecting views so that the mettle of
advocacy can be tested on the anvil of controversy.

CREDIBILITY FROM BEHAVIOR
AS WELL AS FROM THOUGHT

But universities attain credibility by the manner in which they behave
as well as by the thinking that they do. They will find themselves
respected for qualities quite beyond the competence of the intellectual

182 inquiry they pursue. In the chapters that follow, I will examine several
sources of institutional credibility. For instance, an institution's behavior in relationship to its neighboring community may affect its capacity
to influence others. The courtesy of staff toward strangers, its sensitivity toward local feelings, even the manner in which it cares for its
"body" (the campus), may determine an institution's social influence
as much or more as its intellectual accomplishments. The kind of work
to which an institution's graduates gravitate may be a significant
measure of its credibility.

Similarly, the extent to which a school can effectively govern its
own internal affairs will not go unnoticed, especially if those connected
with the school presume to offer advice to those who exercise responsibilities in other sectors of society. If institutions of learning cannot
demonstrate the possibility of reasoned deliberation in the determination of policy, what are the prospects for other groups? Finally, the
fairness with which higher education examines the problems that
confront society becomes yet another ingredient in a complex amalgam
of many factors that give the academy credibility in the entire profile
of its being.

NOTES

1. While the ways in which I am using these two terms are consistent
with much usage, they are tailored especially for this discussion. Clearly there
are forms of power (better called empowerment) that are richer in meaning
than the concept associated mainly with clout, and there are ways of thinking
about credibility that interpret it primarily as the capacity to mount a threat.
It is the contrast as drawn in the discussion which is most crucial to the
argument, not the specific way in which the individual terms are defined.

2. A. Bartlett Giamatti, "Power, Politics, and a Sense of History," in
The University and the Public Interest (New York: Atheneum, 1981), see especially 168f and 172ff.

3. Reinhold Niebuhr, "Is Stewardship Ethical?" in *The Christian Century*, 30 April 1930, 555.

4. The statement from which this excerpt is taken can be found in
Mitchell Cohen and Dennis Hale, (eds.), *The New Student Left*, rev. ed. (Boston:
Beacon Press, 1967), 218.

5. It is probably also the case if political life is reduced to the exercise
of crude, naked, blatant coercion then the foundations of covenanted order
essential to democracy will be rendered all but impossible to maintain.

6. The tendency to make nominations to the Supreme Court primarily
on the basis of political factors—a tendency that has hardly diminished during
the past two administrations—may eventually erode the credibility of the

Court. It suggests that the Court is to be regarded more as an instrument of **183** political power than of judicial deliberation. It is ironic that at the very time President George Bush was so vocal in condemning "political correctness" on the campus he was employing it flagrantly in selecting a nominee for the Court.

7. Peregrine Worsthorne, "Power and Saintly Purity," *New York Times*, 2 July 1974, 35.

8. Jack Boozer, "Morality and the Church-Related University," *Emory University Quarterly*, Summer, 1967, 83.

9. Robert N. Bellah, *The Broken Covenant: American Civil Religion in Time of Trial* (New York: Seabury Press, 1975).

10. John F. A. Taylor, "Politics and the Neutrality of the University," *AAUP Bulletin* Volume 59, No. 4. December 1973, 391f.

11. "Universities Prodded by Gould to Lead Reform in Nation," *New York Times*, 8 October 1967, Late City Edition, 56.

CHAPTER FOURTEEN

The Academy as Neighbor and Citizen

When Daniel C. Gilman was inaugurated at Johns Hopkins in 1876, he expressed the hope that university reform should "make for less misery among the poor, less ignorance in schools, less bigotry in the temple, less suffering in the hospital, less fraud in business, less folly in politics."[1] To hope for such benefits from the educational process is to lay a considerable burden on the academy. While the public benefits that Gilman enumerated may flow from skills in social transformation that the academy can generate in those it graduates, the institution of higher education will have credibility as a source of human well-being to the extent that it also conducts its own affairs in ways that exemplify good neighborliness and the service of human needs.

INSTITUTIONAL RESPONSE TO LOCAL NEEDS

Academic institutions must be intentional about their relationships to surrounding neighborhoods and public constituencies. To be sure, educational institutions as a group lack the resources to mount massive remedial efforts that might by themselves overcome the problems of their surroundings. Peter Drucker noted this limitation with excessive bluntness when he declared, "It is . . . especially tempting for the university to play universal aunt to every community need. But no matter how well meant, it is irresponsibility."[2] Most institutions lack the resources to serve the human needs in their immediate vicinity to any appreciable extent. Facing such insurmountable odds, many of them, understandably, retreat into a self-regarding isolation. But while it is proper to heed Drucker's caution that educational institutions cannot play universal aunt to every good and worthwhile social need, it is improper to dismiss the obligation to be a good neighbor as something beyond the necessary concerns of the academy. Even if an institution cannot be a universal aunt, it has no excuse for being an estranged cousin.

Many colleges provide amenities that can be enjoyed by local residents—concerts and lectures open to the public (either free or at token costs), library facilities generally available for those who can make good use of them, recreational activities, and the infusion of sizable amounts of purchasing power[3]—yet these benefits usually come mixed with annoyances so that appreciation for one is often found alloyed with tension about the other. Loud, boorish, or drunken student behavior undermines the public's appreciation of the educational enclave. Music played in dormitories at ear-splitting levels does not cease to be audible at the campus fence. Learning in the classroom does not consistently translate into decorum in the town. Student needs for off-campus living arrangements drive up rents not only for themselves but also for townspeople. Student cars compound traffic and parking problems. The tax exempt status of most campus facilities is often a source of rancor, since community members pressed by their own tax burdens naturally resent a seemingly wealthy institution that escapes such obligations.

Some of the most difficult and compelling problems confronting institutions of higher education stem from their relationships to crying human needs, especially those needs that are apparent right at their doorsteps. It matters little where those doorsteps are located. Needs may be most obvious in inner cities, but many a college or university in a rural setting does not have to look very far away to see abject poverty and cultural degradation. Nor do the tensions between a campus and its surrounding neighborhood evaporate when affluence surrounds the campus. Many an institution with limited resources located in an affluent suburb finds itself constantly in tension with its community.

Colleges and universities cannot unilaterally provide the resources required to remedy all the problems in their neighborhoods, but they can seek to minimize the disruptions they bring to the communities in which they are located and they can (through both institutional policies and the voluntary activities of their personnel) help to catalyze the efforts of other groups to remedy community problems.

Public feelings about these matters are often born of accidental shifts in mood rather than by accurate assessment of actual policies. Nevertheless, such moods are affected by factors such as institutional behavior, even by institutional attitudes. This means that institutions do well to be sensitive to feelings, to engage in public interpretation of both their own policies and the warrant for public policies such as tax exemption, and to keep their relationships with the public as

186   gracious as possible. Faculty members can help enormously in this by establishing contacts with people in the community who are not officially connected with the institution, and more particularly by avoiding those displays of ill-concealed disdain for the untutored of which, unfortunately, too large a group within the profession are capable. Academic institutions might well regard voluntary leadership roles in the neighboring community as things to commend and encourage in their faculty and staff.

EMPLOYMENT POLICY AND CREDIBILITY

Academic institutions will enhance their credibility not only by being good neighbors, but by being good employers. Many of them often operate under stringent economic constraints, and since they often receive support from philanthropic sources, they are sometimes tempted to consider themselves exempt from the requirements to be fair and just that may appropriately be laid upon enterprises that have larger resources and greater productivity. But to presume that the academic institution is exempt from such responsibilities can lead to a thoughtless disregard of basic rules of good procedure. To the extent this happens educational institutions come under suspicion.

In dealing with finances many institutions follow policies that serve their interests without taking into account the impact of those policies on others. Consider, for instance, a rather common pattern for handling institutional finances. Educational institutions often demand an "up front" payment of a full term's, or a full year's, tuition from students, yet pay faculty on a schedule that lags considerably behind the rendering of services.[4] Since such arrangements are contractually agreed to by the parties involved they involve no bad faith. While they cannot be considered instances of malfeasance, they are revealing of an institutional mind-set. The tendency in much academic management is to give institutional advantage an unquestioned priority in the handling of finances. Fiscal responsibility is certainly necessary, but exercised thoughtlessly can make the pecuniary posture of institutions stringent to the point of fault.

Another widespread practice is to presume that flexibility in working conditions for support staffs, such as secretaries and custodians, legitimizes a pay scale set a notch or two below that provided for corresponding work in other local settings. The flexibility possible in campus jobs does make them attractive, but the university or college that makes this "benefit" into a justification for setting salaries lower than those of comparable work elsewhere is not acting in a responsible manner. Moreover, campus support work has become increasingly hectic and demanding under the pressures of budgetary cutbacks, even as institutional capacity to pay wages comparable to work in other places is harder to come by. Many colleges have squeezed and squeezed support budgets, thereby loading more and more duties on their employees. Such policies will eventually breed discontent, erode morale, and lower efficiency.

One of the truly valuable aspects of many campus working situations is the presence of remarkably capable and dedicated persons who accept responsibilities that are far greater than those spelled out in their job classification and who remain with an institution year in and year out more from a sense of loyalty than from a prudential regard for their own welfare. Most campuses have been served over many years by articulate, able, and imaginative members of support staffs whose contribution to the fullness and adequacy of the educational programs—although different in kind—is surely as valuable as that of faculty. But in most institutions these staff members were too long excluded from benefit packages provided for administrators and professors. In most cases, it was a government ruling affecting the taxable status of unequally awarded benefits, not institutional good will, that caused institutions to include such employees in the range of benefits once reserved for faculty and administrators.[5]

It is never good policy to presume on personal loyalty as a substitute for structural fairness in the treatment of persons. Highly idealistic individuals frequently offer to provide leadership to voluntary and philanthropic organizations at less than the going rate. For instance, out of idealism, a minister may refuse annual salary increments from the local parish. The loyalty and dedication thus expressed is admirable, but the policy itself is unwise. When such persons have to be replaced, the organization that has not budgeted realistically because it has presumed on the continuing generosity of such self-effacing individuals confronts great difficulty. Much the same difficulty can arise with academic institutions whose staffs are retained by the attraction of the amenities rather than by the fairness of the compensation. The prudent policy is to set compensation at a going rate and to let those who wish, and can afford to do so, make contributions for the benefit of the institution.

The presence of faculty members in decision-making and budget processes—which many academics feel is a guarantee of institutional health—does not necessarily ameliorate these problems. Faculty members are not above caring primarily for their own group interest. Moreover, faculty are sometimes the root of much frustration for support staffs—each thinking that the departmental or pool secretary can fulfill the expectations of everyone as though working only for

188 one person. There are too many support staff members in academic institutions who must meet demands laid upon them without any coordinated effort to schedule their work so as to avoid conflicting expectations. It behooves every member of an academic community to be sensitive to such matters.

SCHOLARSHIP PRACTICES AS SOCIAL OUTREACH

American higher education has a long history of trying to educate those who cannot normally afford to pay for college. Some institutions, like Berry College in Georgia, and Berea College in Kentucky, have made the education of the poor a special aim of their entire operation. Oberlin College was founded to improve the conditions of the West, both spiritually and materially. Across the years places like Hampton Institute in Virginia (now Hampton University) and Tuskegee Institute, have provided education for blacks who would otherwise have been unable to afford it. In many institutions scholarships given for need have worked in a more limited way to ensure that institutions of higher education do not function as purveyors of a product available only to the affluent.

Qualified and worthy recipients of scholarship aid have been offered the benefits of an education they could not otherwise afford. Such opportunities have not infrequently been made possible by generous philanthropic gifts, though many institutions also set aside scholarship funds out of current tuition income—a practice that constitutes a limited form of redistributing wealth within a particular group.[6] The principle that educational benefits should be available to persons irrespective of a capacity to pay for them is one that mitigates the harshness of a profit-oriented society, and colleges and universities do well to follow that principle. The financial aid policies of higher education, in so far as they make need a controlling consideration, are important paradigms in a culture marked more typically by the presence of financial tollgates on the way to success. Scholarships have both a functional importance and a symbolic significance. They help those who would not otherwise be able to attend college to do so and they demonstrate that societies are enriched to the extent that they offer benefits to people without always placing a price tag on them.

The idea of giving scholarships for need continues to be an important part of American higher education. But scholarships awarded for merit serve to bring to student bodies persons of special promise and ability whose attendance helps to raise the quality of the intellectual and social life of the campus. Such scholarships are awarded more out of a sense of institutional self-interest rather than from an expression of public concern. There may be warrant for these kinds of scholarships as well scholarships for need, since they serve a rather different role. But, only under the most illegitimate kind of elitism will a program of scholarships granted for need be allowed to fall victim to a program of scholarships given exclusively for merit. In some cases—such as the procurement of top athletes—the idea of scholarships has become less a means of serving human need than of purchasing brawn for the spectator contests with which the college or university entertains (more than it serves) the public. Individuals may be personally advantaged by such scholarships, but the possibilities of corruption have become all too obvious and both the element of social service and that of enhancing the educational environment are all but absent.

THE COLLEGE OR UNIVERSITY'S PHILANTHROPIC ROLES

Universities have, across the years, also found ways to serve the needs of the poor in other ways. Universities, or faculty members within them, have often either sponsored or been closely associated with efforts to serve people in the communities around them. Samuel Barnett pioneered the settlement house idea with the establishment of Toynbee Hall at Whitechapel, England, in 1885; Jane Addams founded Hull House in Chicago in 1889; and Francis Greenwood Peabody and Robert Ely founded the Prospect Union in Boston in 1891. Peabody also established Phillips Brooks House, which was dedicated to piety, charity, and hospitality, and served as a channel through which Harvard students engaged in deeds of philanthropy in the Cambridge area. Union Theological Seminary in New York was connected with Union Settlement until just after the World War II, when students from the Seminary established a more liturgically and socially activistic counterpart, known as the East Harlem Protestant Parish.

Across the years it has not been unusual for college students to serve as tutors to young persons in need, to aid the elderly, to do voluntary work at daycare centers, and to take part in other kinds of activities designed to alleviate the hurts of the communities surrounding the campus. Such efforts have opened the minds and hearts of participating students to dimensions of the social situation which are not necessarily part of classroom awareness, and thus have functioned to underscore the propriety of social outreach as an integral part of the educational venture. Such experiences have served, so to speak, as a form of consciousness-raising that helps the advantaged recognize

190   their social responsibilities—a process as important as raising the consciousness of the oppressed to their rights.

These kinds of community service have suffered under many different pressures. The service dimensions of the collegiate experience often get forgotten during those discussions of educational policy in which cognitive dimensions are given exclusive attention. As a result student involvement in voluntary social service may be all but forgotten on some campuses and considered merely peripheral at others. Narrow academic professionalism and intellectual elitism often ignore matters that belong to the extracurriculum or are sponsored by voluntary and religious student groups. It is dismaying to note that the terms "benevolence," "charity," "philanthopy," "sacrifice," and "service" are all missing from the list of ideas that a prominent book on cultural literacy suggests every American needs to know.[7] Is it any wonder that the pursuit of learning may go its way in many places oblivious to the premise that education should entail the cultivation of compassion?

Then, too, for many years the welfare services needed in the inner cities tended to be taken over by publicly financed programs that came to be almost entirely separated from the educational enterprise. What could amateurs with meager resources do in comparison with public agencies supported by tax dollars? There has also been a tendency to question the very idea of philanthropic charity. What is the value of merely ameliorative strategies when systemic changes that address problems of justice are needed?

But there are signs student volunteerism is reviving on some campuses or growing for the first time at others. At Yale in 1988 close to 40 percent of the students were involved in voluntary service, and at Rice a program had already engaged a fourth of the student body in such activities within a year of its initiation.[8] Several experimental colleges have wisely tied instructional programs to social involvements. Professor Robert Coles of Harvard, who teaches a course on literature dealing with conditions people experience in life, has rightly noted that the learning process is enhanced by having students experience firsthand the problems about which they read in their class work. Ernest L. Boyer, speaking for his study commission, put it this way: "We believe that service constitutes a vital part of an undergraduate education. It offers opportunities that cannot be obtained in any other way. And such an experience may be one of the first truly meaningful acts in a young person's life."[9] Coles and Boyer are saying that only so far as the academic institution attends to its neighborly obligations will it be able to fulfill its educational ones.

Several developments that have taken place in recent years can be interpreted as extensions of the service impulses that have long had a valid place in higher education. For instance, special opportunity programs for students who would otherwise be unable to attend college constitute an updated and expanded idea of the scholarship based on need. Such programs are designed to make learning available not only to students who would not be able to afford higher education, but to those whose situation within the culture had deprived them of opportunities to develop intellectually to the point where they would normally be ready for higher learning. If colleges can rightly offer special financial aid to those without the economic wherewithal to attend, why should they not also provide special pedagogical aid to those who (under conditions they did not control) have not yet developed their intellectual capacities to enter higher learning completely ready to undertake it?

Few programs have proven more controversial among academicians than those designed to extend the availability of collegiate education to a range of cultural groups within which achievement scores are untrustworthy indications of potential. In the eyes of many traditional academicians, special opportunity programs are suspect. Open admissions programs, which extend the special opportunity idea with abandon, are felt by some to lead to an abrogation of standards and to play havoc with excellence. The controversy about these matters has produced a debate in which two different visions of what constitutes the university came into conflict.

The debate over open admissions, in other words, is between two opposing views of the university's role: One, [which the writer of this passage called "the old traditional view,"] assumes college is a privilege granted to a relatively few talented students, the B.A. degree is a rare and coveted prize, and the university is under no obligation to reach larger numbers of people; it is thus the responsibility of the student to meet, on his own, the rigorous requirements for graduation and a degree. According to the new view, it is the university's responsibility to provide an education for as many students as possible, though ideally, not at the expense of standards. To do so it must be active in recruiting students and in helping them live up to its standards. In place of the old "ivory-tower," the university is seen as a force in the struggle for social equality.[10]

192   The contrast drawn in this passage between two views of the university is partially misleading because it calls a purely meritorious aristocracy of intellect "the old traditional outlook." Truly traditional higher education has not been characterized by snobbish disregard for questions of access. In their very earliest days schools such as Harvard and William and Mary offered to open their doors to native Americans.[11] The movement from student aid programs designed to overcome economic inability to afford college to programs that attempt to overcome "readiness inability" to undertake advanced learning is really just a variant of a traditional ideal. It is a thrust for intellectual prestige that prizes achievement as the only significant entrance requirement that represents a departure from the main tradition.

The purposes of special admission plans are admirable. They are intended to make it possible for intellectually able members of our society whose personal odysseys and accidental misfortunes have left them unprepared for collegiate work to make the transition into the strange (to them) new world of the academy. This is not necessarily to argue that such programs work as well as they should or that they are above critical evaluation. All too little effort has been taken to discover the peculiar skills and resources needed to make either type of program as functional as possible. It may be that open-admissions programs—which seek to avoid the possibility of discrimination based on the wrong considerations by repudiating all discriminating judgments—are not entirely wise. They may overload the capacity of some campuses to provide the very kind of guidance often needed. They may be attended by difficulties caused by a failure to recognize the extent of the resourcing necessary to offer such a program successfully, but errors in the implementation of such programs do not provide justification for repudiating their intentions. The college or university says something very important when it deliberately seeks to include within its fold persons whom society has deprived of due development.

The problems that confound many of these programs are not so much with the college that uses them as a way of redressing the social injustices of a society where access to adequate education is grossly uneven, as with primary and secondary educational systems that are tied to localized economic enclaves and segregated housing patterns. The college cannot hope to turn those patterns around through its own efforts alone—but it can say loudly and clearly that it will not allow such patterns to be the primary arbiter of how it composes its own community. Special opportunity programs are the academy's means of saying "No" to the complacent acceptance of debilitating injustices in a society where economic standing is given controlling play, and where individuals are sometimes condemned to lives of squalor by environments imposed upon them by a society that could help to mitigate their presence if only it would do so. It is a significant form of social witness to implement that "No."

These programs do not abandon the measuring of promise, but they relocate the place and manner of measuring that promise to the academy itself—refusing to let some measure of accomplishment (or lack of accomplishment) in other, and often adverse circumstances, be a prior restraint upon opportunity. This calls for a major reorientation of the college agenda, one that is often troublesome and vexing to elitist assumptions and not necessarily economical. Such programs likewise require new explorations of the ways in which persons can adjust to the academic life, and they require an investment of resources that should be viewed as a deliberate opportunity to serve human needs. Nor is it reasonable to demand wide levels of success in such ventures as a precondition for pursuing them. Many a traditional academic program has been carried out without high levels of success—but has not thereby been discredited nor abandoned. Colleges that open their doors to academically ill-prepared athletic scholarship recipients, for instance, and then invest special resources in helping them meet the minimal intellectual demands of their curricular regimens, will not sound convincing if they complain about the special resourcing that is needed to make special opportunity programs work successfully.

Then, too, just as in the past the vision of students was enlarged by relating to settlement houses, so today the outlook of the contemporary campus community will be enlarged by bringing to its fold persons from different backgrounds. The presence of persons of different backgrounds and diverse identifying qualities is crucial to having a campus that prepares persons well to meet the challenges of living in a pluralistic society. On the campus, the tensions and discomforts that sometimes accompany encounters between persons with wide and deep differences can hopefully be dealt with educationally rather than confrontationally—though confrontation may be one way by which the minority group preserves itself from being amalgamated into a majority milieu and thereby preserves its capacity to serve a unique role. Special programs designed to secure student bodies that are more widely representative of our society should not be envisioned merely as a way of making educational benefits available to needy groups, but as a means of broadening the richness of the educational experience for all. Derek Bok sees this as a legitimate reason for the special recruitment of minorities (which he prefers to be done by the exercise of discretion by admission officials),[12] and Justice Powell, who in the

194   Baake case voted against a quota system at the University of California, nevertheless took pains to point out the constitutional right of universities to make discretionary judgments leading to the diversification of student bodies for educational reasons. The effort to include persons from diverse backgrounds within the composition of a student body works toward an important educational goal. Colleges lose a valuable resource for their own ability to prepare people to live in a pluralistic world if they rely entirely on admissions determined by qualifications developed only in privileged secondary educational systems.

THE SPECIAL CASE OF AFFIRMATIVE ACTION

Affirmative action is another strategy that is in part a device for meeting human need; specifically, a device to overcome arbitrary discrimination in employment. It may be to those aspiring to faculty appointment what special opportunity programs are to those seeking admission as students. Both kinds of program offer remedies for analogous difficulties and both create some of the same kinds of controversy over their implementation. Both benefit the institution as well as those they are designed to help.

The moral and legal mandate that overarches all programmatic and logistical technicalities in this area is the duty to overcome discrimination; the educational mandate—which should have at least as controlling a role—is the importance of achieving diversity in the mentoring group. The omission of certain groups from teaching positions on the basis of gender or ethnic identity has been a form of injustice, but it has also been a limiting factor on educational breadth. The presence of persons of both genders and diverse ethnic identity is a way of assuring a breadth of learning perspectives for the classroom and a proper dynamic within faculty deliberations. These twin principles not only rule out exclusion as unfair; they make inclusion pedagogically necessary.

Affirmative action programs, which are designed both to prevent discrimination and also to bring about more desirable diversity in the composition of teaching staffs, can be mandated either as public policy or voluntarily embraced as institutional goals. The primary weight of legally enforced public policy is most appropriately directed at the prevention of discrimination; institutional commitment may well be focused on the goal of achieving diversity. When no applications are submitted by members of the inadequately represented groups, discrimination is technically avoided but the institution has not moved any appreciable distance toward achieving diversity.

Since education is not merely a cognitive matter, and since what we are in the totality of our being is as important to the process as what we know, a cognitive measure of competence is not by itself a sufficient measure of a faculty's potential to contribute to the fullness of the education process—especially if the measure of that competence is determined by standards devised by Euro-males. The presence of women and persons of ethnic diversity within the pedagogical process broadens horizons and helps to overcome stereotypes. Their presence in a faculty also has a monitoring effect upon the way issues are handled in governance deliberations. It is difficult to engage in stereotyping when confronted by the actual presence of members of the groups in question.

But even if the task of affirmative action is defined in the limited sense of precluding discrimination, obtaining assurances of fairness is by no means simple, and public agencies have sometimes resorted to de facto measures to test the absence of any intent to exclude. If a school, or subdivision of a school, has no faculty members from the designated groups (or a proportion greatly lower than the proportion of qualified persons available to the field as a whole) it has, at times, been the policy to rule that the institution has discriminated even if its deliberations have been free of intentional bias on a case-by-case basis.

Externally applied pressures have a place in moving campuses to adopt more inclusive policies, but they are not able to achieve the most valuable educational results of such policies unless accompanied by a rich and genuine moral commitment within faculties and administrations to embrace diversity as an important value. There are fields where the number of available qualified candidates of the desired identity is simply too limited to go around. When this is the case great difficulties arise. Some schools will leave posts temporarily unfilled rather than staff them with persons belonging to the prevalent existing majority. This seems to create what is called "reverse discrimination," and is attended by understandable frustrations. It can leave individuals bitter and subject-matter specialties uncared for. Such consequences can only be avoided if the resolve to overcome social injustice is strong and the patience to persist to the desired ends remains undiminished until the desired consequences are achieved.

It must be realized that any emphasis on affirmative action builds inordinate market demands for persons of limited availability. This may create the possibility that applicants with special identities can work scarcity to their inordinate personal advantage. While such behavior also takes place without respect to gender and ethnic factors in certain subject-matter fields where talent is limited, the problem

196   seems to attract more criticism when it is associated with affirmative action for women and minorities. In either instance, individuals who play their personal advantages callously or contemptuously may be saying something about their own lack of suitability for membership in a faculty community.

For the present time—and given the limited number of minorities entering academic careers this time will not soon come to an end—the achievement of the school as a whole in attracting a diversity of teaching personnel is a more feasible measure of good faith than what is achieved by instructional subdivisions such as individual departments. Even in the larger picture, compromises between what is possible considering the availability of persons and what is desireable for educational reasons will have to be made. Ideally, for instance, a school with half of its students of each gender should have half of its faculty of each gender; a school with a fifth of its students in a minority should have a fifth of its faculty from the same minority group. Not every department can do this under present conditions of availability, nor can every institution. Institutions that do so in effect require others to settle for a lower percentage than they would otherwise be able to attract. The most important affirmative action, therefore, should be at the level of preparation—bringing women and minority students into the professional pipeline. That alone will serve to overcome the tensions created when affirmative action is applied in ways that seem to create reverse discrimination. There is no escaping the importance of manifesting an intense concern about those ways in which a more diverse and pluralistic educational ethos can be established for the benefit both of those slighted by the social process and the life of the academy. Institutions will achieve credibility in these areas by the good faith they show in seeking to do rather difficult and yet necessary things instead of enumerating the reasons why such things are impossible to do. In that way they will be examples to a wider society which also has responsibilities in these matters.

NOTES

1. Quoted in John S. Brubacher and Willis Rudy, *Higher Education in Transition* (New York: Harper and Brothers, 1958), 177.

2. Peter Drucker, *The Age of Discontinuity* (New York: Harper and Row, 1968) 257. The context of this quote makes it clear that Drucker has reservations about the service role of universities, not only on the pragmatic ground that their resources are limited, but also on the grounds that such functions are not within the mandate of the academy.

3. For instance, in the academic year 1979–80 Harvard put more than $100 million into the economy of Cambridge, Mass; See Derek Bok, *Beyond the Ivory Tower: Social Responsibilities of the Modern University* (Cambridge, Mass.: Harvard University Press, 1982), 221.

4. On a twelve month schedule of salary payments that runs from the last day of September to the last day of August for a teaching year that runs from late August to mid-May, a faculty member has normally done half of the teaching and received only one third of the salary at the end of the calendar year! For a new faculty member coming from graduate school into employment with debts and the costs of getting established in new housing such a schedule causes not inconsiderable hardships.

5. For instance, in order for tuition remission plans to be tax-free, it was necessary to make them available to the children of support staffs as well as to children of faculty.

6. The practice mentioned here is primarily found in private higher education. It does have analogies in the pricing of medical services. Many providers set their usual and customary fees at a sufficiently high level to be able to render services to those in need at a greatly reduced cost or at no cost at all. The analogy is only partially valid, however, since the medical system is profit driven while the educational enterprise is not.

In the case of public higher education the situation is somewhat different. Lower costs benefit all who enroll while the main burden is born by society-at-large, not least because society recognizes the value of an educated citizenry. While most societies have moved to finance health care as our society finances public education, the United States has not.

7. E. D. Hirsh, Jr., *Cultural Literacy: What Every American Needs to Know* (Boston: Houghton Mifflin, 1987).

8. "Volunteers in Dual Role on Campus," *New York Times*, 10 February 1988, Late Edition, B9.

9. Ernest L. Boyer, *The Undergraduate Experience in America: The Carnegie Foundation for the Advancement of Teaching* (New York: Harper and Row, 1987), 214.

10. Solomon Resnik and Barbara Kaplan, "Report Card on Open Admissions: Remedial Work Recommended," *New York Times Magazine*, 9 May 1971; 26ff.

11. This offer was refused by the elders of their tribes on the grounds that the classical curriculum offered at these schools was hardly an adequate preparation for survival under the conditions of native American life. They made a counter offer to teach the young men of Cambridge and Williamsburg how to hunt for food. For documentation regarding Harvard, see a talk to the trustees of Hampton Institute by Francis Greenwood Peabody in *Southern Workman and Hampton School Record*, May 1987, 86. For documentation regarding William and Mary see T. C. McLuhan, *Touch the Earth: A Self-Portrait of Indian Existence* (New York: Promontory Press, 1971), 57.

12. Bok, *Beyond the Ivory Tower*, chapter 4.

CHAPTER FIFTEEN

Governance as Communal Responsibility

Academic institutions have a profound responsibility to order their affairs in ways that are consistent with the intellectual life in its broadest sense. The primary purposes of governance in institutions of higher education should be (1) to enhance the possibility of authentic growth and learning; (2) to maintain that openness that enables the exploration of ideas to be free from extrinsic constraint; (3) to ensure fairness and compassion in the treatment of individuals; and (4) to facilitate community in the quest for understanding. In short, it is the place of governance to enhance those protective amenities and that atmosphere of trust which together support human growth and scholarly achievement. Considered in its positive sense, the term "ivory tower" connotes, among other things, an enclave of freedom and reasonableness that constitutes an alternative to the crude exploitations, ruthless hassles, and arbitrary exercises of power that are prevalent in many other places in the culture.

Of course, this is an ideal. Campuses are not always communities of either fairness or trust—and, in some sad instances, not even communities of reason. Across the years, orderly openness has not necessarily been the most distinguishing quality of collegiate life. The campus uproars of the sixties focused attention on student discontent, but behind them lay an even greater erosion of the consensus about purposes and directions of higher education that had already done much to transform the campus into a collection of competing interest groups. Under such conditions campus life works against its main purpose for being. For instance, more psychic energy is sometimes drained from various members of an academic community by the time and attention required to deal with matters of governance than by all the other demands they face. There may be no part of the educational scene more in need of examination, greater thought, or a heavier infusion of meliorative therapy than the ways by which contemporary institutions govern their affairs.

To be sure, conflict will not totally disappear even under the best of conditions. The wolf will not lie down with the lamb until the end of history; it is equally unlikely that total harmony and complete fairness will appear on campuses until learning is no longer a fleshly weariness. Tensions and difficulties are inevitable in academic institutions, but these should be resolved by mediation and resolution in a complex and subtle process, not by imposed fiat or a coercive victory. Governance should be a means of taming conflict so that it ferrets out the most viable alternatives and settles disagreements on the basis of deliberation and negotiation rather than by power struggles. Campus governance should avoid the arbitrary use of authority as well as the purely politicized clash of constituency interests. Those with the functional control need to be challenged: administrators with the question, "What do ye more than tyrants?"; faculty with, "What do ye more than partisan interest groups?"; students with, "What do ye more than mere customers?"

PROBLEMS IN GOVERNANCE OF THE ACADEMY

The governance of academic institutions presents unique challenges. One reason it proves so difficult to govern the college or university is because many contrasting values must be taken into account—values that have to be sustained in different and sometimes even contrasting ways.

An academic institution must be a place in which ideas and values can be freely and candidly examined, yet it is also a place in which canons of competence need to be honored and enforced. Neither administrative decrees nor exercises of faculty or student power can change such things as the currently accepted rules of grammar, the prevailing understanding of physical laws, or warranted historical facts. But institutional governance may well determine whether and how grammar is to be taught, whether physics is to be included in the general requirements, and whether the contributions of blacks, women, and other marginalized groups are to be given greater attention in the teaching of history than they receive at present. One of the important sensitivities that must be developed to govern academic institutions well is to know how to determine the difference between those claims which directly stem from scholarly inquiry itself—which must be protected by academic freedom and left to the intellectual enterprise to determine—and the issues of institutional policy making which require decisions as to the best ways to protect the intellectual

200   enterprise and ensure the integrity of the community in which knowledge is transmitted and even gradually changed by inquiry and reflection.

Another contrast that needs to be considered in governing the academy is the difference between giving due weight to accomplishment and maintaining the right of every member to have equal freedom to explore the truth and argue for a particular way of seeing it. A demonstrated proof or a cogent argument can be as valid when advanced by a student or an instructor as by a full professor. The university is at one and the same time a meritocracy and a community of equals. As a meritocracy it must acknowledge distinctions based upon accomplishment; as a community of equals it must share its learning without respect to standings and be open to the contributions of any and all who will abide by the rubrics of scholarly inquiry. An academic community can neither tolerate prior restraint on the one hand, nor should it be allowed to become the equivalent of "soap-box square" on the other. It must avoid the equal perils of being an intellectual closed shop or of trying to maintain a simplistic egalitarianism. It is neither a public facility available at whim to each and every aspirant, nor is it a privileged club which can block its doors to those whose views do not conform to arbitrary measures of acceptability. Its differentiations should not be drawn merely on the basis of seniority or power, nor can it use a simple abrogation of distinctions to assure its integrity and viability. This means that one of the necessary skills required for governing academic institutions is a sense of when the claims of merit legitimize differentiation of status and when the claims of community require equality of standing.

Finally, a university worthy of respect as a place of personal growth and learning is properly considered the master of its own house—and it must insist upon its autonomy as against subjugation to any external interest group. Yet the life and fortunes of the university intermesh in many ways with those of the society of which it is a special part and by which it is supported. Academic institutions exist to enrich and nurture far more than their own narcissistic curiosities. If they preserve autonomy too vigorously, they jeopardize the support needed to carry on their work, or even to give their agendas significance; if they allow their agendas to be determined too much by the desires or demands of external constituencies, they compromise their most essential reason for being. Thus, one of the most important skills necessary for academic governance is the capacity to balance the autonomous freedom of the campus with the claims of the larger public world.

GOVERNANCE, CONSTITUENCY INTEREST, AND
LEADERSHIP STYLE

Much thinking about the governance of academic institutions is occupied with the question, "Who controls"? Contrasts are drawn, for instance, between institutions controlled by centralized administrations and those in which faculty governance is dominant. The same concern about "who controls" is heard in the rhetoric that demands student power. Such thinking focuses attention on who rules rather than on the purposes that ought to direct the efforts of each and every member of the academic guild.

To be sure, any institution faces the problem of relating constituencies to one another in some agreed-upon pattern. One method for doing this is to determine a ranking among them, thus settling in advance whose authority is controlling. This is the pattern used by such line-command organizations as the military and much industry. Another way to relate constituencies is by covenantal agreements that specify appropriate roles and that allocate responsibilities according to the function and capability of the various constituencies. This is the way constitutional democracies work, particularly those marked by a separation of powers. Still another way to think about these matters is to deny the distinction between constituencies, thinking of each and all as members of a single communitarian gestalt. This is the model that governs the radically egalitarian sect, and lies behind the rally cry "participatory democracy."

Ideal academic life fits none of these models exactly. This can be inferred from a study of academic leadership styles and institutional cultures in which Charles H. Reynolds and David C. Smith identified four types of successful academic president, all of whom seek to develop values from within the premises of the academic process.[1] Their study helps us to understand the complexities that distinguish academic life from that of other organizations. The authors note, for example, that the academic community is characterized by the presence within the structure of "many authorized 'valuers,' persons whose choices and actions make real contributions to the complex of values that is the organizational culture. Colleges and universities [also] differ from more strictly hierarchical organizations in which the organizational values are established only from above."[2]

The four variations of leadership style delineated by Reynolds and Smith include (1) the clinical expert, who utilizes the established principles and procedures that are honored in an institution and which find expression in rationally stated rules and policies; (2) the engaged

202 reformer, who appeals to broader moral principles or a more encompassing vision of the common good that can be accepted by the campus because it is a part of a larger tradition of civility; (3) the campus shepherd, who is guided by institutional lore and history and also utilizes a general disposition toward human affirmation that is honored implicitly by the campus—using the narrative lore by which the institution identifies itself to secure response from the constituencies; and (4) the conscientious exemplar, who is guided by what is an implicit ideal of human virtue—embodied in character and personal virtue. In actual practice few presidents utilize just one of these modalities of leadership on a campus.

Each of the four types of successful academic leadership identified by Reynolds and Smith involves to a significant degree the leader's capacity to symbolize the ideals of the group and to facilitate the dynamics by which it carries on its life together. All of these styles of leadership function primarily on the principle "primus inter pares." A primus inter pares is primarily responsible, not for particular consequences that are to be achieved by forcing various constituencies to do particular things, but for the integrity of the group's life by which all constituencies accept responsibility for the common good. A good academic leader thinks "we" rather than "they." Moreover, such a leader works with a given membership and cannot rely upon a strategy of dismissing members of the community in order to assure cooperation or accomplish objectives.

While no leader does so perfectly, one who nurtures in both a personal and an official way the commitments and values of a purposive group cultivates allegiance on the basis of loyalties that coalesce naturally around a commonly cherished set of ideals and purposes. Moreover, allegiance flows both to and from the primus inter pares, reflecting a combination of commitment to both the individual and to the organization. Usually, only persons who have become acculturated to the group, have undergone its initiations, internalized its values, proven themselves supporters of its goals and defenders of its interests, rise to leadership in this kind of community. Moreover, such persons will be followed only by those who are similarly committed, or who are in a process of becoming committed, to the values of the particular community in question and are at home within its ethos.

Academic institutions have historically been governed by processes basically derived from ecclesiastical models. For all that many academics would cringe at the comparison, they have belonged to something like a monastic order in which leadership comes from within and symbolically represents the purposes of the community. If they would prefer, they can liken the academy to an athletic team that plays together by utilizing the capacity of each member to be completely abreast of the game and to do what is required to advance toward victory on the basis of individual judgments that work together more because purposes are shared than because orders are obeyed. In either of these cases, leadership comes up from within the community and is devoted to the facilitation of the work of a community whose goals it exemplifies. This model is most likely to operate well in small institutions—and as the size and complexity of a college or university increase, this model becomes harder and harder to make operative. Even so, it never ceases to be relevant.

THE ACADEMIC MODEL UNDER SIEGE

There are tremendous pressures at work today that endanger the model just described. Lewis B. Mayhew has indicated that campus governance may be increasingly under siege.

> The question is whether faculty and administration can cooperate and share power or whether they will become adversaries and adopt the techniques of management and trade unionism. There are strong pressures in both directions, but the advocates of antagonism have a slight advantage. Teachers' unions have forced confrontation on campuses, but even more significant, they have forced other organizations such as the National Educational Association and the American Association of University Professors to assume a more militant stand and even to drive out those elements which still believe in professionalism and shared responsibility.[3]

J. Victor Baldridge has expressed similar doubts about the future of traditional patterns of academic governance. He believes that the conflicts of interest that mark the contemporary campus have now become so numerous and great that there is no alternative but to move to a political model of governance, replacing both a collegial and a bureaucratic model.[4] A political model frankly acknowledges the presence of contending constituencies. The leader brokers power among conflicting interests in order to achieve a viable working harmony. The political leader operates with interest groups to fashion ad hoc coalitions that will support specific programs of action or achievements that seem plausible at the moment. Facing a clash of contrary (and sometimes even conflicting) interests among members of a given society, the political leader utilizes ever shifting strategies to affect contingent, revisable, and often unprecedented arrangements that accomplish immediate objectives.

204   It may seem that under contemporary pressures the political model is the most likely alternative. Political pressures both within and upon the university are growing. The pressures stemming from faculty demands have been compounded by the rise of student concerns for a place in the decision-making process. Building upon the premises of the political model, in which the primary question is who will have the power to make a decision, students have asked for (and in many instances, "demanded") a place in the decision making of the campus.[5]

But the political model is not the only one available as a proposed solution for contemporary difficulties. Many people, often including those on governing boards, are looking to another alternative to the traditional view.[6] The alternative model to which they turn is entrepreneurial, and the president is likened to a manager, who operates by setting rationally defined goals and directing the internal operations of institutional affairs with logistical acumen. Management seeks goals that can be set by prudential considerations and are often quantifiable. The manager utilizes power more overtly than does the traditional type of academic leader, and the locus of power and the channels through which it flows can be more clearly described. Often, the manager seeks to dominate constituencies rather than broker between them.

Qualifications for managerial roles are less dependent upon identification with or acculturation to the values of the community than upon raw skill and brilliance. Logistical shrewdness counts more than seniority, an imaginative capacity to innovate counts more than a symbolic power to represent. The leadership skills associated with management reflect the dynamics of productivity. The manager is fully and directly accountable for how things get done and must have an authority commensurate with that responsibility. Moreover, the manager does not necessarily have to fulfill a symbolic role: it is enough for the manager to have access to the tools of command.

Managers as defined in this schema have in the past functioned most appropriately in the supervision of factories and corporations. To be sure, much contemporary thinking about management is broadening the term to denote some additional qualities of leadership not implicit in line command. But the category helps us to understand much that is taking place on many campuses as pressures rise to make institutional governance more functional and to place accountability more specifically on administrations. In private institutions boards of trustees are frequently drawn from people who are most familiar with the managerial mode of leadership. Such boards may have great difficulty understanding the premises of a campus, and they often think of the president as an officer they select and install to make the operation viable. Because the managerial model allows accountability to be specifically assigned, those who are accustomed to using it are dumbfounded when a president who unilaterally imposes policies and gives directives that seem entirely prudent and sensible to persons with a good business sense only breeds resentment and resistance on a campus.[7]

These differences in assumption create a clash between cultures,[8] with the president caught in the middle. To the extent presidents are academicians they have internalized, or presumably have done so, the values and ethos of a guild that considers authority as limited to that of a first among equals; to the extent they are regarded as representatives of a governing board that thinks according to the managerial model, presidents come under pressure to achieve results by logistical shrewdness and are held accountable according to the presumption that leaders have authority to make policy and see that it gets carried out. It is no wonder the tenure of presidents in the educational world has been growing increasingly short.

Responses to a manager tend to be prudent and formalistic. They are explicitly stated in discrete terms rather than vaguely embodied in a symbolic ethos. They may consist of a willingness to do certain required things, but not necessarily to offer a general loyalty. Those who find themselves no longer willing to do what the manager demands are usually expected to sever their membership in the organization. But here is where the managerial way of thinking and the usual assumptions about academic life come into tension. Those who think in managerial terms often have special difficulty understanding academic freedom as a controlling factor in the governance of a campus and tenure as its chief protection. Those who cherish the academic ethos cannot imagine a situation in which disagreements about policy matters would possibly result in punitive sanctions.

REFURBISHING THE ACADEMIC MODEL

If, as I have suggested in chapter 13, academic life must operate on the basis of credibility more than on the basis of power, the presumptive preference is for the facilitator who operates as a primus inter pares. The leader in such a role is an enabler, one who empowers those within the perimeters of the institution and its resources to achieve personal and corporate goals. The alternatives to this model operate on the premises of power—in one instance, economic power; in the other, political power. Managers give orders based on the thrust to maximize productivity; politicians seek to dominate with sanctions

206 that implement policies. To demand productivity or enforce conformity rather than to inspire a freely offered loyalty or whole-hearted allegiance is to shift premises radically. Among the worst conditions that can arise on a campus is one in which its administrators can say to others (often as much by their actions as by their words), "You only work here." However, a politicized situation in which there is little else than a haggling among constituencies over which one will determine policy is hardly much better.

To succeed with governance by communal interaction requires enormous discipline within each of the academy's constituencies. The overriding necessity is commitment to the community's purposes, and a willingness to take responsibility for one's part in furthering those purposes. Faculty members, for instance, must recognize that they are accountable for their actions—that decisions are not endlessly postponable and that policies cannot be shifted too frequently. The case for faculty participation in governance rests upon the credibility that comes from treating matters of educational policy with both skill and dispatch. Likewise, students who aspire to a role in governance should understand their role not as plumping only for their own interests, but as rendering those contributions and raising those issues that are sensed only by those who are the most affected by the way in which the academy directs its affairs. The case for student participation also rests very heavily on the realization that learning is facilitated when all parties are engaged in understanding educational purposes and enriching institutional procedures.

Participatory community depends upon a preparation for the roles that each group plays in the process. In contrast to merely obtaining power in the political sense, acculturation into institutional citizenship depends upon a slow introduction to the agonies of responsibility. It teaches the sobering truth that not every constituency can completely have its own way—even if it gains the political wherewithal to insist that it should. A crisis of credibility is bound to arise if participation in governance is embraced with inflated expectations. Constituencies often suppose that the only thing that stands in the way of achieving their objectives is a failure to share the power. In many situations, and particularly in those characterized by shrinking resources, gaining participation in the actual decision-making process may even become an invitation to serve as the executioner of one's own most cherished dreams. Such experience teaches the sobering truth that the possession of clout does not guarantee achievement. One of the pedagogically important benefits of constituency involvement in institutional governance is to help campus factions come to the point where they realize this truth and learn to accept its implications.

To be sure, there should be a place for the radical idealist who will not become the contented member of the established structure. The radical reminds the citizenry that compromise may purchase viability at too high a price. But those who choose this role contribute to the health of the institution only if they do not suppose that by changing places with those in positions of authority they can suddenly right all ills. For instance, activists of any genre who sit in campus buildings to achieve some objective may force institutions to work out better ways of giving due attention to their aspirations, but they must decide at what point a compromise is preferable to the destruction of the institution they are trying to reform. Their decision will never seem flexible enough to the majority; it will probably always seem too accommodating to those whose vision remains informed only by ideological idealism. Participation in governance becomes a means by which moral idealism is rendered compatible with a worldly wisdom and commitments to important value goals are made humanely tolerable by a common grace.

Alas, the tragedy of so many situations is not that constituencies care too much and thus are irresponsibly demanding, but that they do not care at all. The sickly pale of unconcern can creep over a campus like an odorless gas, putting people to sleep so they no longer realize they have ceased to have a capacity for outrage at injustice or to protest against procedural irregularity. Those who sleep do not grow in loyalty to an institution and its purposes. Although their seeming contentment is often interpreted as a sign of healthy normalcy, it is more like Kierkegaard's "sickness unto death"—a blindness to the fact that one is fatally afflicted.

Only those who have been taught the ideals and premises of institutional procedures are able to see procedural irregularities when they occur. One cannot become a genuinely prophetic voice without having a deep understanding of, and commitment to, the norms and values (as well as cherished working premises) that define the special identity of the covenanted group. Those needed understandings are not bred merely of discontent and disillusionment, but are the deeper products of commitments which cannot bear to acquiesce in the betrayal of deeply cherished loyalties.

In the search for prestige many institutions have sought the services of faculty members whose ties are often almost exclusively to an intellectual discipline rather than to the local community. An institution can include some of these academic stars within its membership without great harm to the viability of its internal life, but if they dominate the

208 composition of a faculty they can significantly affect the institutional ethos. They provide academic prestige but not necessarily credibility in governance. They tend to stay aloof from the dynamics essential to good governance. Some rare persons can be both external stars and campus catalysts, and they are the true crowning glory of the profession. Those who travel away from campus moderately, who maintain ties with other scholars productively, and who stay active in groups that have the general interest of higher education as a center of concern, often manifest just the right balance between intellectual achievement and creative contribution to the health of a local campus. Without some outside contacts, immersion in local concerns can stultify an individual and parochialize the campus; with too many, the contribution of the person can become thin, and perhaps even drop to nil.

The educational institution that manages to achieve the kind of interactional community that combines the many objectives that must be served through academic governance, that is open to a great variety of viewpoints, and that honors the contributions of persons from every group present on campus, can render a contribution to a wider social and communal well-being. It is well to have models of communities such as these. They can stand as demonstrations that not all structural relationships in life are maintained by clout or characterized by haggling between factious groups. They can demonstrate that communities are possible in which reasonableness, common grace, and the search for human values can have priority over productivity and the achievement of only quantifiable results. They can stand as examples that civility can be maintained despite differences of taste and judgment on a variety of lesser preferences and loyalties.

This is not to say that all institutions are good examples of these ideals. Some of them are marked by abysmal controversies that make plausible the disdain that the public sometimes shows toward the academic world. In others, endless deliberations over minutiae create a suspicion about the ability of academic types to translate good intentions into functional accomplishments. But the failure of particular institutions to embody the ideal does not invalidate the vision. It only points to the need for greater commitment to it, and for wiser appreciations of what can be done to move with more dispatch and more success toward the creation of communities that in the quality of their life together would exemplify that free, yet disciplined, quality to community that many other segments of society, despite their suspicions, secretly would like to possess.

1. Charles H. Reynolds and David C. Smith, "Academic Leadership Styles, Institutional Cultures, and the Resources of Ethics." (A paper delivered at the Annual Meeting of the American Academy of Religion, Boston, Mass., December, 1987.)

2. Ibid., 2.

3. Lewis B. Mayhew, "Toward an Unknown Station: Planning for the Seventies," *Journal of the National Association of Women Deans and Counselors*, 32, No.4 (Summer 1969): 150.

4. J. Victor Baldridge, *Academic Governance: Research on Institutional Politics and Decision Making* (Berkeley: McCutchan, 1971), 8.

5. The case for a greater student role in decision making has also been advanced on grounds understandable in the world of the manager—namely, that students are the consumers of educational offerings and thus have a right to determine what is made available to them in exchange for their tuition. But in most cases the political dimension has been more evident. When their pleas for inclusion have met with resistance, or when their requests for changes have not borne fruits, students have resorted to strategies based on the use of power to obtain desired ends—although not usually the power of the consumer.

6. The *New York Times* has reported on a trend in which "universities and colleges, which have traditionally selected their presidents from a pool of academic scholars with backgrounds in the liberal arts, may now be turning to lawyers because the position increasingly requires more political, financial and managerial skills." See "Universities Looking to Lawyers for Leadership," 25 December 1987, Late Edition, B12. Often lawyers are chosen because there is litigation to be dealt with, and they know how to play a political role in public interaction.

7. Rodney T. Hartnett has provided interesting details on the composition and attitudes of the governing board in his study *College and University Trustees, their Backgrounds, Roles, and Educational Attitudes* (Princeton: Educational Testing Service, 1969). While the variations discerned by Hartnett caution against applying the assertion made here without discretion, the general trend is quite apparent.

8. For further examination of this as a general phenomenon see Joseph A. Raelin, *The Clash of Cultures: Managers and Professionals* (Boston: Harvard Business School Press, 1985).

CHAPTER SIXTEEN

Policy Study: Beyond Neutrality and Above Partisanship

The desire to remain neutral on controversial issues often results in a failure to deal with them at all. Many individual scholars and institutions of learning attempt to maintain their academic detachment by bracketing momentous issues of public debate out of their range of attention. Partly in response to this truncating of the academic agenda, a whole new kind of institution has developed, especially in cities (like Washington, D.C.) in which decision making about public policy is very much in the local life-blood. The growth of such policy study centers (or "think tanks") may have come about, at least to some extent, as a result of the failure of traditional academic institutions to do a certain kind of much-needed inquiry.

Some of these centers, particularly older and more established ones that have developed well-deserved reputations for doing careful analysis of controversial matters, are quite like educational institutions (except that they that have few, if any, students and do little or no classroom teaching). Others, particularly those without a track record of fairness or with an all-controlling ideological sponsorship, are little more than lobbying groups dressed in nonpolitical camouflage. Judging where any particular groups lies along a spectrum between policy analysis and partisanship requires subtle discernment.

In order to be considered scholarly, the work of think tanks should not be merely an exercise in pressure politics. It should be distinguishable from lobbying.[1] The work of such centers increases in credibility to the extent that it approaches the academic model. Credibility does not require mere neutrality or disinterestedness, but rather depends on candor in acknowledging ideological perspectives and controlling loyalties. Those who openly declare their premises enable their outputs to be interpreted in light of their agendas. An open acknowledgment of the premises from which any group approaches controversial matters enhances rather than erodes the credibility of the results. Kenneth Keniston makes this truth clear: "the most truly scientific stratagem . . . is a persistent effort to make conscious and explicit one's own motivation and preconceptions; . . . the most objective students of society are those whose own values are most clearly stated, not those who claim that 'as scientists' they have no values. . . . If the writer's preoccupation and values are made explicit the reader is at least allowed to challenge these assumptions as stated and not required to ferret them out as imbedded in 'objective' report and interpretation."[2]

I have already argued that individual perspectives inevitably provide coloration to all intellectual achievements. If scholarly achievement is shaped by the perspectives from which it is undertaken, then we should not be surprised by the fact that findings and judgments that arise in the process of policy analysis also differ, and even result in contradictory results. We ought to be most alert when those differences are not evident in the output of any serious group, either because the issues are discretely ignored or because the spectrum of opinion in a given institute or institution is so narrow as to preclude diversity.

A college or university must seek to build into its life a broader spectrum of opinion and outlook than may characterize the usual "think tank." This does not require the college or university to be neutral, or to shun the examination of controversial issues. It only requires the academic institution to be above partisanship, to see that controversial issues are examined from a plurality of perspectives. The examination of social issues in the university should understand their complexity rather than attempt to advance the fortunes of only one position on them. This does not necessarily draw a clear and unequivocal divide between the think tank and the university. It puts the university onto the same continuum, but at the opposite end from the interest-group lobby. It may require the college or university to devise deliberate safeguards for the balanced pursuit of policy studies but it does not require the academic institution to shun controversial issues.

TOWARD AN UNDERSTANDING OF POLICY STUDIES

The term "policy studies" refers to efforts to bring academic scrutiny to bear on social problems. Such policy study must be distinguishable from partisan activism. The partisan lets the cause determine the agenda; the policy analyst asks what the agenda ought to be. The partisan uses facts and data to bolster a previously taken position; the policy analyst uses all such materials to help judge the merits of a stand or point of view. The partisan is basically a politician hiding behind a scholarly facade; a policy analyst is a scholar who makes the

212   problems of political life the object of critical investigation. The partisan sifts and winnows data with a view to casting aside all signals contrary to the point of view being espoused or advocated; the student of policy will put the pros and cons of an issue alongside each other in order to illuminate the options. Partisanship ignores the importance of objectivity in the espousal of a cause; policy study seeks to legitimize commitments by providing a fair-minded and thoughtful inquiry concerning their warrant. Partisanship reaches its zenith in true believerism and makes the control of power its working aim; policy analysis searches for the responsible foundation of commitment and makes credibility the foundation of its effectiveness.

There is one view of policy analysis—some regard it as the prevailing one—that is primarily concerned with strategy and tactics rather than with moral purposes. It thinks of public policy formation as the ascertaining of the public's wants, government as the process of satisfying the needs and desires of as many people as possible without judging such strategies on moral grounds, and politics as the process of responding to the public's wishes. This view regards social policy formation as primarily instrumentalist and the art of politics as solely strategic. According to one of its critics, this view "disregards the role of ideas about what is good for society and the importance of debating the relative merits of such ideas. It thus tends to overlook the ways such normative visions shape what people want and expect from their government, their fellow citizens, and themselves."[3] This view sees policy study as the analysis of strategy, and may even fear the imposition on public life of arbitrary moral strictures.

An alternative view of policy analysis emphasizes the importance of public deliberation about the aims and purposes of a society at any given juncture in its history. It holds that such deliberation is enriched by the scholarly analysis of the various competing values that strive to capture the public's commitments. It suggests that the "strongest bulwark against demagoguery is the habit of critical discussion about and self-conscious awareness of the public ideas that envelop us."[4] This second view sees policy study as the examination of civic values in relationship to the advancement of the public welfare. It decries the loss of moral ingredients in the making of policy, and abhors the scheming and conniving thrusts for political success by any means that hold constitutional restraints in contempt. While considerations of strategy and policy are germane to any political analysis, the most needed kind of policy study is of the type that takes cognizance of the foundational covenants which give a society integrity. No group—academy or think tank—is precluded from exercising the required disciplines to pursue the second kind of policy studies. Academic institutions, however, may have a greater mandate to do so carefully than institutes set up to further particular agendas.

In thinking about the nature of policy studies, it is helpful to consider the role that religious commitment can play in defining the nature of the university. One of the most extensive and profound examinations of these issues is Kenneth Underwood's Danforth Foundation Study of Campus Ministries. Heavily funded and thoroughly researched, this study considered a new role for religion on the campus—one that goes beyond the pastoral and institutional maintenance functions associated with the traditional forms of campus ministry. To understand the proper role of the campus minister, Underwood felt it necessary to rethink the nature of knowledge. William Kolb has summarized Underwood's thinking about these matters as follows:

> Knowledge, for Underwood, is not divorced from aesthetic and ethical valuation, nor from action within the structures of social life. Rather, together with valuation, it is the indispensable ingredient of social policy which can humanize the quality of modern life. The search for knowledge within this context of valuation, policy formation, and social action is policy research, the kind of research which must increasingly come to characterize the higher learning. Since the primary locus of higher learning is the university, it has become the central institution of the modern world, even though policy research within the context of the higher learning must become an integral part of all professions and institutions.[5]

Underwood stood at the juncture between the educational and the religious worlds. Many people belonging to the first would not normally expect discussions of campus ministry to be a wellspring of profound inquiry about the nature of the intellectual venture, just as some in the second world would not expect a study of campus ministry to focus attention primarily on the functions of the university. But such surprise should not prompt anyone to ignore the critically important vision that was articulated by Underwood just before a premature death precluded further input from his fertile mind and the working out of his vision in further detail. The vision of an objective mode of commitment transcending both neutrality and partisanship, was stated by Underwood himself in this way: "It is crucial that the university recover its understanding of objective involvement in public life as distinct from 'objectivity' as a state of mind. A person is objectively involved with something when his commitment to it demands and inspires the fullest use of his critical powers upon it. Thus 'objective' signifies the 'critical distance,' the breathing space necessary for

214 inquiry and reflection."[6] But, as Underwood goes on to suggest, "One's critical powers are exercised within the "object of commitment." [The scholar] is part of what he judges."

Charles S. McCoy has provided a similar model for scholarship that transcends neutrality, yet does not succumb to partisanship. Holding, as I have done in this book, that aloofness from social concerns is a departure from the main history of education, McCoy calls for ethical inquiry and critical evaluation as a "fourth dimension" of higher education and suggests that the church-related college is in a position to carry out this function more readily than many other kinds of contemporary institution. McCoy declares:

> No change is more needed today than for higher education to discard the pretense of neutrality on important social issues and to participate selectively and self-consciously in the societal process in which all educational institutions are immersed. Such a shift will not be easy for many colleges and universities, for they have made attempts to preserve a dubious and precarious immunity to political and economic pressures by claims to academic freedom based on isolation and nonpartisanship in regard to controversial matters. However difficult the transition, the shift toward overt societal involvement will not only make for greater honesty but will in most instances aid in resolving the identity crisis of the college. It is precisely the pretense of noninvolvement that creates a "credibility gap" between administration and socially aware constituencies, especially students, on the one hand, and between colleges and conservative constituencies on the other.[7]

Similarly, Joseph ben David, who does not flinch from using the phrase "the politicalization of the university," also argues that social involvement and academic inquiry are compatible, and contends this fact has been demonstrated by institutions of learning in the past—both by the medieval and reformation universities of Christianity and universities in traditional Judaism and Islam. He suggests that,

> A politicalized university would be something similar to these historical precedents. In fact, something like this exists in some of the present-day Latin American universities. Of course, the main problem of creating such universities is the absence of a commonly agreed upon intellectual frame of reference suitable for the conduct of such debate. If those who are supposed to participate in it do not share a common religious (or quasi-religious) belief in a doctrine embodied in some traditional knowledge, such as the Bible and patristic literature, or the Bible and

the Talmud (or the writings of Marx and Engels, plus or minus Lenin, Stalin, and Mao), then it is difficult to imagine how such an ongoing debate could be conducted in an intellectually disciplined fashion.[8]

Ben David further argues that the neo-scholasticism found in the Great-Book curriculum at St. Johns College, might have, in the 1930s, furnished the requisite foundation for a learning stance oriented to public responsibility, but since it was not accompanied with a concern to deal with the well-being of society, it has never worked that way.[9]

Many academics will find the religious orientation of the foregoing presentations of policy studies to be a sufficient reason for not taking them seriously. Their feelings at this point are understandable. Religion, at least in many of its popular forms, has not widely commended itself as the most fertile seedbed of socially constructive concern. However, several mainline denominations do, in fact, engage in rather impressive social analysis and critical inquiry in the course of making policy pronouncements. Their accomplishments are not generally well known and are too seldom noticed by the academic community.[10]

Religion may also seem peripheral to the major issues of public life because many campus religious organizations are marginal operations focused on such pastoral matters as personal spirituality and cell-group maintenance. Some of them may even have become more, rather than less, marginal since Underwood's study, although many campus ministers are still significantly engaged in the exploration of social issues—like conscientious objection to military service or the problems related to sexual orientation—which many academic departments simply will not touch. On campuses where this is the case the chaplain or campus minister may be a major leavening influence and play a significant educational role.

A religious grounding for careful policy studies may be more problematic now than when Underwood advanced his suggestions, because some of the most visible and popular theological trends during the intervening years have been driven more by agenda concerns than by a mood of critical inquiry. This is not to discount those concerns, since they represent the cries of the forgotten and dispossessed, and must be taken seriously as a datum for reflection. But such theologies by themselves will not accomplish what more analytical skill can offer in critically addressing the problems of society.

But to discount the significance of the idea of policy study, or to resist the explorations necessary to achieve the kind of inquiry described by Underwood, McCoy, and ben David because these have

216   been advanced in connection with religion, is ill advised. That is to settle for an understanding of the academy's role that is at odds with the educational enterprise in its longer and more enriching heritage. It may also be to let the concerns for social well-being that inevitably have political implications move entirely off the campus and thus be deprived of those benefits which scholarly analysis has to offer.

It is a low view of scholarly potential that does not believe in the possibility of achieving a stance that moves beyond neutrality yet remains above partisanship. It is an equally low view of the possibility of institutional integrity not to believe in the possibility that colleges and universities can engage in a critical study of society without becoming centers of propaganda. Indeed, one of the important features of the traditional basis of support for private universities and colleges has been the willingness of persons with money to make donations for the support of education without seeking to dictate the results of scholarly investigations. They have done this, not necessarily because institutions have been neutral, but because they have been open and fair-minded. Some of the support being syphoned away from regular institutions and used to support activities that narrowly hew to a predefined advocacy represents an unfortunate departure from a premise that has made philanthropy such a valuable part of a free society. Something very important to the viability of that society will be lost if money is treated only as a form of power, and support for undertakings is made so narrowly dependent upon an ideological conformity to the wishes of donor groups as to threaten the underpinning of more balanced forms of inquiry. It is imperative, and possible, both to do more than bracket out socially controversial issues or to treat them merely as causes to be espoused. The academy is best equipped to find the balance in the middle.

TOWARD ENRICHING THE PRACTICE OF POLICY STUDY

Good policy analysis depends, first of all, upon a capacity to make an accurate portrayal of the situation or issue under scrutiny. Most political actions are compounded of a mixture of relevant data and controlling commitments. It is not always easy to sort these out. While the relevant data may not be merely factual—the sociologists of knowledge have shown us how much commitments and ideologies shape perceptions—neither can problems and issues be accurately understood until a statement of the problem can be drawn up in a way that all sides concede as fair. A scholar who does nothing else than demonstrate skillful prowess in accurately defining the nature of a social controversy may go a very long way toward resolving a dispute.

Good policy analysis will also seek to make as accurate and impartial a portrayal as possible of the options that are available for dealing with a social issue. The imaginative construction of alternatives can very well be an exercise in objectivity, particularly when the mandate to delineate all of the possible alternatives is taken seriously. The analyst must listen to the various partisans, hear the case advanced by each, and arrange the possible solutions in a schema that highlights the decisive differences between them. To engage in such a disciplined inquiry requires the most rigorous of scholarly skills.

Policy analysis also involves the capacity to delineate the values and commitments that inform each option. The good policy analyst must be able to suggest both the values served and the values negated by each of the possible ways suggested for dealing with a controversial matter. That can be done most skillfully only by a scholar who understands moral values, as well as the ways in which people appeal to such values both legitimately and illegitimately in the defense of causes. Often this requires the scholar to solicit from the various antagonists within a controversy their own self-understandings, coaching them to recognize their own commitments clearly and to state them with concision. All of these tasks develop scholarly fairness in a crucible more demanding than any purportedly neutral detachment.

Policy study often creates a triadic relationship in which ethicists (those sensitive to the definition of value), social scientists (persons with theoretical awareness of how structures and systems function), and actual practitioners (those with "hands-on" awareness of the problems) are brought together in trialogue. Such combined inquiry—initiated and supported by the academic institution but involving persons with expertise from outside the academic institution—enlarges and enriches the usual academic fare.[11]

Finally, the policy analyst may have to suggest a recommendation. But such a recommendation should come forth only after the relevant data has been gathered, after the available options have been set forth, and after the values served and the values negated by each course of action have been identified. Struggling with these matters in this way is a form of scholarship that utilizes rather than repudiates a commitment to fairness. It is an offering made by a dedicated intellectual for the healing of a broken social order.

POLICY RECOMMENDATIONS AS SOURCES OF SCHOLARLY UNDERSTANDING

In the fifteenth and sixteenth centuries it was the practice of governments to submit problems of current concern for the reflective analysis

218   of university professors. For instance, when the Spanish government was faced with the problems of the New World—how to treat the "Indian," with whom it had to deal, what to do with the silver and gold, whether to treat the new lands as subject colonies or separate nations—it submitted these questions to Francisco de Vittoria of the University of Salamanca. Francisco de Vittoria lectured on these matters and prepared readings about them, and from this process emerged his extensive development of the Law of Nations. What we are now tempted to view as a massive scholarly accomplishment was in its origins a sort of policy report for the government.[12] It may have been fortunate that the kings of those days did not have a chorus of voices echoing the twentieth century professor who declared, "A university ought not to do chores for anyone. . . . Research ought to be generated by curiosity and imagination, not by quasi-scientific problems that are essentially political."[13]

Policy analysis of the kind described should not be the only activity of the scholar nor the only thing that engages the attention of the academy. It will be a contribution to social well-being only in so far as it is the work of a community known and respected for a richly informed concern about the human situation in all that it does. Policy analysis should be one activity among many others in which the academy works out its destiny with a certain humility and perhaps even fear and trembling. While the examination of policy can be done alongside other modes of inquiry, including modes of purely disinterested research, it turns into partisanship only if there is no wider sense of truth and dedication to justice within which it pursues its work. It is unwise, of course, to make the academy an instrument of ideological partisanship, but to avoid partisanship does not demand a neutrality that considers it illegitimate to examine public issues seriously and fairly. The life of the mind should not be cut off from those very matters of society's welfare where its contribution is most greatly needed.

NOTES

1. Even lobbying differs. Lobbying that depends upon the presentation of insights as to how proposed legislation will affect particular segments of society, and which makes such presentations on the basis of research and reflection, cannot be tarred with the same brush as lobbying that merely threatens to use the power of its sponsor as a political ax. Even in the case of lobbying groups those who think clearly deserve to be heard with more respect than those who only shout loudly.

2. Kenneth Keniston, *The Uncommitted: Alienated Youth in American Society* (New York: Harcourt Brace and World, 1960), 12.

3. Robert B. Reiche (ed.), *The Power of Public Ideas* (Cambridge, Massachusetts: Ballinger Publishing Company, 1988), 3.

4. Ibid., 10.

5. William L. Kolb, "Forward," in Kenneth Underwood, *The Church, the University, and Social Policy: The Danforth Study of Campus Ministries, Volume One, Report of the Director* (Middletown, Ct.: Wesleyan Unive.sity Press, 1969), xif.

6. Kenneth Underwood, "The University and Public Leadership," in Scott Fletcher (ed.), *Education: The Challenge Ahead*, (W. W. Norton, 1962), 90.

7. Charles S. McCoy, *The Responsible Campus: Toward a New Identity for the Church-Related College* (Division of Higher Education, Board of Education, the United Methodist Church, 1972), 138f.

8. Joseph ben David, *American Higher Education: Directions Old and New* (New York: McGraw Hill, 1972), 123f. Ben David's position probably depends more upon an orthodoxy than I would consider necessary, but it comes from a thoughtful intellectual who is concerned about the role that higher education ought to play in society.

9. More recently, Alan Bloom has presented the western classical tradition as a intellectual base for overcoming the ills of American higher education. Bloom recognizes the inability of many college students to commit themselves to anything, and he does acknowledge the need for values. However, his seeming opaqueness to the crying needs of a society in which groups suffer continued injustice and deprivation on the basis of sexual, racial, and economic discriminations, as well as his meager attention to the aspirations of many nations that wish to have a share in the achievement of well-being in global terms, prevent his prescription for overcoming the malaise which he has identified from being persuasive.

10. Many of the major denominations do impressive background papers prior to making social pronouncements, but neither the academic community in general nor the rank and file memberships of the churches pay much attention to them. The pastoral letter of the Roman Catholic Bishops, *The Challenge of Peace*, dealing with nuclear warfare did get widespread attention, but an equally well-researched and careful study of the welfare system done only a few years before, attracted almost no public attention.

11. The Center for Ethics and Social Policy in Berkeley California utilizes this kind of procedure for exploring issues. It has more than forty programs in which persons from academic disciplines enter into discussions with persons actually working with particular problems.

12. An account of this is found in Walter Prescott Webb, *The Great Frontier* (New York: Houghton Mifflin, 1951), 326ff.

13. The quotation is from Polykarp Kusch and is reported in John S. Brubacher, *Bases for Policy in Higher Education* (New York: McGraw Hill, 1965), 81.

EPILOGUE

The Public Promise of the Scholarly Ideal

A world without colleges and universities would be a place of contracting possibilities and shrinking horizons. Despite their faults, which are numerous, colleges and universities are custodians of those intellectual resources without which this world would be engulfed in intellectual darkness and its inhabitants culturally dispossessed. Technology depends on science for its continued growth; scientific inquiry is cultivated primarily in the academy. Art and music depend on the mentoring of aesthetic sensibilities for their future enrichment; much of such mentoring is done in academic settings. The public order depends upon a conceptual grasp of truthfulness and justice in order to achieve civility; these ideas are the objects of attention within higher education. Spirituality needs intellectual understanding if it is to attain maturity; ecclesiastical institutions, particularly without the modeling offered by the academy, seldom provide a full measure of what is necessary. A world deprived of its scholars and scholarship would be a world shorn of the most likely possibility of sensing the import of its history, a world without the tools to approach the present with perspective, and a world of immediate preoccupations lacking a vision for the future. Human life is enriched by the examination of ideas; by the articulation of values; by the perceptive awareness of what nature is and how artifacts are created; and by the insights that give identity to selfhood. If colleges and universities do not survive—if they fail to sustain and expand the contributions that they can make to the enrichment of human life—we shall all be impoverished by the consequences.

But the mere survival of colleges and universities is not enough. If their attention is completely absorbed by the pressures of maintaining operational viability, if their freedom to imagine better possibilities is rendered impossible by the tasks of coping with horrendous necessities, if their behavior only encourages an attitude of material aggrandizement but never the yearning to think or dream, our culture will lose the leaven crucial to hope, and will descend into an age of sophisticated nihilism.

Colleges and universities offer a potential for escaping from that fate, but no guarantee. The very promise in education is also a potential danger. While the academy offers the possibility of creating a richer habitat for humanity, if the skills it bestows are placed in the service of the wrong ends life will become worse, not better. If the academic odyssey provides only an operational intelligence but no valuational purposes, it will be more likely to exacerbate than to counteract the social antagonisms that plague us; if the scholarly life pursues only the safe security of routinized inquiry about the factual and the materially productive, it will provide only the tools of submission to the growing horrors of a violent world and not the promise of an alternative; if colleges and universities are the seat of training only to indulge in the narcissistic and not the fount of an impulse to engage in the philanthropic, they will harden the lump in the pit of our stomachs rather than inspire our spirits.

Higher education dares not become merely the avenue to success; it must be the gateway for responsibility. It should not be concerned with competence alone, but with commitment to civic responsibility. An academic degree should not be a hunting license only for self-advancement, but an indication of abilities to seek, cultivate, and sustain a richer common weal. It is not enough to achieve cultural literacy; we must engender social concern. It is not enough merely to open the mind; it is necessary to cultivate moral intentionality in a total selfhood.

If the arguments I have made in this book are correct, these things can be done without in any way threatening what is truly important in academic learning and what is essential to the scholarly life. Learning belongs to the leavening and sensitizing dimensions of public life. It is at its best when it enlarges horizons, magnifies the capacity for empathy, commends the importance of dialogue, and recommits us to the search for life in working viability with others and with an awareness of that which individuals and groups experience as the ground for their most essential being. The importance of practicing the life of learning in that way in the company of a committed guild will never be outdated.